DISENCHANTMENT

Disenchantment Endorsements:

"In this briskly written and keenly observed book, Adrian Furnham and Luke Treglown toss aside the prevailing myths regarding the alleged power of Anglo-Saxon management techniques to explain why 70% of the modern workforce hate the authors' jobs."

Robert Hogan
CEO Hogan Assessments USA

"Adrian's and Luke's work is challenging, practical, thoughtful and accessible. Reading this work stimulates thinking about the challenges and complexities of managing people. It goes way beyond the simplistic solutions posed by many of their contemporaries."

Mike Haffenden
CEO Strategic Dimensions
London

"Superb insight into one of the most difficult areas of the workplace. Adrian Furnham and Luke Treglown offer genuine clarity in areas where critical judgement is needed and often lacking. This book should be required reading for C-suite and HR professionals alike."

David Charters
Author and Founder of PartnerCapital

"This book explores what motivates and demotivates people at work, from a theory of disenchantment, and is extremely topical given the economic and political uncertainties of our time. It is a very engaging, challenging and important book that should read by all interested in managing and caring for people at work. It is a must-read for HR professionals."

Professor Sir Cary Cooper, Alliance Manchester Business School,
University of Manchester

"From grumpy staff to corporate meltdown this book gives valuable insights on how to manage the minefield of the workplace mindset to avoid the pitfalls which trap the less informed. It is a great reference guide for leaders and organisations in understanding why people react the way they do and breaks some popular assumptions about how to get the best and avoid the worst we often see around us or experience ourselves."

Chris Roebuck, Visiting Professor of Transformational
Leadership, Cass Business School London

"Adrian Furnham's and Luke Treglown's work is as timely as it is relevant, providing an analytical framework and practical advice to address disenchantment. Read this book to learn what motivates and what demotivates us at work."

Ernst von Kimakowitz, Director and co-founder
of the Humanistic Management Center

"A thought provoking read and good primer for being able to deal with reality as it unfolds."

Jason Devereux, PhD
Workplace Transformation Consultant, KPMG

DISENCHANTMENT

Managing motivation and demotivation at work

ADRIAN FURNHAM AND LUKE TREGLOWN

Bloomsbury Business
An imprint of Bloomsbury Publishing Plc

BLOOMSBURY
LONDON · OXFORD · NEW YORK · NEW DELHI · SYDNEY

Bloomsbury Business

An imprint of Bloomsbury Publishing Plc

50 Bedford Square	1385 Broadway
London	New York
WC1B 3DP	NY 10018
UK	USA

www.bloomsbury.com

BLOOMSBURY and the Diana logo are trademarks of Bloomsbury Publishing Plc

First published 2018

© Adrian Furnham and Luke Treglown, 2018

British Library Cataloguing-in-Publication Data
A catalogue record for this book is available from the British Library.

ISBN:	HB:	978-1-4729-4972-1
	ePDF:	978-1-4729-4974-5
	ePub:	978-1-4729-4973-8

Library of Congress Cataloging-in-Publication Data
A catalog record for this book is available from the Library of Congress.

Cover design by Anna Berzovan
Cover image © Adam Gault / Getty Images

Typeset by RefineCatch Limited, Bungay, Suffolk
Printed and bound in Great Britain

To find out more about our authors and books visit www.bloomsbury.com. Here you will find extracts, author interviews, details of forthcoming events and the option to sign up for our newsletters.

For Alison and Benedict as always   AF
For Charlie, Dad and Sheona, Mum and Amy   LT

CONTENTS

ACKNOWLEDGEMENTS

We have a number of people to thank for help in writing this book. First and foremost we would like to thank Barry Roche from PGI and John Taylor from JTIP. Both encouraged us right from the beginning to develop our model and measure and to start research on the neglected topic of disenchantment. They have supported us in many ways and we are most grateful.

Next we have to thank many people from our UCL team: Simmy Grover, Zohra Ihsan, Lara Kotobi, Laura Weis, Tony Zarola, Keith Broni and John Hughes. We have enjoyed your insights and practical help in many ways, often over a glass of wine on a Friday. Inevitably we have drawn on previous of our writings in the book.

1

Introduction

The fate of our times is characterized by rationalization and intellectualization and, above all, by the disenchantment of the world.
MAX WEBER

Disenchantment, whether it is a minor disappointment or a major shock, is the signal that things are moving into transition in our lives.
WILLIAM THROSBY BRIDGES

Enchantment lies in everyday moments if you are observant.
AMY LEIGH MERCREE

Introduction

There was a joke told by the few psychologists who were interested in the psychology of happiness that in their local university library there were 197 books about depression, 241 about anxiety, 71 about suicide and 889 about mental illness, but only 3 about happiness. The numbers of course were 'guestimates' but the proportions were true. Psychology has preferred to 'peer into the darkness'.

It certainly was the case that for the whole of the twentieth century psychologists concentrated on various forms of unhappiness, 'unwellness', gloom and despondency. It was not that they thought happiness uninteresting but that it was achieved by getting rid of unhappiness. The absence of unhappiness was happiness. Banish gloom and feel good. But they were wrong.

All the applied psychologists, whether they were clinical, educational or occupational specialists, seem to concentrate on the negative; on general and specific behavioural and emotional problems. They saw their task to understand and then change, eliminate or reduce all things that lead to unhappiness and not fulfilling one's full potential.

Yet nearly fifty years ago, in an early study on well-being, Bradburn (1969) had shown that happiness is not the opposite of unhappiness. Things that cause unhappiness, when changed or removed do not cause happiness. *They were different and unrelated to each other. The lists were distinct. Just because you are not pissed-off, does not mean that you are happy.*

The implication was that to ensure happiness one had to both reduce or remove the factors which caused unhappiness *while simultaneously* increase the factors that caused happiness. Treating unhappiness was not enough. Understanding those things that led to anxiety and depression did not relate in any way to an understanding of how to make people fulfilled, joyful or satisfied.

Of course there was academic controversy about Bradburn's two-factor findings and his conclusions. There are caveats and modifications, but he has in essence been proved right by the increasing group of researchers really interested in happiness as well as motivation. In essence, that which brings joy, happiness and enchantment are different from the factors that lead to gloom, unhappiness and disenchantment.

We believe this to be true and this insight underlies this whole book. The factors that lead to enchantment are different from those which lead to disenchantment. *By disenchantment we mean disaffection, or the reduction and absence of the affect which is emotion.* There is often a lot of passion at work: some positive and others negative. Disenchanted people are disappointed; they are negative. They have often 'gone sour' because of what has happened to them. This book looks in detail at the factors which lead to disenchantment.

Happiness (and enchantment)

Are some people more prone to disenchantment compared to others? Is happiness and enchantment a personality trait that is stable over time and consistent across situations? We all know the *heart-sinking* person, the pessimist, the complainer, the gloom and doom monger. Whatever happens to them they remain negative, helpless and hopeless. By contrast we know the *life-enhancers*. They may be called sunny or bonny or simply optimists. They bounce back from adversity and remain resolutely positive.

They are, for the most part, stable extroverts, while the heart sinkers are unstable introverts. There is not much one can do about one's personality. We know that people do not change much over time: we do become a little neurotic and a little less extroverted but these personality traits are remarkably stable despite what happens to us, be it winning the lottery or a terrible accident leaving us paralysed.

In fact, a longitudinal study of happiness found this unwavering quality of happiness to be true. Psychologists David Lykken and Auke Tellegen (1996) found that external factors – including socio-economic status, educational attainment, income, marital status and religious commitment – made little to no impact on our happiness across the course of our lifetime. Instead, well-being was found to mostly be *inherited*. Our tendency to be happy is determined largely by a genetic lottery, with external factors temporarily pulling us away from that baseline. They boldly concluded that: 'it may be that trying to be happier is as futile as trying to be taller'.

But we also know that the most positive-minded life-enhancer can become unhappy and seriously disenchanted at work. So, what do we know about the psychology of happiness?

Since the 1990s researchers have really looked at this area. The Positive Psychology Centre at Pennsylvania State University has a website dedicated to answering frequently asked questions such as: 'Isn't positive psychology just plain common sense?'

They note thirteen points (abbreviated here) as an example:

- Wealth is only weakly related to happiness both within and across nations, particularly when income is above the poverty level.

- Activities that make people happy in small doses – such as shopping, good food and making money – do not lead to fulfilment in the long term, indicating that these have quickly diminishing returns.

- Engaging in an experience that produces 'flow' is so gratifying that people are willing to do it for its own sake, rather than for what they will get out of it. Flow is experienced when one's skills are sufficient for a challenging activity, in the pursuit of a clear goal, when immediate self-awareness disappears, and sense of time is distorted.

- People who express gratitude on a regular basis have better physical health, optimism, progress toward goals, well-being, and help others more.

- Trying to maximize happiness can lead to unhappiness.

- People who witness others perform good deeds experience an emotion called 'elevation' and this motivates them to perform their own good deeds.

- Optimism can protect people from mental and physical illness.

- People who are optimistic or happy have better performance in work, school and sports, are less depressed, have fewer physical health problems, and have better relationships with other people. Further optimism can be measured and it can be learned.

- People who report more positive emotions in young adulthood live longer and healthier lives.

- Physicians experiencing positive emotions tend to make more accurate diagnoses.

- Healthy human development can take place under conditions of even great adversity due to a process of resilience that is common and completely ordinary.

- Individuals who write about traumatic events are physically healthier than control groups that do not. Writing about life goals is significantly less distressing than writing about trauma, and is associated with enhanced well-being.

- People are unable to predict how long they will be happy or sad following an important event.

Myers (1993), a prolific writer in this area, has suggestions for a happier life:

1 **Realise that enduring happiness does not come from success.** People adapt to changing circumstances – even to wealth or a disability. Thus wealth is life health: its utter absence breeds misery, but having it (or any circumstances we long for) does not guarantee happiness.

2 **Take control of your time.** Happy people feel in control of their lives. To master your use of time, set goals and break them into daily aims. Although we often overestimate how much we will accomplish in any given day (leaving us frustrated) we generally underestimate how much we can accomplish in a year, given just a little progress every day.

3　**Act happy.** We can sometimes act ourselves into a happier frame of mind. Manipulated into a smiling expression, people feel better; when they scowl, the whole world seems to scowl back. So put on a happy face. Talk as if you feel positive self-esteem, are optimistic and are outgoing. Going through the motions can trigger the emotions.

4　**Seek work and leisure that engages your skills.** Happy people often are in a zone called 'flow' – absorbed in tasks that challenge but do not overwhelm them. The most expensive forms of leisure (sitting on a yacht) often provide less flow experience than gardening, socialising or craft work.

5　**Join the 'movement' movement.** An avalanche of research reveals that aerobic exercise can relieve mild depression and anxiety as it promotes health and energy. Sound minds reside in sound bodies.

6　**Give your body the sleep it wants.** Happy people live active vigorous lives yet reserve time for renewing sleep and solitude. Many people suffer from a sleep debt, with resulting fatigue, diminished alertness and gloomy moods.

7　**Give priority to close relationships.** Intimate friendships with those who care deeply about you can help you weather difficult times. Confiding is good for soul and body. Resolve to nurture your closest relationship by not taking your loved ones for granted, by displaying to them the sort of kindness you display to others, by affirming them, by playing together and sharing together. To rejuvenate your affections, resolve in such ways to act lovingly.

8　**Focus beyond the self.** Reach out to those in need. Happiness increases helpfulness (those who feel good do good). But doing good also makes one feel good.

9 **Keep a gratitude journal.** Those who pause each day to reflect on some positive aspect of their lives (their health, friends, family, freedom, education, senses, natural surroundings and so on) experience heightened well-being.

But note: not doing all of the above does not lead to anxiety or depression. Other things do. The data reveal the following:

Compared to unhappy people, but matched on other criteria such as education, experience, skills:

- happier people get better jobs – those with more autonomy, variety and meaning;
- happier CEOs have happier people working for them;
- happier people show better job performance;
- happier people make more money.

These findings occur across jobs from counsellors to cricketers and in different countries studying everyone from German business people to Malaysian farmers.

So what explains these findings? Why is there a connection between positive moods, a sense of well-being, happiness and work success? There seem to be various different factors.

- **Focus and distraction.** Unhappy people are too prone to taking their eye off the ball at work. They tend to be more self-obsessed and not as vigilant about the needs of others, be they colleagues or customers.
- **Memory.** The mood-conjuring effect is well established. People in a good mood recall more positive things and vice versa. Hence we get

virtuous and vicious cycles. Positive people recall happy customers and co-operative peers; unhappy people never let go of their negative experiences. Positive people put in more effort to achieve the positive results they recall.

- **Decision making.** People with sunny dispositions make better decisions: they are faster, more accurate and more inclusive. Unhappy people are too 'hung up' about small, irrelevant issues and alienate those who are trying to help them. Optimistic people believe that problems are solvable and that they can (with help) make good decisions. The pessimists are hapless, hopeless and helpless and often either procrastinate or make poorer decisions than the optimists.

- **Evaluating others.** We all know bosses are best avoided when they are in a bad mood, particularly for annual appraisals. People in a good mood are more encouraging, more forgiving, more tolerant of others and their 'little foibles'. Negative moods are associated with blaming and attacking others rather than helping them. Negative people make bad colleagues and team members.

- **Co-operating.** Good moods make people more generous, more co-operative, more helpful. People in a good mood tend to deflate crises and resolve conflicts. Those in a bad mood increase conflict.

In this book we are interested in both happiness and unhappiness at work, which we shall call disenchantment (see Chapter 3). But the story of job satisfaction and dissatisfaction is not the same. What leads to the one has little effect on the other. The factors that prevent dissatisfaction are not the same as those that drive satisfaction.

Two–factor theory and enchantment

If you ask people to nominate all the psychologists they have ever heard of, you get a familiar list. Everyone has heard of Freud, who many still think a sex maniac. Others mention Jung, particularly because they have done a test (the Myers Briggs Type Inventores (MBTI)) supposedly derived from his ideas. Most have also heard of Maslow and his famous hierarchy of needs.

A surprising number of people have also heard of Herzberg (Herzberg et al. 1959) and his two-factor theory that states that very different things cause job satisfaction and dissatisfaction. Most remember the supposedly counter-intuitive idea that money is not a motivator but only a potential de-motivator at work. But Herzberg and his colleagues pre-dated Bradburn in this all-important discovery.

Over fifty years ago a group of psychologists lead by Herzberg were to develop a theory of great consequence. The two-factor theory states that there are certain factors in the workplace that cause job satisfaction, while a separate set of factors cause dissatisfaction. The researchers found job characteristics that related to what an individual *does* at work have the capacity to gratify specific needs such as achievement, competency and personal worth, leading to happiness and satisfaction. However, the *absence* of such specific job characteristics did not appear to lead to unhappiness and dissatisfaction. However, dissatisfaction resulted from other very specific factors such as company policies, supervision, salary, interpersonal relations on the job and working conditions.

The two-factor theory then distinguishes between:

Motivating factors – such as challenging work, recognition for one's achievement, being given responsibility, the opportunity to do something meaningful, involvement in decision making, a sense of

> importance to an organisation together give positive satisfaction, arising from intrinsic conditions of the job itself, such as recognition, achievement or personal growth.
>
> **Hygiene factors** – such as job security, salary, fringe benefits, working conditions, good pay, paid insurance, vacations – paradoxically do not give positive satisfaction or motivation, though dissatisfaction results from their absence. The term 'hygiene' is used in the sense that these are maintenance factors. These are extrinsic to the work itself, and include aspects such as company policies, supervisory practices or wages/salary.

According to Herzberg, it is the absence of hygiene factors that causes dissatisfaction among employees in a workplace. *In order to remove dissatisfaction in a work environment, barriers to these hygiene factors must be eliminated.* There are several ways that this can be done but some of the most important ways to decrease dissatisfaction would be to pay reasonable wages, ensure employees job security and to create a positive culture in the workplace. Herzberg and his team rank-ordered the following hygiene factors from highest to lowest importance: company policy, supervision, employee's relationship with their boss, work conditions, salary and relationships with peers.

Herzberg distinguished between two types of work: performing work-related action because you feel you *have* to is classed as 'movement', but if you perform a work-related action because you *want* to then that is classed as 'motivation'.

Most importantly, Herzberg thought it was imperative to eliminate job dissatisfaction before going on to creating conditions for job satisfaction because they would work against each other. According to the two-factor theory there are four possible combinations:

1   **High hygiene + high motivation** – the ideal situation where
    employees are highly motivated.

2   **High hygiene + low motivation** – employees have few complaints
    but are not highly motivated and therefore under-productive.

3   **Low hygiene + high motivation** – an unusual situation where
    employees are motivated but unhappy with various aspects of their
    work environment.

4   **Low hygiene + low motivation** – this is the most undesirable
    situation where you have unhappy and unproductive staff.

The theory says nothing about individual differences; some people may be strongly in favour of job enrichment and others strongly against it. Indeed modern writers believe the theory should be laid to rest. This is no doubt attributable to the fact that various methodological errors were introduced into the early theory-testing work. These included the real possibility that all the results were classic attribution errors, such that personal failure is attributed externally (to hygiene factors) and success internally (to motivation factors). Secondly, the theory-testing work was nearly all done on white-collar workers (accountants and engineers) who are hardly representative of the working population.

Essentially, five objections are frequently made:

1   **Selective bias and defensive behaviour.** Responses to critical
    incident questions may 'selectively recall' situational factors and
    project failures to external factors.

2   **Method dependency.** When there are variations in methodology
    (questionnaires, interviews or behavioural observations), different
    results are obtained. This suggests that results are dependent on how
    information is gathered, as much as what that information is.

3 **Assumption about the nature and measurement of satisfaction.** There appears to be substantial evidence questioning the dual-factor argument that hygiene factors lead only to dissatisfaction when absent and motivators are only capable of providing satisfaction.

4 **Individual variations.** Evidence leads to questions of how well the theory applies to all people in different gender, socio-economic, cultural and age categories, and so on.

5 **Organizational differences.** Effects of the two-factor theory vary with the climate of the organization within which it is implemented.

These are 'academic' points, because although we now call the two factors *intrinsic* and *extrinsic* motivation, the above points apply. However there is one point that nearly everyone remembers from Herzberg and which is clearly correct. *Money has more power to demotivate than motivate.* It is a disenchanter not an enchanter.

The essential point for the two-factor theory is that the factors that lead to enchantment are different from those that lead to disenchantment. Those that prevent disenchantment are not the same as those that facilitate enchantment. Moreover it is surprising how quickly a person can be changed from the one to the other.

Money, motivation and disenchantment

One topic that never goes away is money, and more importantly its ability to motivate the average worker. Hard-bitten middle managers believe money is the most powerful motivator. Paradoxically, it is nearly always those who do not have it in their power to be motivated by monetary rewards that believe this to be the case. And by contrast, the people who have control over the purse strings may not regard money as very relevant.

Does money motivate people? Is money a consistent and powerful motivator or work performance? What of economic motivation?

Classical organization theorists assumed that workers had to be driven to work by the carrot and the stick, which may often have been true during the Industrial Revolution. A similar view has been taken by most economists, with their concept of 'economic man'. Occupational psychologists reacted very strongly to these views, and in some books failed to discuss economic incentives at all. The psychologists cite support from surveys in which workers were asked which factors were most important in making a job good or bad – 'pay' commonly came sixth or seventh after 'security', 'co-workers', 'interesting work' or 'welfare arrangements'. This has been confirmed in more recent surveys which have found that pensions and other benefits are valued more.

The basic psychology of incentives is that behaviour can be influenced if it is linked to some desired reward. Speed of work is an example. There is little doubt that people work harder when paid by results than when paid by the time they put in. Other studies have shown the effects of an incentive plan for reducing absenteeism, which fell at once as soon as the plan was introduced, and which rose again when it was discontinued. There is also evidence that money can act as an incentive for people to stay with their organization.

In a pay for performance system, performance may be measured by piecework, group piecework, measured day work or performance/merit appraisal and 'pay' may include profit sharing. Often the competitiveness that characterizes these systems causes problems.

But the simple fact is that money is but one motivator. Job security, a pleasant environment or a considerate boss are all motivators as well. Consider the following: Would you prefer $1,000 (tax free) or a week's extra holiday? $1,000 or a new job title? $5,000 or a job guarantee for life? $1,000 or meaningful and intrinsically satisfying work? Put like that, as a choice between money alone versus other motivators, the power of money declines.

If, indeed, money *is* a powerful motivator or satisfier at work, why has research consistently shown that there is no relationship between wealth and happiness? In fact there are four good reasons why this is so:

1 **Adaptation** – although everybody feels 'happier' after a pay rise, windfall or pools win, one soon adapts to this and the effect very rapidly disappears.

2 **Comparison** – people define themselves as rich/wealthy by comparing themselves to others. However, with increased wealth, people usually move in more 'up-market' circles where there is always someone wealthier than themselves.

3 **Alternatives** – as economists say, the declining marginal utility of money means that as one has more of it, other things like freedom and true friendship seem much more valuable.

4 **Worry** – an increased income is associated with a shifting of concern from money issues to the more uncontrollable elements of life (e.g. self-development), perhaps because money is associated with a sense of control over one's fate.

Money clearly does not always bring happiness. People with ten million pounds are no happier than people with only nine million dollars. Yet, everyone wants more money. Economists are right: money does act as a work motivator, but to a large extent *in the short term, for some workers more than others* and at a cost often to the morale of the organization. Psychologists are also correct – money is only one of many motivators of behaviour.

The main value of money is that one lives in a world in which it is overestimated. It does not buy friends, merely a better class of enemy. The accumulation of money does not end people's troubles, it merely changes them.

The power of money as a motivator is short-lived. Furthermore, it has less effect the more comfortable people are. The famous French philosopher Camus was right when he said it is a kind of spiritual snobbery to believe people can be happy without money. But given earning a modest or average amount, the value of other work benefits become greater. Kohn (1993) offers six reasons why this seemingly backward conclusion is, in fact, the case:

1   **Pay is not a motivator**. Whilst the reduction of a salary is a demotivator, there is little evidence that increasing salary has anything but a transitory impact on motivation. It was pointed out fifty years ago that just because too little money can irritate and demotivate does not mean that more money will bring about increased satisfaction, much less increased motivation.

2   **Rewards punish**. Rewards can have a punitive effect because they, like outright punishment, are manipulative. Any reward itself may be highly desired; but by making that bonus contingent on certain behaviours, managers manipulate their subordinates. This experience of being controlled is likely to assume a punitive quality over time. Thus the withholding of an expected reward feels very much like punishment.

3   **Rewards rupture relationships**. Incentive programmes tend to pit one person against another, which can lead to all kinds of negative repercussions as people undermine each other. This threatens good teamwork.

4   **Rewards ignore reasons**. Managers sometimes use incentive systems as a substitute for giving workers what they need to do a good job, such as useful feedback, social support or autonomy. Offering a bonus to employees and waiting for the results requires much less input and effort.

5   **Rewards discourage risk taking**. People working for a reward generally try to minimise challenge and tend to lower their sights

when they are encouraged to think about what they are going to get for their efforts.

6 **Rewards undermine interest**. Extrinsic motivators are a poor substitute for genuine interest in one's job. The more a manager stresses what an employee can earn for good work, the less interested that employee will be in the work itself. If people feel they need to be 'bribed' to do something, it is not something they would ordinarily want to do.

So pay people market rates and ensure their pay is equitable. That is about the best you can do to achieve happiness. But get it wrong and you are on the path to serious disenchantment

Enchantment and disenchantment

Most people start a job happy enough and determined 'to do a good job.' If they are lucky they have found a job which suits their skills and values. It would be disingenuous to suggest they go to work enchanted. They may be eager, hopeful and willing to be engaged. Some suddenly discover they have made a mistake: the job is not for them. If they are wise they quickly move on. Others discover they have made a very good choice and that the nature of the work and the way they are managed works very well for them.

There is a theory which talks to the concept of fit. It suggests that there are various stages:

Attraction. People are attracted to all sorts of jobs for different reasons. Their personality, their values and their motives might influence this. Clearly some jobs are more attractive than others. Few people want to become a street cleaner and rather a lot an actor. Thus some people want to become a dentist and others a pilot. The better informed they are about their abilities and the skills required to do the job the more likely they are to find a good fit.

Selection. Most selectors have a very clear idea of the sort of person they want for the job. This involves ability, personality and values but might include other factors such as health or lifestyle.

Socialization. Having been selected, job holders are taught implicitly and explicitly how to behave at work. This may involve everything from how the speak and dress to what skills and attitudes they need to develop.

Attrition. People relatively soon discover that the job is not for them. If they wisely and quickly resign, they can start a search for one better suited to their needs and values.

The fortunate ones get into a virtuous cycle. They discover their strengths, they are well managed, they are given reasonable autonomy and they are productive. This can lead to a strong intrinsic motivation, energy, flow and passion (see Chapter 2). This can be witnessed in a number of jobs.

Some stay at their job and work hard because, almost exclusively, of extrinsic factors. This usually means they are very well paid. They might be stressed and even bored but are willing to trade-off extrinsic for intrinsic factors.

Alas, however, it is more common to see disenchantment. Of course, some people are carriers of gloom and negativity and hence fairly easily disenchanted by many things in life, not only their work experiences. For many people things happen along the way to cause temporary disenchantment: the nasty boss, the badly executed merger and acquisition, the sudden threat of redundancy. But there seem to be related and identifiable behaviours that very clearly lead to disenchantment, and this is the topic of this book.

There is a debate in the literature on the dark side of behaviour at work between 'the bad apple' and 'the bad barrel' hypothesis. That is, when 'bad things' happen at work in the form of counter productive work behaviour (such as arson, theft or fraud) it is due to the characteristics of individual (bad apples/people) or bad organizations (bad barrels/firms). The answer is naturally a mixture of the two, though many organizations want to blame the individual. They refuse to accept the possibility that they turn people bad.

The same is true of disenchantment. There have been, and will always be, people in the workplace who are negative, disaffected and dissatisfied. Further, they can spread their gloom and doom among others. But there are probably many more who are not like this but made disenchanted, alienated and dissatisfied by the way they have been treated by those who manage them. This book describes the crucial issues that lead to disenchantment and which can be avoided.

Conclusion

It has been shown that the opposite of happiness is not unhappiness at work, in the sense that (a) because people are not happy (at work) does not necessarily mean they are unhappy and (b) that very different factors seem to cause happiness than unhappiness. Most people start a job with hope and a positive attitude. They are attracted to a particular occupation and a particular organization for many reasons. They, like the selectors, hope for a 'good fit' so that the employee is happy and productive and the employer satisfied with the contribution of the employee. Many factors contribute to a person's satisfaction at work.

However it is the experience of many that 'things go wrong'. These may be major or minor, long- or short-term. Life has its disappointments: you are not promoted as quickly as you would wish; your salary does not match those of friends in other organizations; you and your boss appear not to be 'on the same page'. But occasionally things occur which have more serious consequences and these lead to disenchantment. This book is about what these factors are and how, when and why this occurs.

2

The Nature of Work Motivation: Passion, Energy, Flow and Enchantment

If passion drives you, let reason hold the reins.

BENJAMIN FRANKLIN

When I meet successful people I ask about 100 questions to find out who they attribute their success to. It is usually the same: persistence, hard work and hiring good people.

KIANA TOM

The difference between ordinary and extraordinary is that little extra.

JIMMY JOHNSON

My grandfather once told me that there were two kinds of people: those who do the work and those who take the credit. He told me to try to be in the first group; there was much less competition.

INDIRA GANDHI

Introduction

Noel Coward said that 'work was more fun than fun'. Good work can be the most fulfilling thing that one can do. It can be utterly absorbing: it can give a profound sense of satisfaction.

Some, who are deeply intrinsically motivated to do what they do, often claim that they have never done a day's work in their lives because they have never done anything which even vaguely represents the feeling of doing work. There are few demands, no dullness or drudgery. They are fully engaged, energized and enchanted by the activity. Time flies by because they are fully absorbed. They are doing what they are good at; and getting better at it. They are exploring their strengths.

Of course all work, however enchanting, has its downsides. Things have to be done, bills paid, assignments delivered. But the enchanting job is a low demands, high control job which allows one to exploit and explore personal gifts. Curiously, it is not doctors and teachers that report most enchantment: it is more often artisans who make things. Painters and potters, artists and actors, writers and musicians are amongst the happiest people, though many get very poorly paid.

Most managers are deeply concerned with how to make their staff more motivated. They often want a quick-fix, cheap, magic-bullet solution which ensures they have happy, healthy staff happy and willing to 'go the extra mile', to always pitch-up and pitch-in, and appear happy at work.

The question is why some people are happier than others at work? Are workers happier when they get to work in quirky offices, surrounded by beanbag chairs, coffee machines and high-spec technology? Has it got primarily to do with their personality and values; is it the nature of the job; the perfection of the 'fit' (round peg, round hole); or the way they are managed?

Happy people

Are there happy and unhappy people at, and out, of work. They are called 'life enhancers' vs 'heart-sinking'; or 'radiators' vs 'drains'. As we mentioned in the previous chapter, there are workers who are carriers of optimism or gloom. There is something to this hypothesis as studies have shown that personality is strongly related to job satisfaction and that the former is both heritable and stable. There are the enchanted: by life, work, other people and the world around them. Equally there are the disenchanted: those who seem uninterested and unmotivated by practically everything.

We know that there are very consistent correlations between some personality traits and job satisfaction. Extroverts are optimists, sociable and stimulus speaking. They tend to be happier than introverts, in part because they are able to get more social support. Neurotics or those with low emotional adjustment tend to be unhappy, negativistic and prone to both anxiety and depression. Additionally, agreeable workers are more considerate, co-operative and sympathetic. They tend to give others the benefit of the doubt and are quick to forgive transgressions. As a result, they do not get hung up on negativity, do not hold grudges and are happier with their work and those they work with.

Whilst it is clearly true that there are dispositional correlates of enchantment, it is not enough to explain the issue satisfactorily. Enchantment and disenchantment are temporary phenomenon. The research shows that people can go from one to the other in the workplace quite quickly. To understand enchantment at work, it is necessary to think beyond the individual.

The job itself

There are some dirty, dangerous, boring and badly paid jobs that many imagine nobody could be happy in. Traffic wardens who go out in all weathers and get frequently assaulted and abused; garbage collectors; those who service complaint desks; security staff. Whilst it is true that, quite simply, some jobs are considerably more attractive than others, there is still a lot of variability between people. It is noticeable that some people seem very happy at, and contented by, what others would judge as tedious and monotonous jobs.

Some jobs are well-paid, secure and interesting. They grip the 'spark' of their employees and challenge them each day to fully utilize their skills. Some are the opposite, where workers have many demands and little control. Workers are left feeling devalued and deflated as a result of what they do.

The person–job fit

The central quest of vocational psychology is to help people find work which fits with their abilities, preferences and values. The theory suggests that if indeed you get a round peg in a round whole you will ensure job satisfaction. Whereas that is clearly true, there are people who seem to have no optimal work or job. This particular profile of an individual means they do not fit any obvious job. The following idea is taken from Furnham and Taylor (2011).

Vocational psychology hopes, in part, to help people find the right job for them. The idea is that the individual finds a job that suits their abilities, personality and values; a place where they can thrive.

Box A:　Both employer and employee agree and feel the fit is right. This is the condition to strive for, though it is often based on perceptions and intuition rather than real data. These people may be enchanted, but at least will be happy.

Box B:　The employer feels the employee is good, but the employee is not content. This will lead ideally to the employee's resignation. Problems will develop if the employee stays on and the organization does not change. It feels a poor fit or a far from ideal job.

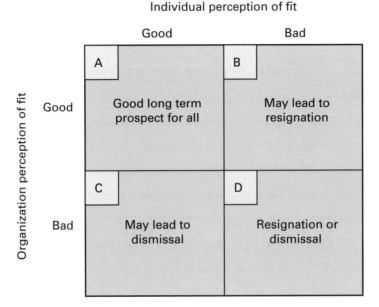

FIGURE 2.1

Box C: Here the employee feels he is in the right job, but this view is not shared by the employer. This should lead to dismissal, but all too often this does not happen; the employee does not receive promotion or similar bonuses as his peers and begins to feel disappointment and then resentment.

Box D: Again both employer and employee agree and there should be an easy resolution. It is probably best to let the employee resign and thus retain dignity. If engineered properly the employee will leave feeling positive about the organization, which treated him well and fairly.

There are various problems with this simple model.

1 **Fit is multidimensional**. Both potential employer and employee see fit of various facets as various levels. Employees are interested in many job features both intrinsic and extrinsic: benefits and compensation, job security, training, maternity and crèche facilities,

etc. The employer is after able, motivated, flexible staff. Thus there may be a perfect fit on one level/facet but not others. Hence both have to compromize in some cost-benefit analysis.

2   **Fit is dynamic.** Just as people find they change their interests, values and attitudes over time, so do organizations. The latter can change radically from their core business to their organizational structure. Many divorces occur because the partners change: once highly compatible they become incompatible. So too, as individuals and organizations change, the more likely fit is to turn into misfit.

3   **Fit is hard to determine.** Neither interviewer nor interviewee are totally honest at interview. Errors of omission and commission mean that neither side are comprehensive in how they present themselves. The tendency is to emphasize the positive. In this sense it can be difficult for both parties to actually determine their degree or level of fit.

4   **Fit may be impossible to articulate.** Neither employer nor employees always have a very good insight into their motives and needs. It is not that they are necessarily hiding something; rather they cannot always accurately and sensitively report on those factors that drive them. In this sense fit or misfit only become clear over time though even then it may be almost impossible for people at work to articulate precisely how this occurs.

Of course this is not the inevitable consequence of selecting the wrong people. People do not easily fit into such neat categories. Employees are often a near fit or near misfit. The issue then becomes one of performance. Where the recruiters have got it right employee performance will be maximized. Where they do not quite make the right choices performance is variable. This is recognized and accepted by organizations. But individuals often feel they are not appreciated and where they are in a high performance business, they often disagree with the labels given them.

In this chapter we will examine various concepts linked to the concept of enchantment. There are indeed many concepts associated with positive emotions at work. For instance, McManus and Furnham (2010) investigated the concept of *fun* and found five clear types of fun labelled: sociability, contentment, achievement, sensual and ecstatic.

Others have used the concept of *thriving at work*, defined as having a sense of vitality and a sense of learning at work. Spreitzer and co-workers (2005) differentiated their concept of thriving from other related constructs such as flourishing, flow, self-actualisation and subjective well-being. They argued that agentic work behaviours – such as being task focused, having a sense of exploration and heeding the well-being of others – leads to thriving at work, which in turn leads to positive outcomes for both the individual and the organization.

Management practices

Psychologists are quite rightly often accused of an attribution error. This involves attributing all sorts of phenomena to the (internal) characteristics of individuals. So, dispositionally happy people are happy at work and vice versa. Yet we know from thousands of exit interviews, people say they leave managers not organizations. They leave managers who are distant, negative or bullying. Equally they stay with, support and feel supported by managers who take an interest in them, who find and nurture their strengths and support their hopes and aspirations. In short, just as a good teacher could enchant pupils ensuring their abiding interest in the subject they teach so some can put off people for life. The same is true of managers. Indeed, we believe it is five core management practices and organisational processes that are primarily responsible for disenchantment. But first, we will examine four well established concepts which give a clue about the nature of enchantment.

Passion at work

Over a twenty-year period Vallerand and colleagues worked on the psychology of passion. Vallerand (2008: 1) defined passion as *a* 'strong inclination toward an activity that people like, find important and in which they invest their time and energy'. The idea is that over time people discover that some activities rather than others seem to satisfy their needs for competence, autonomy and relatedness. These thus become a passionate, self-defining, identity-determining activity into which people put their time and energy. Passion has powerful affective outcomes and relates strongly to the persistence in various activities.

Earlier, Smilor (1997: 342) defined it as 'the enthusiasm, joy, and even zeal that come from the energetic and unflagging pursuit of a worthy, challenging and uplifting purpose'. Passion is not thought of as a primary emotion, though it is conceived as a compelling and overwhelming feeling of desire.

Most importantly Vallerand distinguished between healthy *harmonious* and unhealthy *obsessive passion*. He suggests harmonious passion is the autonomous internalisation of an activity into a person's identity, when they freely accept the activity as important for them. It is done with volition, and not compunction. Harmonious passion for an activity is a significant but not overpowering part of identity, and in harmony with other aspects of a person's life.

On the other hand, the drivers of obsessive passion are essentially specific contingencies, such as self-esteem, excitement or self-acceptance. They feel compelled to engage in particular activities because of these contingencies that then come to control them. Obsessive passion clearly has an addictive quality about it because it is perhaps the only source of important psychological rewards. In this sense workaholism is a sign of obsessive passion, and not harmonious passion.

The theory suggests that harmonious passion leads to more *flexible* task engagement which in turn leads to more employee engagement through the process of absorption, concentration, flow and positive effect. Obsessive passion on the other hand leads to more *rigid and conflicted* task performance, which in turn reduces engagement. Harmonious passion controls the activity; obsessive passion is controlled by it. The former promotes healthy adaptation, while the latter thwarts it.

Vallerand and Houlfort (2003) developed a scale to measure these two dimensions of passion, referring to particular activities such as reading or team sports. Items that reflect harmonious passion include 'I am completely taken with this activity' and 'This activity reflects the qualities I like about myself', while obsessive passion items include 'I am emotionally dependent on this activity' and 'my mood depends on me being able to do this activity'.

Vallerand and colleagues have reported many experimental studies that help explain the process. Vallerand and co-workers (2007) showed that harmonious passion was directly related to activity investment and predicted deliberate practice and mastery goals, which had an important effect on performance outcomes. Thus while harmonious passion ultimately leads to positive performance, the opposite has been true of obsessive passion.

Various empirical studies have confirmed many of Vallerand's hypotheses. For instance, Phillippe, Vallerand and Lavigne (2009) showed that harmonious passion, but not obsessive passion, was related to both *hedonic* (seeking pleasure and avoiding pain) and *eudaimonic* (meaning and self-realisation) well-being. Further, they showed harmonious passion actually increased a person's sense of vitality over time. Similarly, in a study of older adults over time Rousseau and Vallerand (2008) showed that harmonious passion increased activity engagement, which was related to subjective well-being, while obsessive passion had the opposite effect. In a diary study, Mageau and Vallerand (2007) were able to demonstrate how passion moderated the relationship between activity engagement and positive affect.

Lafreniere and co-workers (2011) showed people with relatively high self-esteem experienced higher levels of harmonious passion, given their use of their adaptive self-regulatory strategies. Conversely, people with low self-esteem, given their ego fragility and defensiveness, were found to experience higher levels of obsessive passion.

Vallerand has applied his idea successfully to the world of sport where it has been shown harmonious passion is positively – and obsessive passion negatively – associated with measures of attainment in various sports. The ideas have also been successfully applied to understanding why people persevere with activities that are detrimental to their health, including: cyclists who compulsively train in Quebec during winter, even on icy roads; continually training whilst injured, leading to chronic pain and injury; and sustained gambling behaviour that leads to pathological addiction.

This work has also been applied to behaviour in the workplace. Vallerand and Houlfort (2003) developed a relatively simple model that suggests harmonious passion, but not obsessive passion, predicted psychological adjustment at work. They argue that passion has long-term consequences. Obsessive workers seem akin to workaholics, while harmonious passion workers show greater job satisfaction and performance. Obsessive passion is related to greater negative emotion at work, greater work–family conflict, higher employee turnover and lower performance, as well as reduced physical and psychological health. Vallerand and co-workers (2010) showed harmonious passion was positively correlated with work satisfaction, which in turn was negatively correlated with burnout. Obsessive passion, however, was strongly correlated with conflict, which positively correlated with burnout.

The question is *how* can organizations encourage harmonious passion, rather than obsessive passion? Vallerand (2010: 294) stated that the answer is to: 'provide employees with a healthy, flexible, and secure working environment, one where their opinion is valued, will create conditions that facilitate the development of harmonious passion . . . organizational support seems to foster an autonomous-supportive context that allows individuals to internalize the activity in their identity in an autonomous fashion'.

Others have been inspired by Vallerand's work. Thus, Burke and Fiskenbaum (2009) administered a questionnaire that measured 'feeling driven to work because of inner pressure' and 'work enjoyment', which they called *passion* and *addiction* to different groups in Australia, Canada and Norway. They found that those who scored higher on passion than addiction were more heavily invested in their work, and more job satisfied while showing less work obsessive behaviours and higher psychological well-being. Equally Gorgievski and Bakker (2010) distinguished between *work engagement* and *workaholism*. To be in a job that offers harmonious passion is therefore ideal. It offers the opportunity of enchantment.

Energy and vigour at work

Energy is a very desirable characteristic. It is associated with youth and health and happiness. People remark on the energy of the workplace as a sign of health. The lethargic, flat-battery organization is a very unattractive place to work. Work can drain you, sap your energy, but it can also invigorate. Personal energy is equally important and has various components:

1 **Physical energy.** Older people have less energy than younger people. Sick people have less energy than well people. Sleep deprived people are less energetic than the well-rested.

2 **Psychological energy.** This has been conceived of in different ways. The Freudians conceived psychic energy as: a force, that drives us to want and do things we barely understand. Thus we can be driven to a-rational, irrational or bizarre behaviours because of these unconscious libidinous springs.

3 **Intellectual energy.** The bright have more intellectual energy: more curiosity, more openness-to-new-experience. They use their energy

more efficiently. Indeed, one definition of intelligence is about energy efficient brain processing.

Personality factors are related to energy. Extroverts appear more (socially) energetic but burn up easily with their impulsivity and impatience. Introverts have a much slower burning fuse and are able to sustain longer periods of attentiveness under conditions of poor arousal. Neurotics waste their energy, burning it up on the irrelevant and the imaginary. They can easily become anxious, then depressed, by small things. They fritter away their additional nervous energy rather than conserve it for the long haul or the really important. Paradoxically then, they appear to have more energy than their stable opposites, but waste it on worry.

There is an academic literature on vigour. Shirom (2011) has defined this as physical strength, emotional energy and cognitive liveliness. He argues that genetic, physiological and psychological factors influence vigour which in turn is related to job performance and satisfaction, as well as physical and mental health. He sees vigour as a personal resource, like optimism and self-efficacy related to energy and the way it can be directed in the workplace. His argument is that vigour predicts interaction with others at work, leadership style as well as group processes, and the use of organizational resources to be successful at work.

Flow at work

Over fifteen years ago, Csíkszentmihályi (1975) wrote a book called *Flow*. His research involved watching and talking to people who were creative and successful in various fields from rock climbing to rock music. He also introduced a method called *experience sampling*. People would carry around a beeper, and eight times a day as this went off the carriers were required to write down immediately both what they were doing and how they were feeling.

People felt best, he found, when *engrossed* in some challenging activity. During flow, they lost track of time, felt more capable, more sensitive and more self-confident even though the activities may be work-based challenges. The activity was its own reward: intrinsically motivating. Flow banishes depression, distraction and creeping dispiritedness. So what are the preconditions of flow?

Csíkszentmihályi identified the following factors as accompanying an experience of flow:

1 **Clear goals** (expectations and rules are discernible and goals are attainable and align appropriately with one's skill set and abilities). The challenge level and skill level should both be high.

2 **Concentrating,** a high degree of concentration on a limited field of attention (a person engaged in the activity will have the opportunity to focus and to delve deeply into it).

3 **A loss of the feeling of self-consciousness,** the merging of action and awareness.

4 **Distorted sense of time,** one's subjective experience of time is altered.

5 Direct and immediate **feedback** (successes and failures in the course of the activity are apparent, so that behaviour can be adjusted as needed).

6 **Balance between ability level and challenge** (the activity is neither too easy nor too difficult).

7 A sense of personal **control** over the situation or activity.

8 The activity is **intrinsically rewarding,** so there is an effortlessness of action.

9 **A lack of awareness of bodily needs** (to the extent that one can reach a point of great hunger or fatigue without realising it).

10 **Absorption into the activity**, by the narrowing of the focus of awareness into the activity itself, called **action awareness merging**.

Vallerand (2008) believed flow was the consequence of (harmonious) passion. Thus, for flow to be experienced at work a person needs: a clear goal in mind; reasonable expectations of completing satisfactorily the goal in mind; the ability to concentrate; being given regular and specific feedback on their performance; and having the appropriate skills to complete the task.

One can observe flow in those jobs where people experience greatest work satisfaction. They include mainly artisans – potters and painters, writers and weavers, thatchers and designers. They exercise their talents, work at their own pace, and are the opposite of those 'alienated from the products of their labours'. Indeed they are the products of their labour. They are what they produce. They are bound-up in the product. Their identity, their being, are in the product of their talents.

Drive at work

In 2010 Daniel Pink wrote a book entitled *Drive: The Surprising Truth About What Motivates Us*. It turned out to be a best seller. He acknowledges as a science journalist that most of the ideas are not his but mainly derived from the self-determination theory developed by Deci and Ryan. The book is written and the message clear. Carrot-and-stick motivation does not work anymore.

Pink proposes that businesses should adopt a revised approach to motivation which fits more closely with modern jobs and businesses, one based on the self-determination theory that human beings have an innate drive to be autonomous, self-determined and connected to one another, and that when that drive is liberated, people achieve more and live richer lives. Organizations should focus on these drives when managing their human capital by creating settings which focus on *our innate need to direct our own lives (autonomy), to learn and create new things (mastery), and to do better by ourselves and our world (purpose).*

The three components of the theory with appropriate recommendations are:

1 **Autonomy and empowerment** – provide employees with autonomy over some (or all) of the four main aspects of work:

- When they do it (time) – consider switching to a ROWE (results-only work environment) which focuses more on the output (result) rather than the time/schedule, allowing employees to have flexibility over when they complete tasks.

- How they do it (technique) – do not dictate how employees should complete their tasks. Provide initial guidance and then allow them to tackle the project in the way they see fit rather than having to follow a strict procedure.

- Whom they do it with (team) – although this can be the hardest form of autonomy to embrace, allow employees some choice over who they work with. If it would be inappropriate to involve them in the recruitment/selection process, instead allow employees to work on open-source projects where they have the ability to assemble their own teams.

- What they do (task) – allow employees to have regular 'creative' days where they can work on any project/problem they wish. There is empirical evidence which shows that many new initiatives are often generated during this 'creative free time'.

2 **Mastery and competence** – allow employees to become better at something that matters to them:

- Provide 'Goldilocks tasks' – Pink uses the term 'Goldilocks tasks' to describe those tasks which are neither overly difficult nor overly simple; these tasks allow employees to extend themselves and develop their skills further. The risk of providing tasks that fall short of an employee's capabilities is boredom, and the risk of providing tasks that exceed their capabilities is anxiety.

- Create an environment where mastery is possible – to foster an environment of learning and development, four essentials are required: autonomy, clear goals, immediate feedback and 'Goldilocks tasks'.

3 **Purpose** – take steps to fulfil employees' natural desire to contribute to a cause greater and more enduring than themselves:

- Communicate the purpose – make sure employees know and understand the organization's purpose goals, not just its profit goals. Employees, who understand the purpose and vision of their organization and how their individual roles contribute to this purpose, are more likely to be satisfied in their work.

- Place equal emphasis on purpose maximization as you do on profit maximization – research shows that the attainment of profit goals has no impact on a person's well-being and actually contributes to their ill-being. Organizational and individual goals should focus on purpose as well as profit. Many successful companies are now using profit as the catalyst to pursuing purpose, rather than the objective.

- Use purpose-oriented words – talk about the organization as a united team by using words such as 'us' and 'we', this will inspire employees to talk about the organization in the same way and feel a part of the greater cause.

There is a vast literature on the self-determination theory which, as noted by Pink (above), suggests that three basic psychological needs must be satisfied to foster well-being and health. These needs are universal yet some may be more salient than others at certain times and will be expressed differently based on time, culture or experience.

Despite the theory and research receiving criticism, the self-determination theory has spread to many areas of research. It is, of all the four 'theories/ concepts' noted above, probably the one that is most rigorous and tested.

How to foster passion, energy and drive

There seems abundant evidence that the intrinsically motivated, harmoniously passionate person at work experiences vigour, flow and well-being. The question is how to pick the right people and adopt the optimal management style and corporate culture to maximize it. The literature on intrinsic motivation, passion and flow all suggest similar ideas. These include:

> **Challenge.** Goals need to be set by both worker and supervisor that involve an *optimal amount* of difficulty/challenge in attaining them. People do best when working on meaningful goals where tasks are of intermediate difficulty. They should be *stretching goals* and seen as part of a development plan. Thus, let people set personally meaningful goals and targets which relate to their self-esteem. Give them feedback so that they can see how they are doing.
>
> **Curiosity.** Activities that stimulate an employee's attention and interest are best. This means introducing novelty and stimulating questioning that takes them beyond their present skills and knowledge. Changes and challenges stimulate curiosity. The idea is to foster a sense of wonder. It is about job enrichment.
>
> **Control.** Allowing employees to have a choice in what happens. This sense of actual autonomy is most important. Leadership roles,

even temporary ones, create a higher sense of engagement and recognition. People at work need to understand cause-and-effect relationships. They need to know and believe that their effort and outcomes have real and powerful effects. But most importantly they must be able to freely choose what and how they learn.

Contribution. Most of us like to believe that we are doing something useful and meaningful at work and making a contribution to the welfare of others. People like to have pride in their work in that it shows what they are capable of but also that the products of their labour are recognized as useful.

Fun and Fantasy. Using imagination and games to promote learning in the workplace. The idea is to turn work into play.

Competition. Comparing the performance from one employee to another more as a source of feedback than in the spirit of trying to win a competition. This can however have negative consequences if it reduces co-operation.

Co-operation. Encouraging employees to help each other to achieve goals. This means working in self-organized teams. People enjoy helping as much as being helped. Co-operation improves interpersonal skills.

Recognition. Celebrating employees' accomplishments and successes. This means recognizing employees for a job well done and praise for doing a great job. Where possible, praise should be public; gather your team together for a moment and celebrate an accomplishment. Spend your day looking for and recognizing great performance.

The problem with the above, of course, is that it may not be possible with many jobs. De-skilled, repetitive jobs may not always be economically viable to re-design. However, what does seem to be the case is that management style and philosophy itself can go a long way to increasing passion in the work place, which has benefits for all.

Conclusion

As noted in the first chapter, most researchers have concentrated on the positive side of work. They have been interested in how, why and when some people appear so content, productive, even enchanted with their work. They have come up with similar, but distinguishable, concepts like drive, energy, flow and passion. Some of the researchers have described a dark or negative side to the concept, like obsessive passion or workaholism. The idea is that too much of a good thing could indeed be a bad thing.

But few of these researchers have dwelt on when and why people seem to loose drive, energy and passion. What are the factors that inhibit or indeed prevent these from occurring? This is the topic of the next chapter.

3

A Theory of
Disenchantment

The secret of happiness is not doing what one likes, but in liking what one does.

JAMES MATTHEW BARRIE

Introduction

We have argued that though some people are happier than others, and some jobs are much better than others. People usually start work positive and hopeful that they will have a motivating and pleasant job. However, there are factors that conspire to thwart their hopes; to drive them to despair and long-term disenchantment. The question is, what are these factors and how do they operate? Whilst we believe that some people are more prone to disenchantment than others, the management practices and organizational processes within some workplaces trigger disenchantment quicker and with far greater magnitude than others. The central question is, what experiences at work turn people sour; cause good people to become bad apples? In short, what are the causes of disenchantment? But first, we need to start with definitions.

Definitions

There are many different concepts in psychology that relate to how adjusted and happy people are in the work place. Work psychologists have talked about job satisfaction, job commitment, job involvement and, more recently, job engagement. How are they different and what do they add to our understanding?

Job satisfaction

This is perhaps the oldest term within the psychological literature. It is also one of the simplest to measure. Job satisfaction has usually been measured by asking people the very simple question: 'All in all, how satisfied would you say you are with your job?' However, this does not separate distinct features such that you can be satisfied with some aspects (e.g. colleagues and work hours) but dissatisfied with others (e.g. pay or your boss). Also 'satisfied' is not the same as 'interested in' or 'attracted to'; an employee may be content with their lot, but lack interest or internal drive.

There are validated questionnaires about satisfaction going back seventy years. They are usually divided into measures of general satisfaction and multiple satisfactions. For example, here is a widely used measure devised by Brayfield and Rothe (1951; the (R) means the items are reverse scored so that when totalled all items relate to satisfaction). The scale provides insight into the individual's satisfaction with their job, where higher scores indicate greater satisfaction.

Items

1. My job is like a hobby to me.
2. My job is usually interesting enough to keep me from getting bored.
3. It seems that my friends are more interested in their jobs. (R)
4. I consider my job rather unpleasant. (R)

5. I enjoy my work more than my leisure time.

6. I am often bored with my job. (R)

7. I feel fairly well satisfied with my present job.

8. Most of the time I have to force myself to go to work. (R)

9. I am satisfied with my job for the time being.

10. I feel that my job is no more interesting than others I could get. (R)

11. I definitely dislike my work. (R)

12. I feel that I am happier in my work than most other people.

13. Most days I am enthusiastic about my work.

14. Each day of work seems like it will never end. (R)

15. I like my job better than the average worker does.

16. My job is pretty uninteresting. (R)

17. I find real enjoyment in my work.

18. I am disappointed that I ever took this job. (R)

There are also other measures that try to assess very different features of the job, such as: the work itself; pay; opportunities for promotion; immediate supervisor; colleagues; and the organization as a whole. Some simply distinguish between intrinsic and extrinsic satisfaction. Do employees have a self-driven satisfaction for their work (*intrinsic*) or are they simply happy to clock-in and clock-out in return for a fair days wage (*extrinsic*)?

But it is important to note that research over the years has shown that job satisfaction is highly correlated with stable personality characteristics like neuroticism and conscientiousness. Study after study has shown clear, consistent and big correlations between job satisfaction, as conventionally measured, and personality.

Twin studies have also shown that job satisfaction seems fairly strongly heritable. Thus people are 'carriers' of satisfaction or dissatisfaction. It is not simply a response to a job but a stable disposition. Unhappy, moody, unstable people rarely like any job, whereas those with a sunny disposition like all jobs. People who are satisfied at work tend to be satisfied with other aspects of their life, and vice versa.

The result is that managers and organizations have little insight into what is driving their employee satisfaction, just how much of it there is. Are they fostering a working culture that is making their employees satisfied? Or are employees satisfied simply because they are 'satisfied people'? With the latter, it is unclear how much organizations need to do to maintain their employees satisfaction. For the intrinsically satisfied, it might not take much (or conversely, take a particularly awful) working environment for their happiness to be affected.

Job commitment

Organizational commitment may be differentiated into different types. First, there is *investment* commitment. Over time people invest in organizations not only through buying shares and through compulsory pension plans, but also through their hard work and knowledge. People talk of 'having given their best years' to an organization knowing that beyond a certain age their chances of employment or progression elsewhere become reduced. They make a cost-benefit type judgement and conclude that leaving the organization is more costly than staying in it. Employees leave when the cost of leaving is outweighed by their lack of investment in the organization.

Second, there is *value or goal congruence* and commitment. This essentially means that people perceive that their personal goals are nicely aligned to that of the organization.

Third, there is *social* commitment. For many colleagues, friends at work are very important. One's entire social network may be built around the work-place. Social identity, social support and social contact are latent benefits of the work experience. It is not unusual for the major source of a person's commitment to be other people in the organization.

Essentially organizational commitment has three separate but related components:

1 Acceptance of the explicit and implicit goals and values of the organization.

2 A willingness to work on behalf of, and exert effort for the organization.

3 Having a strong desire to remain loyal to, and affiliated with the organization.

Different authors have defined this topic rather differently. For some it indicates quite simply a sense of loyalty and continuity; a committed employee will stay working at an organization. Others like Buchanan (1974) have distinguished between three facets: job identification (adopting the values of the organization as your own), job involvement (absorption and immersion in the activities at work) and loyalty (allegiance and support for the organization and its people).

A simple scale of job commitment was devised by London and Howat (1978). As with job satisfaction, this gives insight into the level of commitment an employee has to their organization, with higher scores depicting greater commitment. This term seems popular in times of flux and upheaval, when organizations are eager to ensure that their staff remain with them:

Items

1. I would leave this agency if offered the same job with another agency. (R)

2. Barring unforeseen circumstances, I would remain in this agency indefinitely.

3. It is important that we all pull together for the good of our agency because if our agency is successful then we will be successful.

4. Although there are probably reasons for this, it is too bad salaries at our agency are so low. (R)

5. Suppose a young friend of yours has completed his or her training in your field. Even though he or she has also been offered positions of equal work and salary with several other agencies, I would still advise him or her to consider our agency.

Buchanan (1974: 533) devised a three-factor scale to measure commitment defined as 'a partisan, affective attachment to the goals and values of an organization, to one's role in relation to goals and values, and to the organization for its own sake, apart from its purely instrumental worth':

Identification

1. This organization has a fine tradition of public service.

2. If I had my life to live over again, I would still choose to work for this organization.

3. I really feel as if this organization's problems are my problems.

4. I feel a sense of pride in working for this organization.

5. The record of this organization is an example of what dedicated people can achieve.

6. I would advise a young college graduate to choose a management career in this organization.

Job Involvement

1. The major satisfaction in my life comes from my job.

2. I do what my job description requires; this organization does not have the right to expect any more. (R)

3. I don't mind spending a half-hour past quitting time if I can finish a task.

4. The most important things that happen to me involve my work.

5. I live, eat and breathe my job.

6. Most things in life are more important than my work. (R)

Loyalty

1. As long as I am doing the kind of work I enjoy, it doesn't matter what particular organization I work for. (R)

2. I feel a strong sense of loyalty toward this organization.

3. If another organization offered me more money for the same kind of work, I would almost certainly accept. (R)

4. I have always felt that this organization was a cold, unfriendly place to work. (R)

5. Over the years I have grown fond of this organization as a place to live and work.

6. Generally speaking, my career in this organization has been satisfactory.

7. I have warm feelings toward this organization as a place to live and work.

8. Based on what I know now and what I believe I can expect, I would be quite willing to spend the rest of my career with this organization.

But in many ways job commitment is an *intellectual pledge* of allegiance to an organization. People can be committed but not engaged or satisfied because of their personal circumstances (they really need a job), or because they have contractually signed up to the organization and cannot easily escape.

Commitment and loyalty does not necessarily predicate that an employee will be motivated or driven, merely that they are unlikely to abandon their organization.

Job involvement

This refers to the extent to which a person's job plays a central part in their life and in many ways defines who they are. The sort of statements that measure it include 'I am very much personally involved in my work'; 'I live, eat and breathe my job'; 'The most important things which happen to me involve my job'. This has sometimes been called intrinsic motivation.

Below is the well-known job involvement scale of Lodahl and Kejner (1965), which is extensively used in the psychological literature:

1. I'll stay overtime to finish a job, even if I'm not paid for it.

2. You can measure a person pretty well by how good a job s/he does.

3. The major satisfaction in my life comes from my job.

4. For me, mornings at work really fly by.

5. I usually show up for work a little early, to get things ready.

6. The most important things that happen to me involve my work.

7. Sometimes I lie awake at night thinking ahead to the next day.

8. I'm really a perfectionist about my work.

9. I feel depressed when I fail at something connected with my job.

10. I have other activities more important than my work. (R)

11. I live, eat, and breathe my job.

12. I would probably keep working even if I didn't need the money.

13. Quite often I feel like staying home from work instead of coming in. (R)

14. To me my work is only a small part of who I am. (R)

15. I am very much involved personally in my work.

16. I avoid taking on extra duties and responsibilities in my work. (R)

17. I used to be more ambitious about my work than I am now. (R)

18. Most things in life are more important than work. (R)

19. I used to care more about my work, but now other things are more important to me. (R)

20. Sometimes I'd like to kick myself for the mistakes I make in my work.

But job involvement is usually about specific tasks or groups but not the organization as a whole. People can be very involved in their particular job with little or no attention to output relevance, or profitability, or indeed the organization's goals and visions.

Job engagement

The concept of work engagement has emerged from research showing that certain employees find pleasure in work despite strenuous job requirements. This led Schaufeli and colleagues (2006) to propose the theoretical construct of work engagement, a fulfilling and positive work mind-set. Work engagement is not momentary, but is a persistent and continuous affective and cognitive state, comprised of the three dimensions of *vigour* (i.e. being energetic and resilient), *dedication* (i.e. having pride and enjoying work) and *absorption* (i.e. being focused and engrossed in work). One can get a good idea of the concept by looking at the scales:

Scale 1: Vigor/Energy

1. At work, I feel bursting with energy.

2. At my job, I feel strong and driven.

3. When I get up in the morning I look forward to going to work.

4. I can continue working for very long periods of time.

5. At my job, I am very tough mentally.

6. At my work, I can push on, even when things do not go well.

Scale 2: Dedication

1. I find the work that I do full of meaning and purpose.

2. I am enthusiastic about my job.

3. My job inspires me.

4. I am proud of the work that I do.

5. My job is challenging.

Scale 3: Absorption

1. Time flies when I am working.

2. When I am working, I forget everything else around me.

3. I am happy when I am working hard.

4. I feel deeply involved in my work.

5. I become completely absorbed in my work.

6. When not at work, I often think about my job.

Job engagement is now, without doubt the most popular concept in the field. It marries 'heart and head'. Whilst it has attracted a great deal of research, there are still questions to ask. For instance:

- *Is there a distinction between different types of engagement, possibly labelled transactional/transformational, deep/surface, etc.?* Here the questions are how and when these develop and operate. Is it possible or desirable to consider a typological approach to the whole issue of engagement?

- *What is the empirical evidence that shows staff engagement leads directly (or indirectly) to measurable outcomes such as productivity, job attendance, turnover, etc.?* This is about the size of the effects, i.e. the power of engagement to change behaviour. There is very little quality evidence to show the impact of engagement.
- *Are there sector, company size or national culture differences in the extent to which engagement is possible?* That is, is it much easier to bring about staff engagement in smaller rather than larger, in service rather than manufacturing, in culturally homogeneous rather than heterogeneous organizations?
- *What exactly is the process involved?* Is there a process involved, such that management policies, processes and procedures change people at work (i.e. bring about engagement)? To what extent, in turn, does their engagement lead to measureable and sustainable behavioural outcomes?
- *What do business leaders think about engagement?* Are they overall enthusiastic, cynical or sceptical about the claims that various groups make about the power of engagement?

Born from the positive psychology movement, engagement was used to help identify where employees where cognitively, emotionally and behaviourally invested in their work. Gallup, the international management consultancy, has long reported engagement levels among the world's workforce. Their results have consistently found that very few people are actively engaged at work: as of writing this book, only 33 per cent of employees are reported to be actively engaged at work, with a similar number being actively disengaged. Despite engagement being a prominent concept for managers, there has been very little long-lasting change in the number of employees who are engaged at work.

Briner (2012) has written an important and sceptical paper on the concept. This is his conclusion:

'From an evidence-based practice perspective there is something odd going on. Employee engagement proponents hold strong views and offer definitive practical suggestions, which do not appear to be informed by a reasonable quantity of good quality relevant evidence. But why? My best guess is that because proponents and advocates of any cause want to change things for the better and to do it fast, they prioritize getting things done over doing things in an evidence-based way. The question is whether in the longer-term this approach changes things for the better in a sustainable way. My guess is that it does not.

In the end we need to make a choice. Do we want to take employee engagement seriously or not? There are two contrasting approaches. The first is to closely examine definitions, check out the validity of measures, question whether it is new and different, carefully identify the quality of the available evidence and what it is capable of telling us, and to be accurate and explicit about what we know and do not know about the importance and role of employee engagement. The second approach is to be relaxed about definitions, not get too involved in considering the validity of measures of employee engagement, claim it's something new and different without really backing it up, ignore the fact that there is at the present time little good quality evidence, and over- and mis-claim the importance of employee engagement.'

Job addiction

Oates (1971) claimed to have invented the neologism *workaholic*, meaning the addiction to work and the compulsion or the uncontrollable need to work incessantly. But unlike other forms of addiction that are held in contempt, *workaholism* is frequently lauded, praised, expected and even demanded. Signs of this 'syndrome' according to Oates (1971) included boasting about the hours of work, invidious comparisons between self and others on the amount of work achieved, inability to refuse requests for work and general competitiveness:

The workaholic's way of life is considered in America to be one and the same time (a) a religious virtue (b) a form of patriotism (c) the way to win friends and influence people (d) the way to be healthy and wise. Therefore the workaholic, plagued though he is unlikely to change. Why? Because he is a sort of paragon of virtue ... he is the one chosen as 'the most likely to succeed'. (p. 12)

As is customary with popularist expositions of a psychological variable, a taxonomy was provided by Oates (1971) who listed *five types of workaholic:*

1. *Dyed-in-the-Wool* – with five major characteristics: high standards of professionalism; tendency to perfectionism; vigorous intolerance of incompetence; over commitment to institutions and organizations; considerable talent with marketable skills.

2. *Converted* – a person who has given up the above but may behave like a workaholic on occasions for the rewards of money or prestige.

3. *Situational* – workaholism not for psychological or prestige reasons, but necessity within an organization.

4. *Pseudo-Workaholic* – someone who may look, on occasion, like a workaholic but has none of the commitment and dedication of a true *dyed-in-the-wool* character.

5. *Escapist* as a workaholic – these are people who remain in the office simply to avoid going home or taking part in social relationships.

Machlowitz (1980) has defined workaholics as people whose desire to work long and hard is intrinsic. Additionally, workaholics are those whose work habits almost always exceed the prescriptions of the job they do and the expectations of the people with whom, and for whom, they work. According to Machlowitz, all true workaholics are intense, energetic, competitive and driven, but who also have *strong self-doubts*. They prefer labour to leisure and can (and do) work anytime and anywhere. They tend to make the most of their time and blur the distinctions between business and pleasure. All workaholics have these traits, but may be subdivided into four distinct types.

- *Dedicated* workaholic. These are quintessentially the single-minded, one-dimensional workaholics frequently described by lay people and journalists. They shun leisure, and are often humourless and brusque.

- *Integrated* workaholic. This type does integrate outside features into their work. Thus, although work is 'everything' it does sometimes include extracurricular interests.

- *Diffuse* workaholic. This type has numerous interests, connections and pursuits that are far more scattered than those of the integrated workaholic. Furthermore they may change jobs fairly frequently in pursuit of their ends.

- *Intense* workaholic. This type approaches leisure (frequently competitive sport) with the same passion, pace and intensity at work. They become as preoccupied by leisure as work.

To some extent it is thought that workaholism is an *obsessive-compulsive neurosis*, characterised by sharp, narrowed, focused attention; endless activity; ritualistic behaviours; and a strong desire to be in control. It is perhaps linked to perfectionism, pathological ambition and even the OCD personality disorder.

Research in the topic of workaholism and related topics – including burnout and engagement – has been steady for the past thirty years. This stream of research has been attempting to describe and delineate the syndrome of high work involvement and drive to work but low work enjoyment. It is a study of the *joylessness of work*, but almost exclusively with white, as opposed to blue collar, workers. Workaholism is often thought of as working both excessively and compulsively, but with pleasure derived from what is achieved rather than the work itself.

There have been some impressive attempts to build a model of the antecedents, consequences and dimensions of workaholism such as that of Ng, Sorensen and Feldman (2007). The model specifies three types of antecedents (dispositions, socio-cultural experiences and behavioural reinforcements), dimensions of workaholism (affect, cognitive and behavioural), consequences (satisfaction, mental health, career success) and overall long and short term performance.

Much of the research has been concerned with definitions and distinctions using different methodology such as distinguishing between the work enthusiast, the workaholic, the enthusiastic workaholic, the unengaged worker, the relaxed worker and the disenchanted worker (Spence and Robbins, 1992).

Three psychologists, Van Beek, Taris and Schaufeli (2011), in fact conceived of the *engaged workaholic* who did not experience burnout and had many components similar to genuinely engaged workers, like autonomous or intrinsic motivation. Others too have tried to differentiate between passion for work as opposed to addiction at work.

Harpaz and Snir (2003) rejected the 'more than 50 hours at work per week' boundary of workaholism for the idea of work centrality: the ideas that people allocate considerable amounts of time to work-related activities and thoughts because work is more important than leisure, community, family and religion/ spirituality. They believe it stems from the Protestant Work Ethic view that work redeems the believer, because working is seen as a virtue while play or leisure is a sin. As a result, some reviewers want to move on from the concept of workaholism to things like 'heavy work investment' (Snir and Harpaz, 2011) as a descriptor of job enthusiasm.

Many have argued that the essential criteria of a workaholic is a combination of excessive and compulsive working. It is that fun-less and joylessness at work lead to mental and physical ill-health (Gorgievski and Bakker, 2010). It goes beyond working hard due as a result of engagement or involvement, and moves into the darker psychological sphere of compulsion as it becomes 'too much of a good thing'.

The other factors: the dis- and un- concepts

Whilst we have discussed pro-work concepts, there are few psychological concepts that focus on the negative. You can be *un*involved, or *un*committed at work. You can also be *dis*engaged or *dis*satisfied. Researchers have often considered these to be opposite ends of the same spectrum; dissatisfaction is defined as a lack of satisfaction. However, we argue that these *dis-* or *un-* factors are distinct. Instead of appearing in the absence of their counterpart, a separate set of factors drive the *dis-* concepts to appear. Analysing how these *dis-* factors are defined offers insight into this.

Key *dis-* words:
discontent, discontentment, disappointment, disaffection, disquiet, unhappiness, malaise, disgruntlement, frustration, vexation, annoyance, irritation, anger, exasperation, resentment; restlessness, restiveness; disapproval, disapprobation, disfavour, displeasure, grievance, disregard, disgust; regret, chagrin, dismay.

In this book we are going to use the word disenchantment though it is not very different from disaffection. The dictionaries are only partly helpful.

Disenchantment
(*n.*) a feeling of disappointment about someone or something you previously respected or admired; disillusionment.

Synonyms: *disillusionment, disappointment, dissatisfaction, discontent, discontentedness, rude awakening; cynicism, disillusion.*

Disaffection

(*n.*) a state or feeling of being dissatisfied, especially with people in authority or a system of control.

Synonyms: *dissatisfaction, disgruntlement, discontent, restlessness, frustration; alienation, estrangement; disloyalty, rebellion, insubordination, mutiny, sedition, insurgence, insurrection, dissidence; hostility, antagonism, animosity, discord, dissension.*

Three observations can be made about these words. First, they are all affectively, behaviourally and cognitively negative. They suggest an emotional state, a belief system and an inclination to the negative. Second, they are active not passive concepts. They do not imply the absence of something, but rather the presence of something else. Third, they are concepts which seem to imply what psychoanalysts call a 'bad object' or an enemy. They are words that suggest a motivation to engage with a source of frustration. This is the foundation of our theory of disenchantment; what are the factors that *drive* and *motivate* negativity in the workplace?

Disenchantment: a five factor model

In our undertaking to understand what causes negativity in the workplace, we revived the literature on how different situations – particularly organizational processes and management practices – cause an employee to go from engaged to disenchanted; productive to subversive; a friend to an enemy of the organization. Our observations and research identified five distinct yet common factors that drive this process.

1 *Organizational lying/hypocrisy.* This is the perception by the employee that what the organization says about itself in public and

even to its employees is a 'pack of lies.' There is an inconsistency between the words, actions, and decisions in the workplace. The organization is seen as deceitful and lacking integrity. Employees become disenchanted when they realize their workplace is nothing like how it appears on the corporate website.

2 *Perceived inequity.* The idea that some people in the organization are treated very differently from others. The hottest word at work is *fair*: that people are fairly assessed, promoted and rewarded. Yet it can seem to some that loyalty, hard work and productivity have less to do with success than some other attributes such as demography, brown-nosing or particular experiences.

3 *Bullying and mistreatment.* This is the belief that some senior people are callous, uncaring and nasty. The organization is a place where being tough and ruthless is encouraged. Employees feel downtrodden and belittled each day as they fall victim to continuous incivility.

4 *Distrust.* The feeling that the organization does not even trust its own employees. Employees grow suspicious of their managers and colleagues, questioning the genuineness of their behaviour. Employees look over their shoulder, vigilant that a colleague might stab them in the back. Disenchantment grows in two directions: managers are unwilling to let employees work without being monitored or scrutinized, while the colleagues are secretive and unco-operative.

5 *Broken promises.* This is all about expectations not being met, or that the organization has not held up their end of the bargain. For some, the selection interview and the induction period are where people set your expectations about working for the organization. They tell you what they stand for, what they expect and how things work. Employees become disenchanted when these expectations are broken.

These factors can work individually or together to cause disenchantment. What is not clear however is which factor is more important in the 'slide into disenchantment'. In the following five chapters we will consider each of these factors, their causes and their consequences.

One way to understand these factors is at what level they operate: from micro to macro; individual to organizational. We start at the most micro factor and build to the disenchantment factor that operates on the most macro level.

We believe that bullying and disrespect operates primarily on a micro level. With disrespect, it is possible to identify the individual colleague who is to blame for the event. Although there are organizations where bullying is accepted as the 'norm', it is still individuals who are responsible for perpetuating the incivility.

The concept of *broken promises* would also be considered a micro factor. It is individuals who are responsible for making promises they never intend to keep. As a result, the employee becomes disenchanted with failed transactions that stem from individuals. However, there are also groups within the organization – HR, IT, Marketing, PR – who can be equally responsible for breaking promises to employees.

The concept of perceived inequity operates at both levels. There are individual differences in perceived inequity but also the differences in input-output rewards are often determined at an organizational level in the way pay is determined.

The idea that managers and staff distrust each other is the result of corporate culture. There are clearly interesting differences in when employees have different levels of paranoia and distrust, and those who choose not to trust individual managers or peers. However, it is apparent that there is a greater accountability for the procedures and processes that are set in place if an organization does not trust the motives and intentions of its staff.

Finally organizational lying and hypocrisy occurs at the corporate level. Though it might be driven by various groups (e.g. poor communication by the

Macro/
Organisational Level

Organisational
Lying

Distrust

Perceived
Inequity

Broken
Promises

Disrespect

Micro/
Individual Level

FIGURE 3.1

board or marketing), it is a broad perception that affects how the employee pictures the whole organization. It occurs when what organizations say about themselves bares no relation to the experience of individual workers. Employees become cynical of the whole operation (see Figure 3.1).

There is of course a question about process. What is the power, order, frequency and interaction of these factors? Is there a typical domino reaction? Whilst we accept that there may be various different ways in which these factors interact we believe the process illustrated in Figure 3.2 is most typical: Essentially the model is this. A direct process is started by the micro factors. Employees feel that they are inequitably treated or that their expectations are not being met. This then has a cascading effect on how the employee perceives the organization (the macro factor). When managers play favourites or opportunities fail to materialize, employees become suspicious and distrusting of the whole process. They close down, becoming sceptical of the decisions made by managers and their peers. As their disenchantment progresses,

A Progression Model of Disenchantment

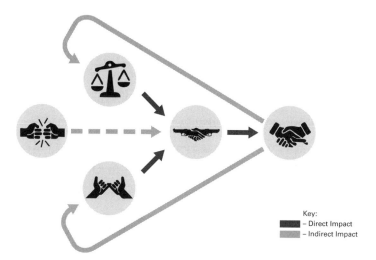

Key:
▬ – Direct Impact
▬ – Indirect Impact

FIGURE 3.2

employees come to believe that the organization is entirely hypocritical and dishonest. Employees notice inconsistencies between the every-day life of the organization and its proclaimed values, job advertisements and public communications. At this stage, the employee's disenchantment with the organization negatively frames the individual and micro events that happen, causing employees to experience greater *perceived inequity* and *broken promises*.

Bullying and disrespect is one of the most commonplace drivers of disenchantment. However, it does not necessarily have a cascading effect. It is the most reactionary driver, with employees looking for immediate retribution or justice as a result. Employees will look to 'balance the scales' in response to acute bullying, targeting the individuals responsible.

However, bullying begins to cause other dominos to fall when it is chronic or institutionalized. Organizations where employees are encouraged to be callous, ruthless and self-serving are ones where bullying is most common. As a result, employees become very distrusting of each other; employees know that they all only have their own self-interest in mind. Employees' distrust grows as colleagues stop co-operating and actively look for ways to undermine and undercut each other. This leads to *organizational hypocrisy* when the organization publicizes that they prioritize respect and integrity above all else. Employees know this to be a blatant lie as they are encouraged to pursue profits above all else. This process can be fast or slow, but is usually emotionally triggered. But the consequences are serious and enduring.

The central question is how workers who become disenchanted react? Some might try to ignore or repress their response hoping that things will get better. Some reactions are short term, and others long term. Of course many things depend on the organization and the individual. Others might try to reinterpret their experience trying to define what occurred. But most will act. They have various options. Some may choose to leave the organization. Some may do that, but also try to exact some revenge on individual managers as well as the company as a whole by stealing, defrauding or sabotaging on their way out. Still others might stay within the system and try some vengeful, even illegal, act in order to balance the scales.

These responses are not alternatives. There may well be a typical pattern of responses to experienced disenchantment based on the acuity and chronicity of the experience. Indeed there has been described elsewhere some famous cases of seriously disenchanted people and how they reacted to their situation (Furnham and Taylor, 2011).

We know that disenchantment *undermines resilience* and *fosters counterproductive work behaviours*. Employees become less able to cope and more likely to act against the interest of the organization. We believe that the acutely and chronically disenchanted person will not 'endure' that state over an extended period. From the literature it seems to us that there are three classic responses.

The first is to leave, resign or go absent a lot to avoid the problem. All organizations have a model of turnover depending on many factors. Some feel a regular turnover rate of say 25 per cent of staff per annum is normal, healthy and desirable. Others see this as far too much. Clearly if there are dramatic changes in turnover this could be seen as a sign of disenchantment. We have labelled this the neurotic of 'flight' response.

The second response is simply to disengage: to show no enthusiasm, energy or flow at work. This has often been termed *presenteeism*; to be physically but not emotionally present, to do the minimal amount of work without being sacked.

The third response is to take revenge on those perceived to be the main cause of the disenchantment. This can take many forms: fraud, theft, sabotage or worse. This we have called the psychotic or 'fight' approach.

We also believe that there are certain personality types that are more likely to engage in certain types of response. We distinguish between the *dark disenchanted*, those employees who are additionally characterized as high on 'dark' personality traits such as psychopathy and Machiavellianism, and the *neurotic disenchanted,* those who are additionally characterized by reserved and neurotic personality types.

The *dark disenchanted* are more likely to disengage or seek revenge. Their callous and often impulsive nature causes them to view this as the most appropriate response. They want to reassert social dominance and right the wrongs they have experienced. Alternatively, the *neurotic disenchanted* are more likely to disengage or leave. Their reserved but worrisome nature will cause them to ruminate on their disenchantment. They will disengage as a result of being preoccupied with avoiding further negativity at work. Only when their disenchantment escalates will they call it quits and find somewhere else to work (see Figure 3.3).

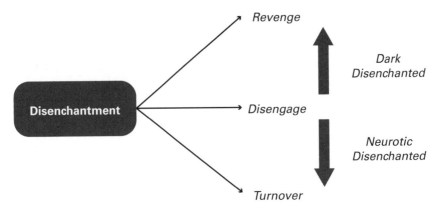

FIGURE 3.3

Conclusion

We have attempted in this chapter and book to introduce our new concept: *disenchantment*. We believe it takes us further than previously used concepts like (job) satisfaction, involvement, commitment and engagement.

We certainly accept that some people are more 'engageable' than others to the extent that personality factors play a role in how people perceive and react to conditions at work. We also accept that it is easier to 'foster staff engagement' in some organizations than others. Where organizations are successful, with a good 'brand' and a history of good management and a healthy culture, it should be relatively easy to avoid staff disengagement.

We believe that there are different identifiable characteristics that interact to produce disengagement. The remainder of this book addresses those factors.FIGURE 3.3

4

The Bad Apple and Bad Barrel Hypothesis

When dealing with people, remember you are not dealing with creatures of logic, but with creatures of emotion, creatures bristling with prejudice, and motivated by pride and vanity.

DALE CARNEGIE

Children imitate their parents, employees their managers.

AMIT KALANTRI

Introduction

It is said that people join organizations, but leave managers. This essentially means that it is the personal experience of bad managers that leads employees to resign: possibly out of anger as well as disappointment and disenchantment. This chapter looks at whether it is bad people or a bad organizational culture that mainly leads to the disenchantment of people who work for an organization.

Some people are carriers of gloom and disenchantment. Indeed, they are the 'Typhus Mary' of disenchantment, carrying it around with them wherever they go. They can be negative or resentful or even disturbed. It is difficult to enchant them and very easy to trigger disenchantment. They are bad apples or bad eggs because of the way they poison the environment.

Psychologists are interested in lay explanations and the attributions of cause. How do you explain the enchanted and disenchanted worker? Are they simply bad apples who infect the barrel or are there bad barrels that cause bad apples? Is disenchantment a function of personality or the way people are treated?

The attribution problem

The *fundamental* attribution error is to explain one's behaviour in terms of contextual and situational pressures, and constraints on others' behaviour in terms of personality. 'I failed because of my teacher; they failed because they were dim.' If you succeed it is attributable to your ability and effort, but if you fail it was due to an unfair exam system. Thus management explains disenchantment in terms of the lack of skills and efforts of workers, while disenchanted people explain it in terms of management practices.

Organizations are happy to admit the occasional selection mistake when employees 'spill the beans' about the organization or take revenge in some way. They prefer to see the individual as angry, disturbed and different: and that they brought their unhappiness on themselves. They are eager to show that they are unrepresentative of the organization; they are a *bad apple.*

On the other hand, those who have experienced all or some of the five causes of disenchantment explain their predicament (and of those around them) in terms of how abusive, unfair or unconcerned the organization is about them. They explain their feeling by the way they have been treated; they are the product of a *bad barrel.*

Politicians play this game superbly. When things are going well they attribute this to their policies but when things are not going so well it is all due to macro-economic forces quite beyond their control.

The clinical psychologists have also noted this behaviour pattern. In the 1930s it was claimed there were three classic behaviour patterns displayed when individuals were faced with anger and frustration, disappointment and failure. They were:

- **Extrapunitiveness** – The habit, tendency or preference to unfairly, unreasonably (but skilfully) blame others.

- **Impunitiveness** – This is to simply deny your role in the failure or to challenge whether the failure was really one at all.

- **Intropunitiveness** – This is the tendency both to exaggerate failure and also to blame yourself too harshly with excessive guilt.

Note that all three are considered types of defence mechanisms. All are ways of dealing with failure. They are *psycho*-logical rather than logical reactions which may be thought of as an attempt to a critically examine the manifold causes of the behaviour.

There are three fundamental questions regarding 'blame-storming.' The first and perhaps most important is what sort of individuals choose to use the strategy. We know that people are pretty consistent in their behaviour pattern. Some blame those who assign, rather than carry out, the task. Some expect failure and therefore, in a self-fulfilling way, actually encourage it.

Extrapunitive – *blame others* – types develop sophisticated theories and language to hand out the blame for anything they may be part of. Impunitiveness is also quite common. They might distort information to avoid blame or attempt to ingratiate themselves with others. Some seem not to care much about failure or to re-frame it. Others expect immediate, total and unmitigated forgiveness for everything, while others prefer complex, near fatalistic explanations for these problems. The intropunitive accept blame, but too readily and too much. They criticize themselves for small errors and shoulder the blame excessively. They are to be distinguished from those who accept blame as an attention-getting device, preferring that to being ignored.

The second issue is the psychological healthiness of these three defences. It is not difficult to see the current cultural answer: there seems to be a cultural endorsement of extra-punitiveness. It is healthy to fix the blame elsewhere; it is good for you. Clearly excessive self-blame leads to martyr-like depression. It is not good to take on the sins of the whole world; to let people off the hook; to be excessively self-critical. That is the road to depression, passivity, and lack of achievement. Impunitiveness is not much help also. Lessons can be learnt from failure, so burying your head in the sand or re-branding your mistakes hardly works.

So third, what advice for people faced with failure? First, have a good look at your preferred habitual style. Second, try a better analysis of the cause of the failure before acting. Treat it as an inquiry to learn lessons for the future.

The quick-fix of extrapunitiveness is very unhelpful at work. Being unfairly blamed can seriously alienate people and cause further failure. Denial does not work, especially when everyone systematically removes themselves from the situation. And being a shock absorber for everything leads to a sense of learned helplessness.

So join the blame-storming session with your eyes open to the three types of blaming behaviour. Recognize who habitually uses which style. And know the consequences of adopting one style over the others.

The bad apple/egg hypothesis

The bad egg hypothesis states that most organizational problems – theft, fraud, sabotage – can be attributed to 'bad people'. These people are morally and ethically corrupt. They are selfish and possibly criminal. They are carriers and spreaders of disenchantment. They are drains not radiators; heart-sinking not life-enhancing.

The difference between a bad egg and a bad apple is that bad eggs do not necessarily affect the eggs around them, whereas this is true of bad apples. Rotting apples cause those around them to also 'go bad'. Thus the bad individual apple in the organization can induce many others to follow their behaviour.

The hypothesis attributes everything to the individual and very little to the organization. What those who favour the hypothesis are not that happy doing is explaining how bad eggs and apples got selected in the first place, often promoted to high positions and undetected by the organization. The motive for the bad egg/apple hypothesis is that the organization can in part *absolve themselves* from serious blame except that they selected poorly. They frequently resist the idea that it was the organization that caused the problem. That is, because of the organizational culture and the behaviours of senior managers otherwise happy, healthy, workers were turned sour, vengeful and retributive.

Take for example the question as to why do people steal? People have tended to focus on five different, but inter-related reasons and various explanations have been suggested:

1 **Financial needs.** Here it is suggested that stealing occurs as a function of financial need. Needs are complicated, such as social or belongingness needs, because people may steal in order to obtain goals/money that allows them to become a 'club member'. However, this explanation does not distinguish the origin or type of need (for example drug addiction, gambling, sick relatives).

2 **Deviant personality/background.** The concept is that there is a person type who is more vulnerable to opportunities to steal, as well

as personally more likely to rationalize stealing behaviour. The theory is weak and tautological – people who steal are the 'stealing type'.

3 **Greed/tempted opportunities.** The idea is that people are inherently greedy and steal when they can: they are inherently untrustworthy. However, it fails to explain why there are systematic differences in greed.

4 **Moral laxity.** Here the theme is that some groups do not possess the same ethical standards or trustworthy qualities as other groups. Again the argument is poor: it is tautological and does not explain individual differences.

5 **Marginality.** People who are marginal have less static jobs with no tenure or social standing and steal as a way of expressing grievances. Because they have had no opportunities to develop commitment – they steal.

These are essentially all 'bad-person theories'. They suggest it is individual demography, morality, personality or psychopathology which explains why individuals steal either at a specific time for a specific purpose or in general.

The dark side of personality hypothesis

It is not clear who first used the term in work psychology, but it was Robert Hogan (2006) who made the concept of 'the dark side' popular. He talked about measuring the *bright* side (normal personality functioning), the *dark* side (the personality disorders) and the *in* side (motives and values). The Hogans (Hogan and Hogan, 1997) argued that it has become possible to describe, explain and predict a good deal of management derailment in terms of the sub-clinical personality disorders conceptual system. Further, by developing a measure called the Hogan Developmental Survey (HDS) they made research in this area possible.

The dark side has come to be known as markers of derailment at work and no doubt disenchantment for their employees. Psychologists are interested in personality traits; psychiatrists in personality disorders. Psychologists interested in personality have made great strides in describing, developing taxonomies of, and explaining the mechanisms and processes in normal personality functioning. Psychiatrists also talk about personality functioning and personality disorders that are typified by early onset (recognizable in children and adolescents), pervasive effects (on all aspects of life) and with relatively poor prognosis (that is difficult to cure).

Both psychologists and psychiatrists argue that the personality factors relate to *cognitive, affective and social aspects of functioning*. It is where a person's behaviour 'deviates, markedly' from the expectations of the individual's culture that the disorder is manifested. The psychiatric manual is very clear that 'odd behaviour' is *not* simply an expression of habits, customs, religious or political values professed or shown by a people of a particular cultural origin.

Psychiatrists and psychologists share some simple assumptions with respect to personality. Both argue for the *stability* of personality. The DSM criteria talk of personality as an 'enduring pattern', 'inflexible and pervasive' and 'stable and of long duration'. The Diagnostic and Statistics Manuals (DSM – a sort of bible of psychiatric disorders) note that personality disorders all have a long history and have an onset no later than early adulthood. Moreover, there are some gender differences: anti-social disorder is more likely to be diagnosed in men, while the borderline and dependent personalities are more likely to be found in women.

The manuals go to great lengths to point out that some of the personality disorders look like other disorders – anxiety, mood, psychotic, substance-related, etc. – but have unique features. The essence of the argument is:

'Personality Disorders must be distinguished from personality traits that do not reach the threshold for a Personality Disorder. Personality traits are diagnosed as a Personality Disorder only when they are inflexible, maladaptive, and persisting and cause significant functional impairment or subjective distress.' (p. 633)

One of the most important ways to differentiate personal style from personality disorder is flexibility. There are lots of difficult people at work but relatively few whose rigid, maladaptive behaviours mean they continually have disruptive, troubled lives. It is their *inflexible, repetitive, poor stress-coping responses* that are marks of disorder.

Personality disorders influence the *sense of self* – the way people think and feel about themselves and how other people see them. The disorders often powerfully influence *interpersonal relations at work*. They reveal themselves in how people 'complete tasks, take and/or give orders, make decisions, plan, handle external and internal demands, take or give criticism, obey rules, take and delegate responsibility, and co-operate with people' (Oldham and Morris, 2000: 24). The anti-social, obsessive, compulsive, passive-aggressive and dependent types are particularly problematic in the workplace.

People with personality disorders have difficulty expressing and understanding emotions. It is the intensity with which they express them and their variability that makes them odd. More importantly they often have serious problems with self-control. Many others have been influenced by the usefulness of the DSM classification of the personality disorders. In order to explain and describe these disorders other writers have changed the names to make them more interpretable to a wider audience. Table 4.1 shows the labels from different authors.

With regard to disenchantment there are two disorders that most clearly lead to management derailment and employee disenchantment: the psychopath and the narcissist.

TABLE 4.1 *Labels from different authors*

DSM-IV Personality Disorder	Hogan & Hogan (1997)	Oldham & Morris (2000)	Miller (2008)	Dotlich & Cairo (2003)	Moscosco & Salgado (2004)	De Haan & Kasozi (2014)
Borderline	Excitable	Mercurial	Reactors	Volatility	Ambivalent	The impulsive loyalist
Paranoid	Sceptical	Vigilant	Vigilantes	Habitual	Suspicious	The brilliant sceptic
Avoidant	Cautious	Sensitive	Shrinkers	Excessive caution	Shy	The simmering stalwart
Schizoid	Reserved	Solitary	Oddballs	Aloof	Loner	The detached diplomat
Passive-aggressive	Leisurely	Leisurely	Spoilers	Passive resistance	Pessimistic	The playful encourager
Narcissistic	Bold	Self-confident	Preeners	Arrogance	Egocentric	The glowing Gatsby
Antisocial	Mischievous	Adventurous	Predators	Mischievous	Risky	The charming manipulator
Histrionic	Colourful	Dramatic	Emoters	Melodramatic	Cheerful	The accomplished
Schizotypal	Imaginative	Idiosyncratic	Creativity and vision	Eccentric	Eccentric	The creative daydreamer
Obsessive-compulsive	Diligent	Conscientious	Detailers	Perfectionistic	Reliable	The responsible workaholic
Dependent	Dutiful	Devoted	Clingers	Eager to please	Submitted	The virtuous supporter

The psychopath

There is an extensive, compulsive and fascinating literature on the psychopaths amongst us. Psychopath is also one of the most commonly psychological terms, and coincidentally one that is most misunderstood. Films have made people think psychopaths are all deranged, axe-murderers and serial killers. But they are also convicts and mercenaries, con-artists and corporate executives.

The term psychopath or sociopath was used to describe antisocial personality types whose behaviour is amoral or asocial, impulsive and lacking in remorse and shame. Once called 'moral insanity', it is found more commonly among lower socio-economic groups, no doubt because of the 'downward drift' of these types. In his famous book called *The Mask of Insanity*, Cleckley (1941) first set out 10 criteria:

1. Superficial charm and intelligence.

2. Absence of anxiety in stressful situations.

3. Insincerity and lack of truthfulness.

4. Lack of remorse and shame.

5. Inability to experience love or genuine emotion.

6. Unreliability and irresponsibility.

7. Impulsivity and disregard for socially acceptable behaviour.

8. Clear-headedness with an absence of delusions or irrational thinking.

9. Inability to profit from experience.

10. Lack of insight.

The book is indeed a classic in psychology and psychiatry because of its insight. Cleckley noted the slick but callous business person, the smooth-talking and manipulative lawyer and the arrogant and deceptive politicians as psychopaths. He made apparent the paradoxical 'normality' or prevalence of this disorder, stressed the personality dimensions of this disorder and clearly believed that most psychopaths are not violent. While he acknowledged that a substantial proportion of incarcerated individuals exhibit psychopathic traits, he asserted that the majority of psychopaths are not incarcerated. As with all psychiatric illnesses there have been discussions and debates about definitions and terms. Babiak and Hare (2006) clarified the distinction between the overlapping terms:

> Psychopathy is a personality disorder described by the personality traits and behaviours. Psychopaths are without conscience and incapable of empathy, guilt, or loyalty to anyone but themselves. Sociopathy is not a formal psychiatric condition. It refers to patterns of attitudes and behaviours that are considered antisocial and criminal by society at large, but are seen as normal or necessary by the subculture or social environment in which they developed. Sociopaths may have a well-developed conscience and a normal capacity for empathy, guilt and loyalty, but their sense of right and wrong is based on the norms and expectations of their subculture or group. Many criminals might be described as sociopaths.

The defining characteristics of psychopathy tend to fall into two dimensions. The first is socio-emotional where the psychopath is superficial and lacking in empathy, guilt or remorse. They are also deceitful and manipulative while being prone to egocentricity and grandiosity. The second is their social deviance associated with boredom, susceptibility, impulsivity and lack of self-control. In children they show evidence of behaviour problems and in adulthood anti-social behaviour.

Oldham and Morris (2000) call these types 'Adventurous'. They describe the psychopath in popular terminology which makes it easier for non-specialists to spot. The following eleven traits and behaviours are clues to the presence of the 'Adventurous' style. A person who reveals a strong 'Adventurous' tendency will demonstrate more of these behaviours more intensely than someone with less of this style in his or her personality profile.

1 **Non-conformity.** Men and women who have the 'Adventurous' personality style live by their own internal code of values. They are not strongly influenced by other people or by the norms of society.

2 **Challenge.** To live is to dare. 'Adventurous' types love the thrill of risk and routinely engage in high-risk activities.

3 **Mutual independence.** They do not worry too much about others, for they expect each human being to be responsible for him- or herself.

4 **Persuasiveness.** They are silver-tongued, gifted in the gentle art of winning friends and influencing people.

5 **Adventurers relish sex.** They have a strong sex drive and enjoy numerous, varied experiences with different partners.

6 **Wanderlust.** They love to keep moving. They settle down only to have the urge to pick up and go, explore, move-out, move on.

7 **Freelance.** 'Adventurous' types avoid the nine-to-five world. They prefer to earn an independent, freelance living, do not worry about finding work, and live well by their talents, skills, ingenuity and wits.

8 **Open purse.** They are easy and generous with money, believing that money should be spent and that more will turn up somewhere.

9 **Wild oats.** In their childhood and adolescence, people with the 'Adventurous' personality style were usually high-spirited hell-raisers and mischief makers.

10 **True grit.** They are courageous, physically bold, and tough. They will stand up to anyone who dares to take advantage of them.

11   No regrets. 'Adventurers' live in the present. They do not feel guilty about the past or anxious about the future. Life is meant to be experienced now.

Hogan and Hogan (2001) call the anti-social person 'Mischievous'. They note that these types expect that others will like them and find them charming and they expect to be able to extract favours, promises, money and other resources from other people with relative ease. However, they see others as merely to be exploited, and therefore have problems maintaining commitments and are unconcerned about social, moral and economic expectations. They are self-confident to the point of feeling invulnerable, and have an air of daring and sang-froid that others can find attractive and even irresistible. In industries where bold risk-taking is expected they can seem a very desirable person for senior management position.

Miller (2008) calls psychopathic bosses 'predators'. He claims they think: 'It's a dog-eat-dog world. Look out for number one. Rules are for losers. I'm smarter than all these suckers ... My needs come first. I can get over anyone. Miller notes that psychopathic bosses are prototypically cut-throat, chainsaw-type entrepreneurs. The interpersonal inquisitiveness is more about getting to know how to manipulate people than befriend them. Is the person useful to them or not? They revel in outsmarting 'suckers' to reinforce their personal sense of cleverness and powerfulness. They can easily become experts, cheats, embezzlers or harassers. Curiously they often risk a lot for a little because of their love of thrills and excitement. According to Hogan and Hogan (1997: 34):

'They tend to be underachievers, relative to their talent and capabilities; this is due to their impulsivity, their recklessness, and their inability to learn from experience. These people handle stress and heavy workloads with great aplomb. They are easily bored, and find stress, danger and risk to be invigorating – they actively seek it. As a result, many of these people become heroes – they intervene in robberies, they rush into burning buildings, they take apart live bombs, they volunteer for dangerous assignments, and they flourish in times of war and chaos. Conversely, they adapt poorly to the requirements of structured bureaucracies.'

Hare (1999), in a chapter on white-collar psychopaths, noted how many were 'trust-mongers' who, through charm and gall, obtained, then very callously betrayed, the trust of others. He notes how they make excellent imposters and how they frequently target the vulnerable. They target and exploit people's gullibility, naivety and Rousseau-ian view of the goodness of man.

He calls them *subcriminal psychopaths* who can thrive as academics, cult-leaders, doctors, police officers and writers. They violate rules, conventions and ethical standards always just crossing legal boundaries. He also gives a rich case study description of what he calls a *corporate psychopath*. He notes that there is certainly no shortage of opportunities for psychopaths who think big. It is lucrative. 'They are fast talking, charming, self-assured, at ease in social situations, cool under pressure, unfazed by the possibility of being found out, and totally ruthless.'

Babiak and Hare (2006) believe most of us will interact with a psychopath every day. But their skills and abilities make them difficult to spot. Often they tend to be charming, emotionally literate and social skilled. Next they are often highly articulate. They are brilliant and chameleon-like in their impression management.

Oldham and Morris (2000) offer tips on dealing with the *adventurous* person in your life. First, have fun but be careful: your partner seeks excitement through charming, disarming adventurousness. Next, have no illusions about changing him or her: they will not or can not, so you have to be the flexible one. Third, do not crowd them or try to keep them on the traditional 'straight and narrow' path. Fourth, you have to be responsible for your own safety and others' welfare – because they will not be. Next, know your limits for excitement, risk, drugs, etc., because he/she will draw you into their world. Sixth, do not expect much support and help from them, because they will not provide it, so you need to be strong, resilient and tough.

The term psychopath is much used but more misunderstood. Psychopathy lies on a continuum from low to high. Successful, subclinical, industrial psychopaths can be very successful at work. If they are clever and presentable their superficial charm and boldness may suit them well, particularly in business situations that are rapidly changing. Further, it is stress that may push people 'over the line' from people with 'weak conscience' and taste for excitement into subclinical and even psychopathic behaviour.

One test of whether a person is a subclinical psychopath lies in their biography. From the age of adolescence onwards it may be possible to detect early signs of delinquency, brushes with the law and a string of people lining up to testify, quite happily, about the way they were lied to, cheated and 'conned' by a particular individual they trusted.

The narcissist

Psychologists use three related concepts: hubris, narcissism and overconfidence. Clinicians talk about Narcissistic Personality Disorder and some social psychologists the dangers of post-success hubris (Furnham, 2015). There are moral, social and clinical debates about narcissism. The moral issue concerns the evils of hubris; the social issue, the benefits or otherwise of modesty; the clinical debate is about the acute and chronic mental health consequences of misperceptions.

Dotlich and Cairo (2003) list narcissism-arrogance in their terms as the first (probably major) cause of why business CEOs fail. They note four common symptoms:

- A diminished capacity to learn from others or previous experience.

- An off-putting outright refusal (ever) to be accountable and hence responsible.

- Resistance to change because they know 'their way' is best.

- An inability to recognise their (manifold) limitations.

Oldham and Morris (2000) have noted that narcissists never seem defensive or embarrassed about their ambition and supreme confidence. However, because they are so aware of, comfortable with and grateful for their supposed gifts and strengths, they are easily and profoundly wounded by any suggestion that they have serious weaknesses or shortcomings. Oldham and Morris summarise the psychiatric diagnostic criteria as a 'pervasive pattern of grandiosity (in fantasy or behaviour), lack of empathy, and hypersensitivity to the evaluation of others, beginning by early adulthood and present in a variety of contexts', as indicated by at least five of the following:

1 Reacts to criticism with feelings of rage, shame or humiliation (even if not expressed).

2 Is interpersonally exploitative: takes advantage of others to achieve his or her own ends.

3 Has a grandiose sense of self-importance, e.g. exaggerates achievements and talents, expects to be noticed as 'special' without appropriate achievement.

4 Believes that his or her problems are unique and can be understood only by other special people.

5 Is preoccupied with fantasies of unlimited success, power, brilliance, beauty, or ideal love.

6 Has a sense of entitlement: unreasonable expectation of especially favourable treatment, e.g. assumes that he or she does not have to wait in line when others must do so.

7 Requires constant attention and admiration, e.g. keeps fishing for compliments.

8 Lack of empathy; inability to recognise and experience how others feel, e.g. annoyance and surprise when a friend who is seriously ill cancels a date.

9 If preoccupied with feelings of envy.

But narcissism is a *disorder* of self-esteem: it is essentially a cover-up. People with Narcissistic Personality Disorder (NPD) self-destruct because their self-aggrandizement blinds their personal and business judgement as well as their managerial behaviour. At work they exploit others to get ahead yet they demand special treatment. Worse, their reaction to any sort of criticism is extreme, including shame, rage and tantrums and they aim to destroy that criticism, however well-intentioned and useful. They are poor empathizers and thus have low emotional intelligence. They can be consumed with envy and disdain of others, and are prone to depression as well as manipulative, demanding and self-centred behaviours; even therapists do not like them.

The earlier fourth version of the DSM has nine diagnostic features for narcissism. Narcissists are boastful, pretentious and self-aggrandizing, over-estimating their own abilities and accomplishments while simultaneously deflating others. They compare themselves favourably to famous, privileged people believing their own discovery as one of them is long overdue. They are surprisingly secure in their beliefs that they are gifted and unique and have special needs beyond the comprehension of ordinary people.

Paradoxically, their self-esteem is fragile, needing to be bolstered up by constant attention and admiration from others. They expect their demands to be met by special favourable treatment. In doing so they often exploit others because they form relationships specifically designed to enhance their self-esteem. They lack empathy being totally self-absorbed and they are also envious of others and begrudge them for their success. They are well known for their arrogance and their disdainful, patronising attitude.

The two dimensions of narcissistic personality disorder are often referred to as *grandiose* and *vulnerable narcissism*. Grandiose narcissism primarily reflects traits related to aggression and dominance, while vulnerable narcissism reflects a defensive, insecure grandiosity that obscures feelings of inadequacy, incompetence and depression. The primary feature shared by both dimensions of narcissism is a tendency to act antagonistically towards others. Vulnerable narcissists have grandiose fantasies but are timid, insecure and consequently do not appear narcissistic on the surface. Grandiose narcissists have higher levels of happiness, life satisfaction, and are more exhibitionistic than vulnerable narcissists.

Most individuals with narcissistic personality disorder are preoccupied with fantasies of unlimited success, power, brilliance and money. They believe that they are 'special' and unique and can therefore only be properly understood by, or should associate with, other special or high-status people (or institutions). They may try to 'buy' themselves into exclusive circles. They often require excessive admiration and respect from people at work for everything they do. This is their most abiding characteristic. They usually have a sense of entitlement – that is, unreasonable expectations of especially favourable treatment or automatic compliance with their manifest needs. Worse, they take advantage of others to achieve their own ends, which makes them inefficient and disliked as managers.

They are unsupportive but demand support for themselves. All are unwilling to recognise or identify with the feelings and needs of others in and out of work. They have desperately low emotional intelligence though are apparently unaware of this. Indeed they may assume they have superior emotional intelligence. Curiously they are often envious of others and believe that others are envious of them. In this sense they are deluded. They show arrogant, haughty behaviours or attitudes all the time and everywhere at work (and home) (Hogan, 2006).

Narcissists are super self-confident: they express considerable self-certainty. They are 'self-people' – self-asserting, self-possessed, self-aggrandizing, self-preoccupied, self-loving – and ultimately self-destructive. They seem to really believe in themselves: they are sure that they have been born lucky. At work they are out-going, highly energetic, competitive and very 'political' depending of course on their normal personality profile. Thus the extroverted conscientious narcissist may be rather different from those more neurotic and open. They can make reasonable short-term leaders as long as they are not criticized, or made to share glory. They seem to have an insatiable need to be admired, be loved and be needed. This can appear amusing or pathetic to outside observers. They are often a model of the ambitious, driven, self-disciplined, successful leader or manager. The world, they believe and demand, is their stage. There are various aspects to narcissistic leadership. Ouimet (2010) has identified five:

1   **Charisma**: the ability to seduce others in their entourage through various mechanisms.

2   **Self-interested influence**: with a sense of entitlement, the relentless striving to construct, and protect a (false) strict self-image, and the attribution of humanizing traits to oneself as opposed to others.

3   **Deceptive motivation**: using bold actions and a sensationalism (attention getting acquisitions) trying to cover up their real motives of aggrandisement.

4   **Intellectual inhibition**: the hypersensitivity to criticism, the exaggerated need for admiration, and the remorseless perceived threats to integrity leading to very poor decision making.

5   **Simulated consideration**: the callous and superficially charming manipulation and exploitation of employees and colleagues.

Clever, articulate, good-looking narcissists can be energetic, charismatic, leader-like and willing to take the initiative to get projects moving. They can be relatively successful in management, sales and entrepreneurship, but usually only for short periods. However, they are arrogant, vain, overbearing, demanding, self-deceived and pompous. Yet they are so colourful and engaging that they often attract followers. Their self-confidence is attractive. Naively, people believe they have to have something to be so confident about.

Narcissists handle stress and heavy workloads badly; they are also quite persistent under pressure and they refuse to acknowledge failure. As a result of their inability to acknowledge failure or even mistakes and the way they resist coaching and ignore negative feedback, they are unable to learn from experience. In a very accessible, almost self-help book written as a collaboration between a psychiatrist and a journalist, Oldham and Morris chose the more neutral term *self-confidence*.

There remains considerable debate about the treatment of, and prognosis for each of the personality disorders. Until relatively recently it was argued that they were particularly difficult to treat and that prognosis was therefore poor.

The business world often calls for and rewards arrogant, self-confident, self-important people. They seek out power and abuse it. They thrive in selling jobs and those where they have to do media work. But, as anyone who works with and for them knows, they can destabilize and destroy working groups by their deeply inconsiderate behaviour. Management and self-help books stress how to cope with clinical or subclinical narcissism. Few take a very negative view or report case studies where narcissists personally destroy whole organizations, but it is not difficult to imagine how the deeply egocentric, narcissistic manager causes long-term disenchantment in their staff. Working for someone only interested in their own welfare becomes deeply alienating.

The fatalist

The *perceived control* personality variable or *locus of control* relates to beliefs about internal versus external control of reinforcement (i.e. the cause of behavioural outcomes). It assumes that individuals develop a general expectancy regarding their ability to control their lives.

People who believe that the events that occur in their lives are the result of their *own* behaviour and/or ability, personality and effort are said to have the expectancy of *internal control*. However, people who believe that events in their lives are a function of luck, chance, fate, deities, powerful others or powers beyond their control, comprehension or manipulation are said to have an expectancy of *external control*.

It is without doubt one of the most extensively measured individual difference or dimensions analysed in the whole of psychology. Indeed, various different scales exist, all of which purport to measure this general dimension, as well as scales designed to tap beliefs with respect to specific settings such as health, educational, political and religious settings. In each instance, locus of control has been significantly, consistently, and predictably related to beliefs and behaviours – nearly always indicating the psychologically adaptive features associated with inner locus of control. Locus of control is related to desire for control, conceived of as a trait reflecting the extent to which individuals are generally motivated to control the events in their lives. People with high desire for control tend to have higher aspirations, to be more persistent and responsive to challenges, and to see themselves as the source of their success.

Beyond psychological health, the locus of control concept has been applied to *behaviour in organizations*. In a review paper, Spector (1988) noted that locus of control is related to motivation, effort, performance, satisfaction, perception of the job, compliance with authority, and supervisory style, as well as an important moderating factor between incentives and motivation, satisfaction and turnover. For instance, 'internals' tend to prefer piece-rate systems, whereas 'externals' tend to be more satisfied with direct supervision, to comply more with demands of coercive supervisors, and to be more compliant with social demands than internals. Spector concludes that much more organizational theory may be applicable to internals.

Essentially the fatalist tends to be gloomy and passive, rather than proactive and positive. Those with an external locus of control tend to see themselves as victims of forces and helpless to change many issues. As a result, they feel victim to what is happening around them, and become more prone to disenchantment.

The unstable stress prone person

Stress at work is as inevitable as death and taxes. We all get stressed; amen. But what is really interesting is how often we get stressed. How significant (acute and chronic) is that stress; what are the usual causes of that stress; and what essentially can we regularly do about it?

Stress affects the body, decisions and judgements, relationships and work performance. We now know a lot about the physiology of stress and how cortisol, noradrenalin and adrenalin impact on people over time. Stress is bad, so we need to know how to deal with it. Being stress resistant and stress-coping is good. That is at the heart of resilience. It is about coping and bouncing back after significant as well as minor setbacks. Resilience is a prophylactic against failure: a way of adapting and thriving, rather than ruminating or falling into depression. Resilient people can self-regulate: they can control their impulses and emotions. And they tend to be optimistic. Employers want resilient staff. And most people want it too.

It has been argued that resilience has various component parts. It has to do (in part) with realistic *self-confidence* which is a realistic appraisal of achievements and choices. It is also about *self-esteem*, which is having a sense of one's purpose and contribution. Next, there is *self-efficacy*, which is the belief in one's own abilities and strengths. And also, *self-control* or the belief that one is in control of one's life: captain of your ship and master of your fate.

Resilience is also about thinking straight. The power of Cognitive Behaviour Therapy has shown how thinking errors or styles can have both powerful positive and negative effects. These include frequently 'catastrophizing' or getting things out of proportion; externalizing which is blaming others for your own behaviour; generalizing to believe that small things always have large consequences; and black-and-white thinking.

The bad barrel

Why are some organizations so disheartening and disenchanting? Many have pointed out that just as you need three components for fire (namely heat, oxygen and fuel) similarly you are unlikely to get leadership derailment if you do not have the needed components. In this case, the three factors are: leaders with a derailment profile; people who are prepared to follow derailing leaders; and environments that allow it to happen.

Many people have tried to moderate the simple-minded and individualistic trait approach to leadership derailment by stressing the nature of organizational culture and leader–follower dynamics. Canadian psychologist, Gilles Ouimet (2010), noted three particularly salient factors:

Cultural factors. There are national and corporate cultural factors that favour the dark-side manager making it to the top. First, individualistic cultures (mainly in the West) more than collectivistic cultures (mainly in the East) value personal achievement over group success. Thus in these cultures it is more natural to look for, and select, people who draw attention to themselves and have significant self-belief.

Further, if the organisation promotes and trumpets values like immediate results, audacity, ambition, individual initiative, financial success, professional prestige and social celebrity they become a breeding ground for dark-side leaders. Thus inevitably dark-side types are drawn to organizations in which they can thrive. This is particularly the case for organizations in sectors that are fast moving and poorly regulated.

Environmental Factors. There is considerable historical evidence that dark-side leaders emerge in times of political and economic crisis. Where people perceive an imagined or real and significant threat to their well-being and livelihood they are often drawn to the 'superman, heroic' leader who promises them he or she can save them. People are drawn to the rhetoric, the self-confidence and the bravado of leaders who can mobilize people and give them confidence.

Crises occur for all sorts of reasons. Political crises can trigger economic crises and vice versa. Sudden changes in technology or international law can have an immediate and massive impact on organizations of all sizes who look for immediate solutions. If at this point the bold, mischievous, Machiavellian steps forward the emergence of a dark-side leader is usually guaranteed.

Organizational Structural Factors. All organizations for historical but also legal reasons have processes and procedures that can, in effect, facilitate or frustrate the emergence of a dark-side leader. Some place serious restrictions on an individual's power and freedom to make decisions. Some organizations have strict rules and procedures about group decision-making and the keeping of records. Others are more relaxed.

Furthermore, most organizations have rules about corporate governance. There may be non-executive directors whose explicit task it is to 'keep an eye on' maverick leaders and their decisions. There also may be rules about reports and statements and shareholder's meetings that make all sorts of procedures public. In short, the better the corporate governance the less chance the dark-side leader has to emerge.

There is a great deal of literature that supports the idea that some environments inhibit and others almost encourage illegal behaviour. Thus Baucus and Near (1991) showed that large firms operating in a dynamic, munificent environment, with a history of prior violations and in certain industry sectors, were more likely to take part in illegal acts.

Peck and Slade (2007) tried to understand why organizations allow bad people to succeed. At the heart of the problem is *organizational process, structural and system complexity.* Essentially this means all the bad behaviour can be hidden: incompetence, mistakes, shadowy alliances, bullying and the development of sycophantic in-groups. Better still for the toxic manager is to be part of a multinational on various sites in a quick moving market. Even more desirable for them is a poorly regulated environment. Any organizations come to mind?

Organizational structures encourage domination and legitimization. This can trap people in subordinate roles that render them unable to speak out against injustice. The toxic leaders allocate power and resources. To understand and then manipulate organizational systems is often the goal of the corporate psychopath, described by Paul Babiak and Robert Hare so clearly in their book *Snakes in Suits,* simply subtitled *When the Psychopath Goes to Work.* But toxic tyrants in small, regulated and specialist organizations are soon found out. The grapevine spreads the message, eventually reaching those who are in a position to do something about it.

Then there is the pervasive problem of reward systems (money, promotion) reinforcing aggressive and ambitious behaviour. Outsiders are often struck by the mismatch between the proudly trumpeted values of 'integrity', 'customer care' and 'respect for people' and the blatantly obvious cut-throat competitiveness inside the organization.

The smart employee soon picks up the signals: what is really important and what really counts? What the organization really values and rewards is often easily measured in terms of money: reduce costs, increase revenue; hence the dubious sales techniques we read about every day. Thus, paradoxically, the culture of superficial charm, disregard for others, little or no shame or remorse, is rewarded. Worse, if occasionally some punishment is meted out, it leads to cabalistic cunning to avoid being caught. This in turn can lead to a dulling of the conscience. Whole groups follow processes that require the inefficient and complex 'interference' from the individual conscience. There is a state of disinhibition that discourages the exposing of organizational deviance, even violence. The organization can be quick to rationalize and then legitimize behaviours that are later exposed as shockingly hypocritical.

There are other factors, including delegation, which facilitate control. To be able to build up teams is the ideal situation for the toxic tyrant whose largesse is all-powerful. They can establish a situation where team members are grateful for their inclusion, eager to be accepted and recognized and therefore happy to follow the directive of the tyrant. Thus, they fall ever more into the controlling clutches of the rewarder. This is in essence a 'mate-ocracy' where success allows political networks to be established that serve no one but the leaders.

A further factor helping the tyrant remain hidden and often thrive lies in vague and abstract Key Performance Indicators (KPIs) or Key Result Areas (KRAs). If the goal is to 'manage relationships', 'steer the project' or 'ensure customer delight', it is very unclear how these can be measured. As all those in Performance Management know well, the really hard part is coming up with a series of reliable, objective, behavioural measures of success. The more vague the goal or objective, the more room for devious impression management. The tyrant can therefore, with relatively little effort, create an impression of an exceptional manager who is essential to the team's, indeed the whole organization's, success.

Finally, organizational complexity and flux can seriously distort and disrupt information flow to and from the decision makers. Employees often report that they did not know whom to tell what when they were faced with the toxic tyrant. Deviants can easily find ways to block or manipulate information, ensuring it is only positive, if often bland. This can make them, in time, more audacious and bold.

So why do arrogant, greedy, narcissistic opportunists thrive in some organizations? Often it is because the bureau-pathic organization allows, and even encourages, them. These *bad apples* can thrive in a *bad barrel*.

This is much to think about with all the hype around mindfulness at work. Organizational policies and practices can cause individuals considerable stress, which their managers hope to cure by a couple of hours of mindfulness training. Others call in consultants to sprinkle 'magic resilience dust' to make their tired and stretched staff more able to cope. Perhaps reducing the stress in the first place is a better solution.

Conclusion

It can be very disheartening, disenchanting and demotivating to work for bad people and bad organizations. Managers that cause disenchantment can be crudely divided into three groups: bad, mad or sad. Some of these characteristics are described above. Equally it is possible to find good managers in bad organizations that allow or even encourage bad behaviour.

While it is possible to frame this as a bad person versus bad organization issue, this is essentially a false dichotomy. It is not a matter of 'either/or' but 'both/and'. Bad, disenchantment-producing managers only really thrive in an environment (*barrel*) that allows, turns a blind-eye to, or even encourages it.

5

Organizational Honesty, Lying and Hypocrisy

The essence of immorality is the tendency to make an exception of myself.
JANE ADDAMS

All of us are experts at practicing virtue at a distance.
THEODORE M. HESBURGH

Hypocrite: the man who murdered both his parents . . . pleaded for mercy on the grounds that he was an orphan.
ABRAHAM LINCOLN

A man generally has two reasons for doing a thing. One that sounds good, and a real one.
J. PIERPOINT MORGAN

Introduction

All organizations know the power of Public Relations (PR). Many have PR departments whose job it is to make sure their public image and reputation is very positive. They want to be seen as honest and open, fair and just, and a good employer. Many trumpet their values through mission statements or value proclamations where they seek to state what they stand for. They are usually little more than a wish-list than an actual reflection of reality.

Organizations may spend a lot of time and money on these proclamations of their beliefs, values and mission. Not surprisingly most organizations have very similar values: integrity, honesty and justice are a few that appear with high frequency. But what happens when an employee walks past every day the guided values and mission-statement in the company headquarters and knows they are patently not true? What occurs when you see the CEO on television or in a newspaper article say things about the organization that are blatantly false? How does the employee respond to the massive gap between the PR and the reality?

What happens when a boss recommends what is essentially dishonest dealings with customers and competitors and yet the company says it supports openness, honesty and integrity? What happens when workers are asked to fudge and hide facts and figures when the company says it is always totally law-abiding, honest and transparent? What of colleagues who talk of win-win, when you know it is always win-loose? They say they prize co-operation when you know it is competition; they talk of ability and talent when you know it is nepotism and networks.

Hypocrisy is all about assuming a false appearance of goodness, morality and virtue while covering up, or lying about, real beliefs and behaviours, intentions and inclinations. It is about pretence and sham. It is essentially about inconsistency but also about blame and complacency.

The hypocrite is disingenuous. We have all been hypocrites at one time or another. People publicly 'take up' popular positions on socio-political issues but frequently do not believe in the cause. This could be seen to be a form of 'virtue signalling'. People very publicly espouse a position or cause which they know (or believe) to be essentially virtuous, though they might not believe it, or even believe in its opposite.

To be called a hypocrite is an insult. To work with one is often a very unpleasant experience. But what is the effect when hypocrisy occurs at a more macro level; working for a company that is deeply hypocritical in the sense that what they say they believe in (their values) are quite different from how they behave?

Most people are acutely aware of the reputation of the organization for which they work. Some feel that working for a tobacco or drug company elicits so much negativity to them that they even disguise or lie about where they work. Others will complain about whole sectors like banking being unfairly thought of as greedy cheats and liars. Equally some people are very pleased about the fact they work for a high profile organization, like a charity that overtly does good. The ethics of your company effects how you are seen. It can be a major source of pain or pleasure.

Most companies realise the importance of their reputation management. Indeed some hire external professionals or have entire departments dedicated to purely managing the reputation of their organization. It is an important role: the share price can take a major tumble if word gets out about tax evasion or avoidance, discrimination, or unethical practices with foreign subsidiaries. For instance, United Airlines, an American airline, learned this the hard way in April 2017. They lost $255 million in market value after a video emerged of them forcibly dragging (and consequently injuring) a passenger off an overbooked plane.

How the organization both promotes and conducts itself, and the congruence between these, can have a profound impact on an employee's disenchantment. Disenchantment can very easily follow if you see senior members of the organization hypocritically espousing positions they clearly do not believe in.

Mission statements

President Bush Senior, who did not have a high tolerance for 'management speak', once talked about 'the vision thing'. Wikipedia tells us that this oft-cited quote became a shorthand for the charge that Bush failed to contemplate or articulate crucial policy positions in a compelling and coherent manner. Visions inspire: he did not apparently have one.

Not long ago organizations were encouraged by consultants to think through and articulate their unique and important mission and vision. They had to write, display and glorify their purpose in these statements of meaning and intent. They were supposed to have all sorts of benefits ranging from clarifying strategy to customer satisfaction.

The story went that a mission statement is a statement of the purpose of a company or organization; it succinctly articulates the organization's primary reason for existing! It is a sort of guide for all the actions or decision making of the organization. It is the framework or context within which the company's strategies should be formulated.

The gurus at the time advised the statement should cover things like the main aim of the organization, its essential stakeholders and how the organization provides value to these stakeholders. It could include a declaration of an organization's sole core purpose. Mission statement writers were encouraged to ask: who is your target client/customer? What product or service do you provide to that client? What makes your product or service unique, so that the client would choose you?

But the result is usually little more than bland humbug. Below are sixteen relatively big and famous organization's mission statements taken from their publicity material, though these might have changed. See how many you can guess:

1   'We shape a better world.'

2   'Helping people achieve their ambitions – in the right way.'

3   'Our purpose is to create long-term shareholder value through the discovery, acquisition, development and marketing of natural resources.'

4   To Refresh the world; Inspire moments of optimism and happiness; Create value and make a difference.

5   'We are working to create an environment that naturally enables [our] employees, suppliers, dealers, and communities to fully contribute to the pursuit of total customer satisfaction.'

6   'The priorities are: grow a diversified global business, deliver more products of value, and simplify the operating model.'

7   'To be the preeminent global hospitality company – the first choice of guests, team members, and owners alike.'

8   'We want to ensure that our employees feel empowered to do the right thing and that we meet the expectations of society, customers, regulators, and investors.'

9   Purpose – 'Nourishing families so they can flourish and thrive.'

10 Core values: – 'putting people first, pursuing excellence, embracing change, acting with integrity and serving our world.'

11 'To help businesses throughout the world realise their full potential.'

12 'Our goal is to build the iconic professional services firm, always at the front of people's minds, because we aim to be the best.'

13 'To be the consumer's first choice for food, delivering products of outstanding quality and great service at a competitive cost through working faster, simpler and together.'

14 'Our aim is to meet the energy needs of society, in ways that are economically, socially and environmentally viable, now and in the future.'

15 'To inspire and nurture the human spirit – one person, one cup and one neighbourhood at a time.'

> **16** Core Purpose – 'We make what matters better, together.'
>
> **The answers in order:** Arup; Barclays; BHP Billiton; Coca-Cola; General Motors; GlaxosmithKlein; Hilton Hotels; HSBC; Kellogg's; Marriott Hotels; Microsoft; PWC; Sainsbury's; Shell; Starbucks; and Tesco.

What does this tell us? First, most people are in business much for the same thing. So why not a generic mission statement such as: 'To maximize return for our stake-holders.'

Second, it should teach us that all this crypto-metaphysical talk is rather pointless. Mission statements are often filled with abstract terms that amount to not a lot. It is a form of *circumlocution*; using too many words to express an idea, especially in an attempt to be vague. You need to know what business you are in, and as they used to say, 'stick to the knitting'. But deciding that is a task for the strategic planners and the board. You do not need management consultants designing bland statements.

Third, slogans do matter. It is easy to know these: 'Every little helps'; 'Good with Food'; 'Finger-licking good'; 'I'm Loving it'; 'Just do it'. They do not mean much but they are instantly recognisable. That is good marketing.

The issue is this: if an organization wants to use mission statements as PR and brand identification that is fine. But the process can backfire if they take 'the high moral ground' when people who work in the organization know it is completely untrue. That is a certain start on the route to disenchantment.

The values fad

Values are enduring beliefs or basic convictions that guide action. They provide a relatively permanent framework for shaping behaviour. They can be seen as a conscious or unconscious guide to the way we behave.

Psychologists often try to measure motivation by finding out what people value. So people who value hedonism and fun choose rather different jobs from those who value altruism. Some values seem to be opposites, others quite compatible. There are terminal values and instrumental values. One is about ends; the other is about ways to that end.

Academics have come up with many different models and theories. Some are interested in cultural differences in values and others in how parents try to instil certain values in their children. But values-statement are all the rage now for the HR community. Deciding on core company values helps them in the decision-making processes. They are yard-sticks or guiding lights and principles. These core values educate clients and potential customers about what the company is about and believes. They say what the product, processes and company stands for. Core values are even primary recruiting and retention tools. People choose and stay in companies with values that they admire and support. Typical values include: accountability, balance, caring, committed, customer service, diversity and integrity.

But the old cynics and sceptics say 'we have been here before'. They point to the following:

1 Every company has essentially the same values; and so they should. If you read any particular set of corporate values, you could often not guess the identity of the organization. They all do integrity/trust/ honesty/fairness/transparency. Fashions change so when a new 'issue' is in it becomes part of the values. A new fad may be diversity of race, age, ability as well as sexual orientation. So the values change over time: but not a lot.

2 Values statements are too abstract; they are too pie-in-the-sky wish lists to be of any use other than for PR purposes. As all parents and teachers know, you have to pre- and pro-scribe specific behaviours to get people to act in a particular way. One person's openness and honesty is not the same as another's. There is all the difference in the

world between *core* values that are manifest in behaviour and *espoused* values that appear in corporate documents.

3 The best statement for all organizations is: 'To maximise return for the organization's stakeholders.' If you want to know your real values, hire some anthropologists to observe the corporate culture; 'the way we do things around here'. But they are likely to give you a nasty shock. We respond to real motivators; to 'carrots and sticks'. And if neither is clearly linked to values, no one really cares much about them.

4 It is pointless to invest in a Chief Values Officer. Use your existing managers to openly talk about, model and reward the behaviour you desire. It is wiser to target observable and changeable behaviours not abstract values.

5 There is always (although often hidden) value conflict. Different parts of the organization and different individuals hold fundamentally different values: e.g. equity vs equality; marketing vs production. There are values about means and values about ends. It was ever thus and is not unhealthy. In this sense, different parts of the organization value different things. Value clashing is normal, even productive.

6 The relationship between attitudes or values and behaviour is very weak. It is unwise to believe that by targeting values you are going to radically or fundamentally change behaviour. Change behaviour and you change values: seat belts, drink driving and smoking are the classic examples. It turned out impossible to persuade individuals to wear safety belts, or stop drinking and driving, by appealing to their better nature. You change the law, threaten fines, and over time people begin to internalize those values. Reinforcing the behaviour you want your values to emulate is the fastest and surest way to embed values.

7   Organizational change is more effectively brought about by restructuring, recruitment and performance management than it is by fiddling around with values. There are various routes to bringing about organizational change. Hiring and firing takes a long time. Moving sites or buying new equipment can be expensive. But both have impact. Having talking-cure, value workshops may look like a soft option, but that is because it is one. Whatever effect is achieved evaporates at a great speed.

8   Unless value-informed behaviour is modelled and rewarded by senior management, the whole concept will fail. Top-down 'value work' is only effective if senior staff *really* live all the values, all the time. The 'little people' are very observant about the grown-ups. Many are super-sensitive to hypocrisy about transparency, fairness and honesty. So, if the board-level managers and their equivalents are not seen to be 'living the values', you might as well give up immediately.

9   There is a lot of hypocrisy in organizations. If you challenge the process or the values, you will be labelled a cynic, a fifth-columnist, or simply not on board. So employees keep silent and you have false consensus and pluralistic ignorance. If you act like some religions, that in effect forbid the questioning of the 'great truths', you will encourage an underground of disbelievers who will form their own powerful counter cults.

Individual and corporate values at work

Researchers on the topic of social values have conceived of them as a system of beliefs concerned with such issues as competence and morality, and which are derived in large part from societal demands. These value systems are organized summaries of experience that capture the focal, abstracted qualities of past encounters; have an *ought-ness* (specifying prescribed and proscribed behaviours) quality about them and which function as criteria or a framework against which present experience can be tested. Also, it is argued that these act as general motives.

A value is considered an enduring belief that a specific instrumental mode of conduct and/or a terminal end state of existence is preferable. Once a value is internalized, it consciously or unconsciously becomes a *standard criterion* for guiding action: for *developing* and *maintaining attitudes* towards relevant objects and situations; for justifying one's own and others' actions and attitudes; for *morally judging* self and others; and for comparing oneself with others.

Research by Feather (1975) and others has demonstrated that these value systems are systematically linked to culture of origin, religion, chosen university discipline, political persuasion, generations within a family, age, sex, personality and educational background. These values in time may determine vocational choice and occupational behaviour. Feather has argued that social attitudes precede values that emerge as abstractions from personal experience of one's own and others' behaviour. These values in time become organized into coherent *value systems*, which serve as frames of reference that guide beliefs and behaviour in many situations, such as work. He has argued that values, attitudes and attributions are linked into a cognitive–affective (thinking–feeling) system. Thus, people's explanations of unemployment are 'linked to other beliefs, attitudes and values within a system in ways that give meaning and consistency to the events that occur' (p. 805).

Thus, it may be expected that there are coherent and predictable links between one's general value system and specific work-related beliefs. What are the things people want and consider important in their lives?

Values list 1
(1) EQUALITY (equal opportunity for all)
(2) INNER HARMONY (at peace with myself)

(3) SOCIAL POWER (control over others, dominance)

(4) PLEASURE (gratification of desires)

(5) FREEDOM (freedom of action and thought)

(6) A SPIRITUAL LIFE (emphasis on spiritual not material matters)

(7) SENSE OF BELONGING (feeling that others care about me)

(8) SOCIAL ORDER (stability of society)

(9) AN EXCITING LIFE (stimulating experiences)

(10) MEANING IN LIFE (a purpose in life)

(11) POLITENESS (courtesy, good manners)

(12) WEALTH (material possessions, money)

(13) NATIONAL SECURITY (protection of my nation from enemies)

(14)SELF RESPECT (belief in one's own worth)

(15) RECIPROCATION OF FAVOURS (avoidance of indebtedness)

(16) CREATIVITY (uniqueness, imagination)

(17) A WORLD AT PEACE (free of war and conflict)

(18) RESPECT FOR TRADITION (preservation of time-honoured customs)

(19) MATURE LOVE (deep emotional and spiritual intimacy)

(20) SELF-DISCIPLINE (self-restraint, resistance to temptation)

(21) DETACHMENT (from worldly concerns)

(22) FAMILY SECURITY (safety for loved ones)

(23) SOCIAL RECOGNITION (respect, approval by others)

(24) UNITY WITH NATURE (fitting into nature)

(25) A VARIED LIFE (filled with challenge, novelty and change)

(26) WISDOM (a mature understanding of life)

(27) AUTHORITY (the right to lead or command)

(28) TRUE FRIENDSHIP (close, supportive friends)

(29) A WORLD OF BEAUTY (beauty of nature and the arts)

(30) SOCIAL JUSTICE (correcting injustice, care for the weak)

Values list 2

(31) INDEPENDENT (self-reliant, self-sufficient)

(32) MODERATE (avoiding extremes of feeling and action)

(33) LOYAL (faithful to my friends, group)

(34) AMBITIOUS (hard-working, aspiring)

(35) BROADMINDED (tolerant of different ideas and beliefs)

(36) HUMBLE (modest, self-effacing)

(37) DARING (seeking adventure, risk)

(38) PROTECTING THE ENVIRONMENT (preserving nature)

(39) INFLUENTIAL (having an impact on people and events)

(40) HONOURING OF PARENTS AND ELDERS (showing respect)

(41) CHOOSING OWN GOALS (selecting own purposes)

(42) HEALTHY (not being sick physically or mentally)

(43) CAPABLE (competent, effective, efficient)

(44) ACCEPTING MY POSITION IN LIFE (submitting to life's circumstances)

(45) HONEST (genuine, sincere)

(46) PRESERVING MY PUBLIC IMAGE (protecting my 'face')

(47) OBEDIENT (dutiful, meeting obligations)

(48) INTELLIGENT (logical, thinking)

(49) HELPFUL (working for the welfare of others)

(50) ENJOYING LIFE (enjoying food, sex, leisure, etc.)

(51) DEVOUT (holding to religious faith and belief)

(52) RESPONSIBLE (dependable, reliable)

(53) CURIOUS (interested in everything, exploring)

(54) FORGIVING (willing to pardon others)

(55) SUCCESSFUL (achieving goals)

(56) CLEAN (neat, tidy).

Schwartz (1992) and his collaborators wanted to understand whether there were values that transcended culture. Schwartz identified what values people held in eighty-two countries and found that people's values can be broadly organized into ten types. Schwartz called this the Theory of Basic Human Values, which are:

- **Benevolence** – active protection of others' welfare.

- **Universalism** – equality and justice.

- **Self-direction** – independence in thought and action.

- **Stimulation** – excitement.

- **Hedonism** – sensuous and emotional gratification.

- **Achievement** – personal success through competence.

- **Power** – status and respect.

- **Security** – safety and harmony of self and social groups.

- **Conformity** – restraint of actions and impulses likely to harm others or violate norms.

- **Tradition** – respect, acceptance, and commitment to cultural customs.

Personal values can be reflected in the values at work, which may be categorized into two facets. The first facet is whether the work value concerns an *outcome* of work (e.g. recognition, pay) or a *resource* that one shares merely by being associated with the work organization (e.g. working conditions, company reputation). The second facet categorizes work outcomes into *instrumental* (e.g. benefits), *affective* (e.g. relationship with co-workers) and *cognitive* (e.g. achievement, contribution to society). Some values are associated with the work ethic – achievement and hard working – whereas others are related to interpersonal relationships at work (Hui, 1992).

Employees who score highly on these work values focus on the *content* of their work. They are intrinsically motivated, achievement-orientated and hardworking, striving to move upwards, and seek challenges. They usually have higher education and occupy senior positions in organizations and tend to be higher in organizational commitment.

There are other values which are associated with the *context* of work: high salary, job security, pleasant physical working environment and many fringe benefits. These are more related to a person's basic survival needs than are the content-orientated values. People who have strong context-orientated, and thus extrinsic, work values ascribe much importance to social status, comfort, salary and benefits. They view work not as an end in itself, but as a means to attain other, more desirable, ends. It is quite possible that a fairly large proportion of workers in developing countries are context-orientated, as they strive to better the livelihood of themselves and their families: work is primarily a chance for them to move up the social ladder. Employees who hold these values are often lower in organizational commitment than other employees (Hui, 1992).

The important issue is first that personal values may not be the same as company values. The second is that people differ in their values. It is these differences that can lead to all sorts of problems. Consider one that can lead to various problems: equity vs equality. For instance, some trade unions oppose performance management systems because they believe in equality: equal pay for equal work. People in the same job should receive the same pay. But those who believe in equity (see Chapter 6) argue that you should be paid for productivity at the job and because people with the same job title have very difference performance levels so their rewards should reflect this. So what if the company stresses equity and rewards equally?

Ethics and social responsibility at work

Business ethics is primarily about people at work resolving conflicting interests between different groups such as customers, directors, employees, investors and suppliers. It is usually concerned with applying tests of fairness and integrity which is essentially about rights, duties and a shared sense of moral values. Business ethics pervades all aspects of business life. It concerns the avoidance and evasion of taxes; following legal processes and procedures; the hiring and firing of people; dealing with trade unions; marketing and sales policies; and respect for intellectual property.

Business ethics and practices are often culturally specific: what is thought of as desirable or acceptable in one culture may be quite different in another. Business ethics questions apply at very different levels:

- At the *societal level*, questions concern the ethics of dealing with certain countries, the desirability of capitalism versus socialism and the role of government in the marketplace. At this level the discourse is about societies and principles.

- At the *stakeholder level*, questions concern the employees, suppliers, customers, shareholders and those related to them. Ethical questions here are about the company's obligation to these various groups.

- At the *company policy level*, the questions concern all the company's rules and regulations, the ethical implications of lay-offs, perks, work rules, motivation, leadership, payment schemes and so on.

- At the *personal level*, the ethical questions are about how people in the organization should and do behave with each other.

Business ethics are concerned with values, rights, duties and rules. To a large extent, companies are interested in the definition and application of rules covering things such as keeping promises, and mutual respect for persons and property. Many organizations even try to enshrine their ethics in the company mission statement.

The topic of business ethics has become high profile with so many cases of corrupt business practices, dishonest CEOs and rogue traders. Ethics are relative judgements: business ethics is a journey rather than a destination. Many people face ethical dilemmas regularly: the conflict between tax avoidance and social responsibility; between protecting friends who are immoral and about the rationing of scarce resources.

Firstly, why is business ethics so high on the business agenda? The answer seems to be the numerous headline financial scandals and the fact that consumers and investors appear to be losing trust in business people. According to Edelman's 2017 Trust Barometer, 55 per cent of British people have little to no trust in the financial sector. People in business understand the importance and value of 'reputational risk' which many see as higher than credit, market or operational risk.

Secondly, it is uncertain whether 'ethical organizations' do better (make more money, are more stable) than a-ethical or non-ethical organizations. The data is weak and difficult to obtain and the vested interest in the answer too high. But there is research in support of the basic contention. There is enough evidence to suggest 'being good is good business' – that ethical corporations financially outperform less ethical organizations.

For some, the concept of *caveat emptor* (let the buyer beware) was enough. It was, so many believed, the duty of companies to serve their shareholders, employees and customers by maximizing profits and staying within the law. But, over the past decade or so, for a variety of reasons, businessmen, academics and writers have been considering in more detail the relationship and responsibility between companies and society. As a result, the sub-discipline of business ethics has arisen. Its questions include the following:

- Should a company place the interests of its shareholders before that of its employees or of the environment?

- Should a company be responsible for all the social consequences of its operations?
- When is regulation necessary, when excessive and when counter-productive?
- What does a corporation 'owe' its employees?
- To what extent should an organization be accountable for their products?
- Is there an ethical difference between tax avoidance and evasion?
- Is the only social responsibility of business to maximize profits?

Johannes Brinkman, a business ethics scholar at the BI Norwegian Business School, argues that there are at least four distinguishable approaches to professional ethics:

First there is the *moral conflict* approach which sees ethics as primarily a way to analyse, handle and prevent conflict by addressing or introducing a moral dimension to decision making.

The second is the *professional code* approach that sees professional ethics as essentially a question of developing and implementing rule sets of desirable behaviour.

The third is the *professional role morality* approach which focuses on conflicting rights and duties between multiple parties at work.

The fourth is the *moral climate* approach which stresses the collective conscience of the organization and the predominant ideology with respect to ethical behaviours. It is recognized that these approaches are indeed linked and that organizations will employ more than one at a time.

Researchers have tried to find universal moral standards which they may be able to use to develop robust international corporate codes of ethics. Schwartz

(2004) believed it is possible to identify six universal moral standards: trustworthiness, respect, responsibility, fairness, caring and citizenship. Thus it was argued it is possible to develop specific principles:

- Be honest to stakeholders.

- Stick to values despite financial loss.

- Fulfil commitments.

- Avoid conflicts of interest.

- Respect the rights of others.

- Take responsibility for actions.

- Treat stakeholders fairly.

- Avoid unnecessary harm.

- Act benevolently.

- Obey the law.

- Protect the environment.

Friedman (1980) argued that businesses should concentrate on producing goods and services efficiently and legally, in open and free competition and without deception and fraud, but socio-ethical problems should be left to concerned individuals and government agencies.

Corporate Social Responsibility (CSR) is in essence a self-regulatory strategy that complies with some social norms and aims at social good. Organizations often focus on specific themes such as environmental protection and sustainability, community involvement and ethical marketing. There are various mantras used like 'people, planet and profit'. We are a carbon neutral, diversity sensitive employer.

Critics have always called it window dressing and hypocrisy. They claim that companies often have CSR programmes for very cynical reasons such as brand differentiation, reduced scrutiny from authorities and better supplier relations. Their motives are to misdirect criticism, also to get good PR. But it can easily have the opposite effect if the hypocrisy and cynicism is exposed.

Arguments for social involvement of business

- Public needs have changed, leading to changed expectations. Business, it is suggested, received its charter from society and consequently has to respond to the needs of society.

- The creation of a better social environment benefits both society and business. Society gains through better neighbourhoods and employment opportunities; business benefits from a better community, since the community is the source of its workforce and the consumer the source of its products and services.

- Social involvement discourages additional government regulation and intervention. The result is greater freedom and more flexibility in decision making for business.

- Business has a great deal of power that, it is reasoned, should be accompanied by an equal amount of responsibility.

- Modern society is an interdependent system, and the internal activities of the enterprise have an impact on the external environment.

- Social involvement may be in the interests of stockholders.

- Problems can become profits. Items that may once have been considered waste (e.g. empty soft-drink cans) can be profitably used again.

- Social involvement creates a favourable public image. Thus, a firm may attract customers, employees and investors.

- Business should try to solve the problems that other institutions have not been able to solve. After all, business has a history of coming up with novel ideas.

- Business has the resources. Specifically, business should use its talented managers and specialists, as well as its capital resources, to solve some of society's problems.

- It is better to prevent social problems through business involvement than to cure them. It may be easier to help the hard-core unemployed than to cope with social unrest.

Arguments against social involvement of business

- The primary task of business is to maximize profit by focusing strictly on economic activities. Social involvement could reduce economic efficiency.

- In the final analysis, society must pay for the social involvement of business through higher prices. Social involvement would create excessive costs for business, which cannot commit its resources to social action.

- Social involvement can create a weakened international balance of payments situation. The cost of social programmes, the reasoning goes, would have to be added to the price of the product. Thus, companies selling in international markets would be at a disadvantage when competing with companies in other countries that do not have these social costs to bear.

- Business has enough power, and additional social involvement would further increase its power and influence.

- Business people lack the social skills to deal with the problems of society. Their training and experience is with economic matters, and their skills may not be pertinent to social problems.

- There is a lack of accountability of business to society. Unless accountability can be established, business should not get involved.

- There is not complete support for involvement in social actions. Consequently, disagreements among groups with different viewpoints will cause friction.

Ethics committees

Many kinds of public institutions have found it necessary to appoint ethics committees.

Ethics committees are formed usually to facilitate decisions as to whether a course of action – such as conducting a research project – fulfils certain criteria. The theory is that a group of (wise) individuals can perform a disinterested evaluation of a proposed course of action that minimizes harm to any and maximizes benefits to many.

Ethics committees are in some senses like juries. One crucial difference is how people get into these groups. Juries are usually co-opted, conscripted and many fight, kicking and screaming, to be exempt. On the other hand, ethics committees are often staffed by happy volunteers eager to take part. The jury system of ethics committees has come under increasing critical scrutiny not only for their expense and inefficiency but their record of poor judgements. But at the same time ethics committees appear to be mushrooming in schools and hospitals, universities and businesses.

There are three major problems with the way people use and think about ethics committees. The first is about ethics itself. The assumption is that, just as one does not have to have any detailed knowledge or understanding of the law to join a jury, so one need know nothing of ethics to join an ethics committee. This analogy is wrong for a number of reasons. First, there are competing ethical systems. What is right and just for the situational ethicist is simply not true for the absolutist. Different rules may be seen to apply; hence ethics. One may have different interpretations of the law, but one legal system. Consider the following very different ethical positions that one may take with regard to the allocation of scarce medical resources:

Lottery: the random allocation of interventions, through drawing recipients blindly.

First-come, first-served: allocating interventions based on the order of request, or requirement.

Sickest first: prioritizing those with the worst future prospects if left untreated.

Youngest first: prioritizing those who have had the least life years, and thus have the potential to live longer if cured.

Save the most lives: aiming to save the most individual lives possible, through offering all people treatment.

Prognosis or life-years: aiming to save the most life-years, thus prioritizing those with positive prognoses, and excluding those with poor prognoses.

Instrumental value: prioritizing those with specific skills and usefulness – e.g. those producing a vaccine, or those who have agreed to improve their health following treatment and thus requiring fewer resources (stop smoking, lose weight, etc.).

Reciprocity: prioritizing those who have been useful in the past – e.g. past organ donors.

Second, it is the role of the judge not only to control the court but when necessary to explain the law. Judges are experts and highly knowledgeable in the way that the chairperson of a committee is not. Indeed it is not always clear how and why one person is elected to chair an ethical committee

Third, jurors are vetted in the way volunteers for ethical committees are not. Indeed it has been suggested that the motives for people volunteering for ethical committees are far from ethical themselves. Researchers will tell you time and time again about the massive delays that committees cause, but more that people in these groups seems to have little or no knowledge about research like the point of double blind, randomized control trials. It is not unusual to hear deeply frustrated researchers postulating that some people try to get elected to committees precisely to prevent their more successful research colleagues doing more work.

It would therefore be desirable, perhaps necessary, for someone to know something about ethics and to have a view on what system they intend to follow. Are they Utilitarians or not? What principles should be followed? Rather than select amateurs, select people who really know something about ethics, which is an interesting and sophisticated research area.

The fallacy is that groups of individuals make more considered cautious and wise decisions than individuals alone. But in fact there is a wealth of evidence suggesting the opposite, namely that groups nearly always make more extreme decisions. That is, they can be excessively cautious or excessively risky. There are well-documented reasons as to why this may occur.

For ethics committees it is too easy to say no. To default on the negative certainly decreases their chances of being blamed. It is not difficult to find reasons for not doing something. In this sense ethics committees can be extremely conservative and pro the status quo.

The third problem concerns the real reason why we have seen a tremendous increase in the number of ethics committees in the first place. The answer is litigation. This is a growing and massively complicated area. Ethics committees may or may not help the problem of litigation. Unless of course it is their explicit remit and there is a lawyer on board. Once one has incurred legal fees with respect to being sued over some ethical issue most organizations see the wisdom of having all protocols not sent to an ethics committee but to a sharp lawyer.

To make ethics committees function, the following seem useful requirements:

1   Have a chair who knows about ethics.

2   Decide on a system or code that is to be implemented.

3   Choose and vet committee members carefully and do not have too many.

4   Have a lawyer on board.

5   Ensure this process and dynamic is functional not dysfunctional.

6   Ensure the committee knows precisely its function and duties.

7   Have an appeals procedure that is open and fair.

8   Ensure people have a set period on the committee and do not automatically renew to become stale, entrenched and out-of-date.

9   Give the committee feedback on their earlier decisions so that they learn from their possible mistakes.

10   Consider changing the name from ethics committee to something else.

Corporate culture

Companies have a culture, defined succinctly as 'the way we do things around here'. How is it that so many individuals within an organization share basic attitudes, behaviour patterns, expectations and values? In other words, how does a culture form and how is it maintained? What is the origin of corporate culture? Corporate culture is based on the needs of individuals to reduce uncertainty and to have some reference to guide their actions. This uncertainty-reducing need is resolved by the evolution of behaviour standards (*do's* and *don'ts*) and norms of perceiving events.

Firstly, organizational culture may be traced, at least in part, to the *founders of the company* or those who strongly shaped it in the recent past. These individuals often possess dynamic personalities, strong values and a clear vision of how the organization should be. Since they are on the scene first, and/or play a key role in hiring initial staff, their attitudes and values are readily transmitted to new employees. The result is that these views become the accepted ones in the organization, and persist as long as the founders are on the scene, or even longer. Given the length of time over which cultures become established, the reasons why people do things may well be forgotten, yet they perpetuate the values and philosophies of founders.

Secondly, organizational culture often develops out of, or is changed by, an *organization's experience with external exigencies*. Every organization must find a niche and an image for itself in its sector and in the marketplace. As it struggles to do so, it may find that some values and practices work better for it than others – for example, one organization may gradually acquire a deep, shared commitment to high quality, and another company may find that selling products of moderate quality, but at low prices, works best for it. The result is that a dominant value centring on price leadership takes shape.

Hence, the pressure to change the corporate culture to 'fit' the external environment is constant, particularly in turbulent times. Indeed, it is because the business environment changes more rapidly than the corporate culture that many managers see culture as a factor in business success.

Thirdly, culture develops from the *need to maintain effective working relationships* among organization members. Depending on the nature of its business, and the characteristics of the person it must employ, different expectations and values may develop. Thus, if a company needs rapid and open communication between its employees, and informal working relationships, an open expression of views will probably come to be valued within it. In contrast, very different values and styles of communication may develop in other organizations working in other industries with different types of personnel. Just as groups go through a well known sequence in their development, remembered as *forming, storming, norming* and *performing*, so do corporate cultures. Indeed, it is the development of behavioural norms that is at the very heart of culture.

For Schein (1990) culture is created through two main factors. *Firstly*, there is norm formation around critical incidents, particularly where mistakes have occurred; that is, the lessons learnt from important corporate events (often crises) are crucially important factors in the formation (or change) of culture. *Secondly*, there is identification with leaders and what leaders pay attention to, measure and control; how leaders react to critical incidents and organizational crises; deliberate role modelling and coaching; operational criteria for the allocation of rewards and status; operational criteria for recruitment selection, promotion retirement and excommunication. The role of unique visionary leaders cannot be understated. Understanding the factors that lead to the establishment of corporate culture are important because they also serve to highlight the factors that need to be concentrated on when changing that culture. So why does culture relate to work motivation and demotivation? Consider the work of Cooke and Lafferty (1989) who developed a measure of corporate culture with three domains and twelve facets.

The four constructive styles

The corresponding cultural styles allow the employees to act constructively and in a self-determined manner (Cook and Lafferty, 1989). 'Task related aspects' and 'humanistic aspects' are equally considered in decision making processes. These kinds of behaviour are particularly important for the success of the company. Successful corporations score high in this area.

- **Achievement** – attaining high quality-results on a continuous basis.
- **Self-actualizing** – finding unique and individual solutions.
- **Humanistic-encouraging** – coaching and counselling others and providing them with support and encouragement.
- **Affiliative** – developing and sustaining pleasant relationships.

The four aggressive/defensive styles

These styles reflect self-promoting thinking and behaviour used to maintain one's status/position and fulfil security needs through task related activities.

- **Oppositional** – emphasising flaws, looking for confrontation.
- **Power** – equating self-worth with controlling others.
- **Competitive** – viewing even non-competitive situations as contests and win–lose situations.
- **Perfectionistic** – needing to attain flawless results and placing excessive demands on oneself and others.

The four passive/defensive styles

These styles represent self-protecting thinking and behaviour that promote the fulfilment of security needs through interactions with people.

- **Approval** – being accepted and liked by others through pleasing them, making good impressions, being agreeable and obedient.
- **Conventional** – conforming and 'blending in', relying on established routines and securing a predictable work environment.

- **Dependent** – allowing others to make decisions for oneself, depending on others for help and obeying orders willingly.

- **Avoidance** – withdrawing from threatening situations, minimizing risks and reacting in an indecisive and non-committal way.

In many ways it may be possible to describe a hypocritical corporate culture, where the corporate culture is quite clearly oppositional and competitive but 'pretends' to be supportive and competitive. It is particularly galling to employees to hear senior staff saying how much the organization values openness, social support, and being caring when their personal experience is exclusively of secretiveness, competiveness and selfishness.

There is a big business in culture change which usually involves assessing the current culture, describing the ideal culture and attempting to reconcile the gap. It is a long and difficult process and involves coming to terms with a great deal of hypocracy.

Office politics

We have national politics and local politics, but we also have office politics. Office politics seem to be a catch-all, supermarket trolley of wickedness. 'He plays politics all the time'; 'Office politics caused the failure'; 'She was only promoted because of office politics.' If you ask any person to rate their organization on a 10-point scale as to how political it is (0 low; 10 high) people often will say 11. That is, they believe their organization is not what it seems: what is on the surface and said is very different from what is under the surface.

Ask people: 'When you think of "organizational politics", what words come to mind?' They tend to respond: 'backstabbing, brown-nosing, bootlicking, style-over-substance, manipulative, hidden agendas, old boy networks, deals under the table, turf struggles, testosterone overload.

What are the key features of the concept of office politics? First perhaps is the *secrecy*, the covert agendas, and the under-handedness of it all. Politics conducted in smokey rooms, behind closed doors, in private clubs, on the golf course. There are the insiders and the outsiders. The players and the pawns. Those in the know and those in the dark. Politics are exclusionary. Office politics are about processes, procedures and decisions that are not meant to be scrutinized. Politics are about opaqueness, not transparency.

Secondly, there is an *impression management* to office politics. Another word for this may be hypocrisy. Office politicians speak with forked tongue. The clever ones understand the difference between sins of omission and commission. The others just dissimulate. What you see, hear and read is not what you get. Internal communications (except those carefully encrypted) are half truths, little more than management propaganda. Office politics are about censorship; about disguise.

Third, office politics are is about *self-interest*. They are concerned with power and all of the trappings like money and prestige; about select groups high-jacking activities, processes and procedures to secure their (and only their) interests. Covert groupings of individuals based on clan, ideology or simply greed, co-operate with each other to obtain an unfair share of the resources of an organization. In this sense office politics act against long-term organizational interests at least from a shareholder perspective.

Those who like to categorize people suggest there are essentially two dimensions relevant to office politics: how aware people are and how manipulative they are. This yields four types as shown in Figure 5.2.

The negative view is clear. Politics cause distrust, conflict and lowered productivity. People do not openly share, they are guarded. They spend too

Baddeley & James, 1987

Adapted from Haddeley & James, 1987

much time and energy ingratiating themselves to the in-group and try to work the system. The in-group are as much concerned with increasing or holding onto power as steering the company. The opposition is internal not external. Office politics are dysfunction.

But there is another perspective and it is much more positive. Office politics are about building and strengthening networks and coalition. About getting together movers and shakers prepared to do the hardest thing of all; making change happen; about driving through necessary but unpopular strategies; about identifying those with energy and vision – those who command various constituencies.

The researchers in this area have identified four dimensions to the positive side of office politics, often called *Office savvy*:

1 **Social awareness** – a leader's ability to astutely observe others to understand their behaviours and motives.

2 **Interpersonal influence** – a leader's ability to influence and engage others using a compelling and charismatic interpersonal style.

3 **Networking** – a leader's ability to build diverse relationship networks across and outside of the organization.

4 **Apparent sincerity** – a leader's ability to be forthright, open, honest and genuine with others.

Why are some organizations more political? Organizations at the high end of the scale (and probably the ones with problems in this area) are likely to be those where some or all of the following apply:

- Excessive competition at the top: this can lead to all sorts of 'sculdugery' to first achieve and then maintain high positions.

- Complex structures; these can hide all sorts of bad behaviour.

- High (or very low) level of change; the ambiguity of the former and the frustration with the latter can lead to much politics.

- Refusal by powerful people to change; this may lead less powerful people to attempt to oust those above them who they do not respect.

- Punishment culture; (see above).

- Limited resources; fights over scarce and valuable resources of many sorts often causes considerable problems.

- Jobs at risk; this really encourages people to act in devious and underhand ways to preserve their jobs.

Politics are about power – the power to influence, persuade and cajole. Most organizations seek out and admire a CEO who is well respected and connected. One who knows how to play-the-game; how to get people (investors, journalists and 'real' politicians) onside. In this sense being political is about being shrewd, pro-active and strategic. CEOs have to present a positive picture of their organization. They have to align, steer and change the organization, so they turn to those who have a reputation for doing so.

You can not outlaw office politics. You might want to blame everything from personal failure to falling share price on office politics, and there is no doubt that some offices are dysfunctional places to be. But better to study and try to understand management power than condemn it.

Conclusion

Every organization likes to think of, and portray itself, in a very positive light: a company where the workers are happy; the goods and services are fairly supplied and priced; where they pay their taxes but keep all their shareholders happy. Some are prepared to pay relatively large sums of money on public relations and internal communications to achieve this end. Indeed many put a lot of stress on honesty, integrity and transparency. They often compete for awards and certification of the organization passing some (semi-rigorous) test to 'prove' the above.

However, for many people in these organizations the reality is somewhat different. What they experience on a day-to-day basis can be the precise opposite of the well-trumpeted values and mission of the company. The company proclaims its honesty and integrity while staff are encouraged to fool naive customers into paying more. Bullying is hushed up and various help-lines for whistle-blowers are powerless.

Imagine what it is like for the employee to walk past, everyday, large signs that proclaim the company values which are untrue; reading job advertizements which describe the organization in terms that are patently false; hearing a senior manager on the media talk about the company in words and concepts that are dishonest lies. It is the outrage that goes with witnessing this continual and deliberate dishonesty that starts the process of disenchantment.

DISENCHANTMENT CASE 1: LENNON BROWN

The following comments are from former and current employees of large organizations, sourced from Glassdoor.

'They say the right words, but there is no substance behind them or there is blatant dishonesty.'

'The pay scale is ridiculous with some cabin crew earning four times what others do for doing exactly the same job.'

'You get treated like dirt.'

'I have been let down by this company.'

THIS CASE OF DISENCHANTMENT REACHED its climax on 23 December 2013. Brown was a computer engineer for Citibank, where he was responsible for researching, designing, developing, and testing the technological systems within the company.

The IT systems that Brown governed were the lifeblood to Citibank's internal workings, including everything from telecommunications to computer software. Brown started working for Citibank as a contractor, but was brought on as a fully fledged employee at their campus in Texas early in 2013.

With two days to go until Christmas, Brown was scheduled for performance appraisal with his manager. Needless to say, it did not go well. Brown had only fully been with the company for nine months, and his performance in that time had been lacking. Brown's manager did not hold back in letting him know how poor his work had been.

Later that day, Brown was reported to have waited for working hours to finish for the day. After everyone had gone home, he was looking for a way to respond to what had been said (as well as how it had been said) during his appraisal. He was disenchanted and looking for revenge.

Brown swiped his ID badge to enter the building at 18:03 that evening. He logged into his computer and sent a code and command to ten of the core Citibank Global Control Center routers. In doing so, Brown had erased the running configuration files in nine of the routers. The result: 90 per cent of Citibank's North American operations were completely shut down. Brown swiped his ID badge at 18:05 and left the building.

In those two minutes, Brown had managed to cause massive financial and reputational damage to his employer. In the successive fallout, Brown sent the following text to his co-workers to explain what he had done:

'They was firing me. I just beat them to it. Nothing personal, the upper management need to see what they guys on the floor is capable of doing when they keep getting mistreated. I took one for the team.

Sorry if I made my peers look bad, but sometimes it take something like what I did to wake the upper management up.'

Whilst the consequence was extreme, the motivation behind Brown's action was not. Brown was a severely disenchanted employee and felt driven to cause damage in response to how his manager had treated him.

The question is this: how did Citibank respond to this case of disenchantment? Information security specialists use Brown's case as an example of how companies should protect against the potential insider threat by implementing greater IT restrictions, monitoring employees for 'unusual' activity, and putting new policies in place for IT and human resources.

The reality is that this was not a technological problem, but a human one. The solution therefore needs to be a human one as well. Not all disenchanted employees would have taken the extreme measures that Brown did. Most disenchanted employees engage in more passive forms of retaliation: higher absenteeism, deliberately doing work slowly and badly, and eventually they will leave to join a competitor. But that is not to say that some disenchanted employees will not try to take revenge along the way. Understanding how, where and why employees are becoming disenchanted is key to reducing the motivation for insider threat.

Brown was arrested shortly after 23 December. He pleaded guilty to intentional damage to a protected computer, and has since been sentenced to twenty-one months in prison and to has been ordered repay $77,200 in restitution.

6

A Sense of Fairness: Perceived Equity and Inequity

Fairness is man's ability to rise above his prejudices.
WES FESLER

Win or lose, do it fairly.
KNUTE ROCKNE

Justice is a certain rectitude of mind whereby a man does what he ought to do in circumstances confronting him.
SAINT THOMAS AQUINAS

Introduction

Without doubt, the 'hottest' word in the workplace is the F-Word: *Fairness*. Listen to any politician for the consistent overuse of the word. Both politicians of the right and the left claim that their policies will ensure 'a fairer society'. The same is true for many CEOs. They want to be 'fair' to all their stakeholders. However, as we shall see, one person's definition of fairness may be quite different from another's.

What is very clear is that perceptions of unfairness at work are immediately and powerfully related to disenchantment. Nearly everyone assumes that they will be fairly treated at all levels: that pay is fair and related to skills and effort; that promotion policies and practices are fair and that service and ability are the main factors; and that people are treated fairly with discipline issues. Fairness is about justice.

Once evidence of unfairness and the dirty 'D' word – *Discrimination* – occurs, a person can pass very quickly into a state of *deep disenchantment*. To suddenly find that, despite what your boss or organization has assured and promised you, the distribution of rewards and punishments that is patently not just and deeply unfair can cause a disenchantment wound from which it may be very difficult to recover.

A person's sense of justice and fairness is based primarily on comparisons. It is less about how much people earn *absolutely* than how much they earn *comparatively* that determines their pay satisfaction. Hence issues with pay secrecy (see below). People who work together know better than anyone else their relative contributions to effort and outcome. Some people always 'pitch up and pitch in'; others are much less happy to pull their own weight. The sense of *a fair wage for a fair day's work* is very comparative.

Equity theory

Equity theory views motivation from the perspective of the comparisons people make among themselves. It proposes that employees are motivated to maintain fair, or 'equitable', relationships among themselves and to change those relationships that are unfair or 'inequitable'.

Equity is not the same as *equality*. People assume equal opportunity but differences in effort and ability. This is not an argument against equal pay for equal work, but rather the extent to which people really work equally hard. It has been argued and demonstrated that the top 10 per cent of workers in any group typically produce two- to four-times the output of the bottom 10 per cent. The question is whether to reward them equally or equitably in terms of their output.

Equity theory is concerned with people's motivation to escape the negative feelings that result from being, or feeling that they are, treated unfairly. They engage in a continual process of *social comparison*. Equity theory suggests that people make social comparisons between themselves and others with respect to two variables – *outcomes* (benefits, rewards) and *inputs* (effort, ability):

1 **Outcomes** refer to the things workers believe they and others get out of their jobs, including pay, fringe benefits or prestige. Some are more easy to compare than others: pay is, of course, the easiest.

2 **Inputs** refer to the contribution employees believe they and others make to their jobs, including the amount of time worked, the amount of effort expended, the number of 'colleagues helped', or the qualifications brought to the job.

Equity theory is concerned with outcomes and inputs as they are *perceived* by the people involved, not necessarily as they *actually* are. Thus workers may disagree about what constitutes equity and inequity in the job. Equity is therefore a subjective, not objective, experience, which makes it more susceptible to being influenced by personality factors and other individual differences. Employees compare themselves to others. Essentially they have four choices:

1   **Self-inside** – an employee's comparison to others in a different position inside his or her current organization.

2   **Self-outside** – an employee's comparison to the experiences of others in a situation, job or position outside his or her current organization.

3   **Other-inside** – comparisons with another individual or group of individuals inside the employee's organization.

4   **Other-outside** – comparisons with another individual or group of individuals outside the employee's organization.

Equity theory states that people compare their outcomes and inputs to those of others in the form of a ratio. This can result in any of three states: *overpayment*, *underpayment*, or *equitable payment*:

- **Overpayment inequity** occurs when someone's outcome:input ratio is *greater than* the corresponding ratio of another person with whom that person compares himself or herself. People who are overpaid are supposed to feel *guilty*. There are relatively few people in this position.

- **Underpayment inequity** occurs when someone's outcome:input ratio is *less than* the corresponding ratio of another with whom that person compares himself or herself. People who are underpaid are supposed to feel *angry*. Many people feel under-benefited.

- **Equitable payment** occurs when someone's outcome:input ratio is *equal to* the corresponding ratio of another person with whom that person compares himself or herself. People who are equitably paid are supposed to feel *satisfied*.

According to equity theory, people are motivated to escape these negative emotional states of anger and guilt. We are deeply motivated to achieve equity or fairness. Further we are easily rendered disenchanted when the organization or particular people institute, cover-up or even try to justify unfairness. This can include discrimination against various groups of individuals.

Equity theory admits two major ways of resolving inequitable states:

1   **Behavioural** reactions to equity represent things people can do to change their existing inputs and outcomes, such as working more or less hard (to increase or decrease inputs) or stealing time and goods (to increase outputs).

2   **Psychological** reactions are essentially cognitive. People may resort to resolving the inequity by changing the way they think about their situation.

Inequitable states may be redressed effectively by merely *thinking* about the circumstances differently. An underpaid person may attempt to *rationalize* that another's inputs are really higher than his or her own, thereby convincing himself or herself that the other's higher outcomes are justified.

There are various reactions to inequity: people can respond to overpayment and underpayment (i.e. being under-benefited) inequities in behavioural and/ or psychological ways (i.e. being over-benefited), which help change the perceived *inequities* into a state of perceived *equity*. Another way of seeing this is to point out that people have six possible reactions to perceived inequality:

1   Change their inputs (e.g. exert less effort, go absent).

2   Change their outputs (e.g. individuals paid on a piece-rate basis can increase their pay by producing more 'widgets' of lower quality, or they could steal).

3 Distort perceptions of self (e.g. 'I used to think I worked at an average pace; now I realise that I work a lot harder than everyone else.').

4 Distort perceptions of others (e.g. 'Her job isn't as easy and desirable as I previously thought it was.').

5 Choose a different referent (e.g. 'I may not make as much as my brother, but I'm doing a lot better than my next-door neighbour.').

6 Leave the field (e.g. quit the job; take early retirement).

The more unusual position is the overpaid individual who one could describe more as *uncomfortable* than *disenchanted*. Specifically, a salaried employee who feels overpaid may raise his or her inputs by working harder, or for longer hours or more productively. Similarly, employees who lower their own outcomes by not taking advantage of company-provided fringe benefits may be seen as redressing an overpayment inequity. Overpaid persons may convince themselves psychologically that they are really worth their higher outcomes by virtue of their superior inputs. People who receive substantial pay rises may not feel distressed about it at all because they rationalize that the increase is warranted on the basis of their superior inputs, and therefore does not constitute an inequity. The theory establishes four propositions relating to pay:

1 **Given payment by time, over-rewarded employees will produce more than equitably paid employees**. Hourly and salaried employees will generate high quantity or quality of production in order to increase the input side of the ratio and bring about equity.

2 **Given payment by quantity of production, over-rewarded employees will produce fewer, but higher-quality units, than will equitably paid employees.** Individuals paid on a piece-rate basis will increase their effort to achieve equity, which can result in greater

quality or quantity. However, increases in quantity will only increase inequity since every unit produced results in further overpayment. Therefore, effort is directed towards increasing quality rather than increasing quantity.

3 **Given payment by time, under-rewarded employees will produce less or poorer quality of output**. Effort will be decreased, which will bring about lower productivity or poorer-quality output than equitably paid subjects.

4 **Given payment by quantity of production, under-rewarded employees will produce many low-quality units in comparison with equitably paid employees.** Employees on piece-rate pay plans can bring about equity because trading off quality of output for quantity will result in an increase in rewards with little or no increase in contributions.

There are many studies on equity theory that show how people react to inequity. In one study a researcher hired male clerical workers to work part-time over a two-week period and manipulated the equity or inequity of the payment their employees received. *Overpaid* employees were told that the pay they received was higher than others doing the same work. *Underpaid* employees were told their pay was lower than that of others doing the same work. *Equitably paid* employees were told the pay they received was equal to that of others doing the same work.

People who were overpaid were more productive than those who were equitably paid. People who were underpaid were less productive than those who were equitably paid. Moreover, both overpaid and underpaid employees reported being more dissatisfied with their jobs than those who were equitably paid.

In another study, insurance company employees were temporarily and randomly assigned to offices of co-workers who were considered to be of equal, higher or lower status. Some employees remained in their own offices (the control group). Compared to employees who were transferred to offices with equal-status co-workers, those who were assigned to offices with higher-status co-workers raised their performance, and those who were assigned to offices with lower-status co-workers lowered their performance (as measured by number of life insurance applications).

In yet another study, theft rates among employees in manufacturing plants were studied during a period in which pay was temporarily reduced by 15 per cent. Because two large contracts were lost, the host company temporarily reduced its payroll across the board for the two plants. In plant 1, the president met with all employees and explained the causes of the pay cut and of its duration (10 weeks). Plant 2 had only a short meeting with employees; the amount of the cut was announced, but no other information or explanation was offered. No pay cuts were made in plant 3, and it was used as a control group.

Both the plants in which pay was reduced had significantly higher theft rates than the control plant did. However, plant 1 had a significantly lower theft rate than plant 2. Employees in plant 2 experienced the highest degree of perceived inequity. Workers whose pay reduction was adequately explained to them did not express greater payment inequity while their pay was reduced.

Equity theory has its problems: how to deal with the concept of negative inputs; the point at which equity becomes inequity; and the belief that people prefer and value equity over equality (see Equity sensitivity below).

The management implications are twofold: firstly, that comparative pay and benefits between different groups, sections and levels in an organization are a major source of motivation or demotivation; secondly, employees need to feel they are fairly dealt with – that they and their colleagues are rewarded equitably for their efforts. Of all the things that leads most quickly and powerfully to disenchantment, perceived lack of fairness at work is perhaps the most powerful.

Justice at work

The concept of fairness and justice at work in organizations can be traced back to the 1960s. Organizational justice is usually thought of as people's (manager and employee) *perceptions of fairness* in an organization's policies, pay systems and practices. The concept of justice and how justice is meted out in any organization is, nearly always, fundamental to that organization's corporate culture and mission.

The psychological literature tends to be *descriptive* (focusing on perceptions and reactions), whereas moral philosophy writings are more *prescriptive* (specifying what should be done). References to questions of justice and fairness occur whenever decisions have to be made about the allocation of resources, whatever they are in a particular business. Most, but by no means all, fairness-at-work issues focus on pay, but also include selection, promotion and the granting of particular privileges.

Organizational justice researcher's have, for forty years, carried out research on the economic and socio-emotional consequences of perceived injustice. In doing so, researchers have distinguished between various types of justice:

- **Distributive justice.** The allocation of outcome rewards in accordance with implicit or explicit norms like equality and equity.

- **Procedural justice.** The consistency, accuracy, lack of bias, correctability and representation in all decision-making processes at work.

- **Interpersonal justice.** The way people are treated (i.e. with respect, sensitivity, dignity) as justice procedures are enacted.

- **Informational justice.** The accuracy, timing and comprehensiveness of explanations for all justice procedures and distribution.

- **Retributive and retaliative justice.** The attempt to take revenge or retaliate against individuals, groups or organizations that have been perceived as treating one unfairly.
- **Restorative justice.** The attempt to restore justice to victims and their network.

It is possible to see two dimensions (proactive–reactive and process–content) which revealed four types of theory: *reactive content* (How do workers react to inequitable payments?), *proactive content* (How do workers attempt to create fair payments?), *reactive process* (How do workers react to unfair policies or legal procedures?), and *proactive process* (How do workers attempt to create fair policies or procedures?). Of these different types of justice, the following three are perhaps most relevant to disenchantment.

1   *Distributive justice.* Concern about the outcomes of justice decisions is called *distributive* justice. Research in distributive justice draws on the concept of 'rules of social exchange'. It is argued that rewards should be proportionate to costs, and the net rewards should be proportionate to investments. Most of the current research focuses on employees' perceptions of the fairness of the outcomes (both rewards and punishments) they receive. Results show clearly that fairness perceptions are based on relative judgements – that is, comparisons with salient others. Thus, how happy one is with fairness decisions (such as decisions about pay) is dependent on the perceptions or knowledge of *others'* pay. It is not the absolute amount of reward people focus on but their relative rewards compared to salient others

The question is *who* does one compare oneself to, on what *criterion* of one's job, and for *how long*? It seems that most employees are able to distinguish between unfavourable outcomes (not as good as one had hoped) and unfair outcomes. Clearly, employees react much more strongly and angrily to unfair, compared to unfavourable, outcomes. There may be cultural factors that relate to distributive justice; for example, in collectivist cultures equality decisions may be seen as more important than equity decisions; whereas the reverse is true of individualistic cultures.

2   *Procedural justice.* Procedural justice concerns *the means* rather than *the ends* of social justice decisions. These are questions about how fair decisions are made and the procedures and processes each organization has in place to make those decisions. Researchers have found that employees are more likely to accept organizational decisions on such things as smoking bans, parental leave policies, pay, and even disciplinary actions, if they believe the decisions are based on fair procedures. The evaluation of procedural justice issues depends on both the environmental context within which the interaction occurs and the treatment of it.

Although there are, or should be, general context-independent criteria of fairness, there are always special cases. Various factors are considered to be crucial in building a justice procedure that is characterized by consistency, non-partiality, accuracy, correctability, representative and openness. These include:

- Adequate notice for all interested parties to prepare.

- A fair hearing, in terms of giving all parties a fair chance to make their case.

- A perception that all judgements are made upon good evidence rather than on intuition.

- Evidence of two-way (bilateral) communication.

- The ability and opportunity to refute supposed evidence.

- Consistency of judgement over multiple cases.

Quite simply, procedures matter because a good system can lead people to take a long-term view, becoming tolerant of short-term economic losses for long-term advantage. Research has demonstrated many practical applications or consequences of organizational justice. Using fair procedures enhances employees' acceptance of institutional authorities. Further, staffing procedures (perceptions of fairness of selection devices) can have pernicious consequences. People at work often talk of particular types of injustice: unjustified accusation/ blaming; unfair grading/rating and/or lack of recognition for both effort and performance; and violations of promises and agreement.

3 *Interpersonal justice.* All employees are concerned with interactional justice, which is the quality of interpersonal treatment they receive at the hands of decision makers. Two features seem important here: *social sensitivity*, or the extent to which people believe that they have been treated with dignity and respect, and *informational justification*, or the extent to which people believe they have adequate information about the procedures affecting them.

Restorative versus retributive justice at work

Restorative justice has become a familiar concept in the context of rehabilitating prisoners by making them face their victims. There are various calls for victims to be more involved in setting punishments rather than leaving it up to the law enforcers. Few crimes are victimless. The question is how best to reduce this type of crime.

It has become fashionable to contrast two very different approaches to crime, delinquency and deviance, be they at school or work. The contrast is between *retributive* and *restorative* justice. The former sees 'misbehaviour' in terms of breaking the law, the rules or the conventions; the latter sees it as adversely affecting many other people. Restorative justice focuses on the needs of victims and offenders, rather than legal principles or calculating and exacting punishment. It aims at repairing harm and reducing recidivism. It follows a very different set of procedures.

The retributive approach focuses on establishing blame or guilt, often through some adversarial process. It is believed that the evidence argued over by prosecution and defence will (hopefully, usually) establish *who* did *what* and *when,* and perhaps *why.* There may be, as part of this model, a lot of attention to due processes: following carefully and openly the proper procedures that ensure justice. It is a model that emphasizes head over heart: where argument and conflict of description and explanation are portrayed as abstract, impersonal and logical.

The restorative justice model involves many more people: usually those who were affected by the behaviour – the 'victim', their friends and family, witnesses even. Their task is twofold – to express their feelings but more importantly to undertake a problem-solving attempt to prevent recurrence. The objective is to fully attend to the victim's needs; to help re-integrate the offender and to get them to take real responsibility for their actions; to recreate a healthy community and avoid escalating the costs of traditional legal justice.

The retribution model aims to deter by some sort of *punishment*: pain, exclusion, firing. The restitution model aims for the restoration of property and well-being by *reconciliation.* The latter approach is usually more about relationships, respect and feelings. It is not about the pain that the perpetrator should receive, but the pain the victims feel. It is less about meting out the exact and appropriate amount of pain for that inflicted, and more about *repairing* the damage, hurt or injury to others.

Restorative justice assumes that people learn and change when they have a say in their behaviour: that is when things are done *with* them, rather than *to* or *for* them. Restorative justice is about engaging with the various parties involved: it is participatory.

The retributive model of the community within which the problem has occurred sees justice done by being on a jury or being spectators to the whole process. Hence, the importance of the representativeness of juries. The restoration model is rather more vague. Any, and all, of those in the community can and should be involved in the restoration project because all are affected.

Finally, there is the role of the wrong-doer. In the retributive model it is they who accept the punishment as a 'fair exchange' for their crime and a deterrent to others. In the restorative model it is all about fully understanding the impact of their actions – all of the consequences of the act – and deciding how best to put things right.

In summary, the more traditional model is about apportioning blame, the analysis of motives and decisions about punishment. The restorative approach is about establishing who has been affected, how to put things right and what can be learnt from the process.

How an organization deals with misdemeanours sends very powerful messages. The disenchanted are very sensitive to this. Some prefer a cover up, others a very public display of retribution. Some misdemeanours seem more abstractly victimless than others, such as theft or fraud, while others, such as interpersonal violence, have clear victims. Some people are traumatized for long periods. Which type of process would best help their recovery?

It may be possible for organizations to give offenders a choice in the type of justice that is served. For example, organizations could ask wrong-doers if they would prefer to do a week or a month of community service or to meet their victims and their families face-to-face. Offer them a chance to repair and restore goodwill, or be sacked or go to prison. There are reviews on all aspects of restorative justice. There is also a growing research base which looks at outcomes including a victim's satisfaction and recovery, criminal recidivism and the costs of this method. But most of the work appears to have been done in schools and small communities not in the larger, more corporate workplace. The question that requires further investigation is how well the method applies across a variety of workplaces and how successful it is.

Pay fairness and secrecy

There is an extensive literature on fairness-of-pay perceptions. These are related to sex, age and ethnicity as well as work-related motives and type of job. Studies have clearly demonstrated that satisfaction with pay is related to such things as the understanding of the pay plan and its perceived effectiveness as well as organizational commitment.

What is well established however is that nearly everyone makes remunerative comparisons; that is, they compare their salary with their peers. Previous research has shown a person's satisfaction with their salary is predominantly determined by a comparative process (references). Indeed it has been suggested that the single most powerful determinant of a person's satisfaction with their salary is the perceived salary of colleagues. More importantly, there is abundant evidence that if remunerative comparisons result in a discrepancy this usually leads to a sense of injustice which in turn leads to demotivation, lower productivity and turnover.

One way in which some employers have tried to deal with the problems of pay comparison processes has been to insist on secrecy: the idea that salaries are kept secret and staff are strictly forbidden to share pay information. Just after the First World War a big American company put out a 'policy memorandum' entitled 'Forbidding discussion among employees of salary received'. It threatened to 'instantly discharge people' who disclosed their 'confidential' salary in order to avoid invidious comparison and dissatisfaction.

The staff in this instance rejected the order and protested by marching with large signs showing their exact salaries.

The same issue continues to this day with employers worrying that pay discussion fuels 'hard feelings and discontentment'. Pay secrecy is complex. An organization may withhold information about an individual or their pay levels and/or they may provide pay ranges or average pay rises rather than the specifics. An organization may also restrict the manner in which pay information becomes available. It may threaten heavy sanctions for disclosure and discussion. There may be secrecy about pay level and structure as well as the basis and form of pay. Some employers very actively restrict the way pay information is made available. There is a continuum from complete secrecy to complete openness. For many pay secrecy is about respectful privacy and about individualism.

Colella and co-workers (2007) looked at the costs and benefits of pay secrecy. They argued that there were various costs:

First, employee judgements about fairness, equity and trust may be challenged. If people do not know exactly what amount individuals are paid and why, they surely infer or guess it. Yet uncertainty generates anxiety and vigilance about fairness. People believe that if information is withheld, it is for a reason. This in turn affects three types of justice judgements: *informational* (it being withheld); *procedural* (lack of employee voice and potential bias); and *distributional* (compressing the pay range).

Second, judgements about pay fairness will often be based on a general impression of the fairness in the organization. People see and remember all sorts of things (hiring, firing, perks) that are vivid examples of 'fairness'. So even if they have a 'fair but secret' pay policy it will be judged to be unfair if other (perhaps unrelated) actions do not look fair.

Third, secrecy breeds distrust. Openness about pay signals integrity. Secrecy may exacerbate views about organizational unfairness and corruption. Further it signals that the organization does not trust its employees. Secrecy reduces motivation by breaking the pay for performance linkage.

Fourth, people need to have, and perform best when given goals/targets/KPI and rewarded for them. But if they do not know the relative worth of the rewards (i.e. in pay secrecy) they may be less committed to those goals.

Fifth, pay secrecy could affect the labour market because it could prevent employees moving to better, more fitting, and rewarding jobs. Pay secret organizations may not easily lure or pull good employees from other organizations. Secrecy makes the market inefficient.

On the other hand, secrecy can bring real advantages to the organization:

First, secrecy can enhance organizational control and reduce conflict. Pay differentials can cause jealousy so that hiding them may prevent problems in *corps d'esprit*. Making pay open often can reduce differences, that is, the range distribution is narrower than the performance distribution. So, paradoxically, secrecy can increase fairness in the equity sense because people can more easily be rewarded for the full range of their outputs.

Second, secrecy prevents 'political' behaviour, union involvement and conflict. Openness is both economically inefficient and likely to cause conflict.

Third, pay secrecy allows organizations more easily to 'correct' historical and other pay equity. So, paradoxically, one can both minimize unfairness and discrimination as well as perceptions of those matters more easily by secrecy.

Fourth, secrecy benefits teamwork particularly in competitive individuals, organizations and cultures. It encourages interdependence rather than 'superstardom'.

Fifth, secrecy favours organizational paternalism in that organizations can (and do) argue that employees themselves want secrecy, and that this can reduce conflict, jealousy and distress. One can even suggest that workers might make irrational decisions if they know how much their colleagues are paid. So paternalistic secrecy can increase control and the 'feel good' factor.

Sixth, secrecy is another word for privacy, an increasing concern in a technologically sophisticated surveillance society. Perhaps this is why surveys show that employees are generally in favour of secrecy because they do not want their salaries discussed by their co-workers. Many employees are willing to trade-off their curiosity about the pay of others in exchange for not having their own package revealed (Collela et al., 2007).

Seventh, secrecy may increase loyalty or, put more negatively, labour market immobility. If employees can not compare their salaries they maybe less inclined to switch jobs to those which are better paid. So you get what is called continuance commitment through lack of poaching.

Clearly the cost–benefit ratio depends on different things. Much depends on the history of the organization. It is pretty difficult to 're-cork' the genie once it has escaped the bottle. It also depends on whether good, up-to-date, accurate industry compensation norms really exist. What does – on average – a senior partner in a law firm, a staff-nurse, or a store manager get paid? The public industry norm information can have a powerful effect on organizations that opt for secrecy or privacy.

The next issue is how the organization determines, or claims to determine, criteria for pay allocation. Does it allocate payment for years of service, for level, for performance on the job or for some combination of these? The more objective the criteria (number of calls made, number of widgets sold), the more difficult it is to keep pay secret. Next, appraisal systems should strive to be objective, equitable and fair. The fairer they are, the less need for secrecy.

When objective criteria are used, staff have less concern for secrecy. So subjectivity and secrecy are comfortable bed-fellows. When pay is secret, employees have to guess how they rank relative to others at the same level. That may be why high performers want secrecy more than low performers; they believe they are equitably being paid more and want to avoid jealousy and conflict. So if you believe you are well paid because of your hard work, secrecy is acceptable.

But what if they do not believe this? When pay secrecy is abolished, some people not only feel angry but also humiliated by exposure to relative deprivation. They feel unfairly dealt with and their easiest means of retaliation is inevitably to work less hard. Pay secrecy is not just a human resources issue. It relates to the organization's vision and values as well as to individual job motivation. Secrecy can lead to more management control, bigger differentials and less conflict. But can you enforce it? Paradoxically, the more enthusiastically an organization tries to enforce secrecy the more employees are likely to challenge the notion. Individuals and groups choose to, or not to, talk.

Once an organization has abolished or reduced secrecy the path back is near impossible. Next, if competitors have openness they might undermine secret systems. For openness to work, an organization needs to be clear in explaining how pay is related to performance at all levels and to defend the system.

However, the situation seems to be complex. The impact of pay secrecy on an individual's task performance is mediated and moderated by other factors, particularly a person's tolerance for inequity. It is because money is such a simple and 'objective' comparator that it excites such attention at work.

Equity sensitivity

There is evidence that some people can be more sensitive to equity issues than others. Most of us pay attention to input-output equity (i.e. what you give to and get from an organization), though some really take it very seriously. They are called *equity sensitive*. They adjust their inputs to those of others to ensure equity of effort and reward. However, there are two other groups. First, those who appear not to mind giving more than they receive. They are the *benevolents*.

There are also those called the *entitled,* who are pretty determined to ensure others do the lion's share.

A recent study examined the properties of the benevolent 'givers' and the entitled 'takers'. Many of these studies use the Equity Sensitive Instrument, though there are now others to choose from. *Benevolents* are those who are always socially useful. They think always more about giving than receiving and are prepared always to contribute and co-operate. They are prototypic altruists with the philosophy of 'service above self'. This is the tradition of maximum effort, high input without thought of reward. It is empathy and self-sacrifice; and the central message of various religions. Cynics and sceptics however believe that *benevolents* are disguising their real motives. These may be to gain social approval or to enhance their self-image or their reputation.

The *entitled* on the other hand believe they have a right to others' total, continual and unconditional support. They have a high threshold for feeling indebted. They seem to demand help and support from all around them as their due and feel little or no obligation to reciprocate. In this 'cloud cuckoo land', all are debtors but themselves. *Entitleds* are exploiters and manipulators. They employ charm, or temper tantrums, intimidation or attention seeking to achieve their end. They seem insatiable, they are 'getters'.

Entitled people seem to always be worried that they are not getting a better deal. They can be difficult to manage unless, of course, they have been paired up with *benevolents*. If work is being carried out on a piece-rate system *entitleds* tend to produce a lot, but usually at subsistence levels rather than achieving high quality. *Benevolents* tend to produce more and better work. This is particularly true under salaried work conditions. *Benevolents* are consistent and low in their absenteeism and turnover, regardless of the level and equity of reward. *Entitleds* are the opposite and will demonstrate high absenteeism and turnover if equity is not ensured. There is also evidence that *benevolents* and *entitleds* define work outcomes quite differently. Thus, doing 'challenging work' may be seen as a privilege by *benevolents* but as a source of stress by *entitleds*.

The origin and cultural normativeness of equity sensitivity remains to be investigated. Manfred Schmitt has worked extensively in this area and has devised the scale below to measure many of these issues (Schmitt et al., 2010).

People react quite differently in unfair situations. How about you? First, **we will look at situations to the advantage of others and to your own disadvantage.**

		not at all				exactly	
1	It bothers me when others receive something that ought to be mine.	0	1	2	3	4	5
2	It makes me angry when others receive a reward which I have earned.	0	1	2	3	4	5
3	I cannot easily bear it when others profit unilaterally from me.	0	1	2	3	4	5
4	It takes me a long time to forget when I have to fix others' carelessness.	0	1	2	3	4	5
5	It gets me down when I get fewer opportunities than others to develop my skills.	0	1	2	3	4	5
6	It makes me angry when others are undeservingly better off than me.	0	1	2	3	4	5
7	It worries me when I have to work hard for things that come easily to others.	0	1	2	3	4	5
8	I ruminate for a long time when other people are being treated better than me.	0	1	2	3	4	5

	not at all		exactly
9 It burdens me to be criticized for things that are being overlooked with others.	0 1 2	3	4 5
10 It makes me angry when I am treated worse than others.	0 1 2	3	4 5

Now, we *will look at situations in which you notice or learn that someone else is being treated unfairly, put at a disadvantage or used.*

	not at all		exactly
11 It bothers me when someone gets something they don't deserve.	0 1 2	3	4 5
12 I am upset when someone does not get a reward he/she has earned.	0 1 2	3	4 5
13 I cannot bear it when someone unilaterally profits from others.	0 1 2	3	4 5
14 It takes me long time to forget when someone else has to fix others' carelessness.	0 1 2	3	4 5
15 It disturbs me when someone receives fewer opportunities to develop his/her skills than others.	0 1 2	3	4 5
16 I am upset when someone is undeservingly worse off than others.	0 1 2	3	4 5
17 It worries me when someone has to work hard for things that come easily to others.	0 1 2	3	4 5
18 I ruminate for a long time when someone is being treated nicer than others for no reason.	0 1 2	3	4 5

	not at all		exactly
19 It gets me down to see someone criticized for things that are overlooked with others.	0 1 2	3	4 5
20 I am upset when someone is being treated worse than others.	0 1 2	3	4 5

Now, we *will look at situations which turn out to your advantage and to the disadvantage of others.*

	not at all		exactly
21 It disturbs me when I receive what others ought to have.	0 1 2	3	4 5
22 I have a bad conscience when I receive a reward that someone else has earned.	0 1 2	3	4 5
23 I cannot easily bear it to unilaterally profit from others.	0 1 2	3	4 5
24 It takes me a long time to forget when others have to fix my carelessness.	0 1 2	3	4 5
25 It disturbs me when I receive more opportunities than others to develop my skills.	0 1 2	3	4 5
26 I feel guilty when I am better off than others for no reason.	0 1 2	3	4 5
27 It bothers me when things come easily to me that others have to work hard for.	0 1 2	3	4 5
28 I ruminate for a long time about being treated nicer than others for no reason.	0 1 2	3	4 5

	not at all		exactly
29 It bothers me when someone tolerates things with me that other people are being criticized for.	0 1 2	3	4 5
30 I feel guilty when I receive better treatment than others.	0 1 2	3	4 5

Finally, *we will look at situations in which you treat someone else unfairly, discriminate against someone, or exploit someone.*

	not at all		exactly
31 It gets me down when I take something from someone else that I don't deserve.	0 1 2	3	4 5
32 I have a bad conscience when I deny someone the acknowledgement he or she deserves.	0 1 2	3	4 5
33 I cannot stand the feeling of exploiting someone.	0 1 2	3	4 5
34 It takes me a long time to forget when I allow myself to be careless at the expense of someone else.	0 1 2	3	4 5
35 It disturbs me when I take away from someone else the possibility of developing his or her potential.	0 1 2	3	4 5
36 I feel guilty when I enrich myself at the cost of others.	0 1 2	3	4 5
37 It bothers me when I use tricks to achieve something while others have to struggle for it.	0 1 2	3	4 5
38 I ruminate for a long time when I treat someone less friendly than others without a reason.	0 1 2	3	4 5

	not at all				exactly
39 I have a bad conscience when I criticize someone for things I tolerate in others.	0	1	2	3	4	5
40 I feel guilty when I treat someone worse than others.	0	1	2	3	4	5

Schmitt has found that individuals differ in how readily they perceive and how strongly they react to injustice. These differences are consistent across types of injustice and are stable across time. Thus, these patterns are seen as a personality trait called justice sensitivity. This trait can be differentiated into four facets that match with corresponding roles individuals take on in a justice conflict: victim sensitivity, observer sensitivity, beneficiary sensitivity and perpetrator sensitivity. Several studies have shown that observer, beneficiary and perpetrator sensitivities are highly correlated with each other and only weakly correlated with victim sensitivity.

Observer-, beneficiary- and perpetrator-sensitive individuals seem to be primarily concerned with justice for others. In this sense, these sensitivities represent potential factors that help in constructive conflict resolution and in the prevention of conflict escalation. By contrast, victim-sensitive people seem to have a predominant interest in justice for themselves. Accordingly, several studies have shown that victim sensitivity promotes antisocial behaviour. The antisocial behaviour of victim-sensitive people seems to serve two functions. First, having suffered from innocent victimization previously, victim-sensitive individuals commit selfish behaviour in order to balance their personal justice account. Second, in fear of being cheated, they engage in preventive strikes against those who might cheat them. Both of these motives and mechanisms are potential risks for social, organizational, and ecological conflicts.

Conclusion

One of the major causes of disenchantment at work is the perception of unfairness. This is made even worse when the organization hypocritically proclaims the very opposite. There have been many cases of whistle-blowers who have been deeply motivated by a sense of unfairness.

Fairness and unfairness is however a subjective judgement. Furthermore, there are those who seem particularly sensitive to any form of injustice. Life is not fair: but companies that do not try to ensure equity as much as possible risk the problem of major employee disenchantment.

For some life is unfair: the rain falls on the just and the unjust alike. Most of us would like to believe that we live in a fair and just world where people get what they deserve in every sense of the word. Indeed there is an extensive psychological literature on what is called the 'just world hypothesis' (Furnham, 2010). Just as in the equity sensitivity literature it is clear people are differently sensitive to, as well as rather idiosyncratic in, the sense and definition of fairness and justice. But what all the theories are clear about is the emotive power of the experience of unfairness and injustice and attempts to change the situation. This may, and often does, include attempts to punish those who are seen to have caused the problem.

The moral of the story for organizations: beware of trumpeting the *f-word* as a virtue if you cannot justify your claims very thoroughly.

DISENCHANTMENT CASE 2: VITEK BODEN

The following comments are from former and current employees of large organizations, sourced from Glassdoor.

'Values, ethics and culture are talked about and written about in catch phrases but do not genuinely exist in my experience.'

'Politics is absolutely at the core of everything, even senior managers spend most of the day networking and very little time making change happen.'

'"Zero tolerance policy to bullying" is like many impressive value statements at BA: is not in my experience genuine at all.'

'There is always a promise of "new development opportunities" which support staff never see.'

VITEK BODEN LIVED IN QUEENSLAND, Australia, where he worked for Hunter Watertech, a company that installed radio controlled sewage equipment. In the late 1990s, Boden and his team had replaced the entire sewage network for one of their clients, the Maroochy Shire County Council in Queensland.

Boden hated his job, and hated his manager in particular. They did not get along well. Boden thought that his manager was a tyrant and a bully, whilst his manager thought Boden was a stuck-up and self-righteous contractor. Boden was becoming increasingly disenchanted and decided that it was time to leave Hunter Watertech.

In early December, he did just that and handed in his resignation. He had decided that he wanted to work for the Maroochy Council instead. During his project, he had got to know the team there and had decided that was the type of culture he wanted to work in. Later on in December, Boden contacted one of his associates at the Council and enquired about a job.

The reality was that Boden had not thought about the notion that he would not get a job there. In January 2000, the Council decided not to give Boden the job he had enquired about. He was left feeling disgruntled and cheated out of what he thought was a guaranteed job. He decided that none of this could be his fault, and that someone had to pay for the predicament he was in.

When Boden left Hunter Watertech, he decided that he would keep some of the technology they had lent him as a part of his job. This now gave him access to the whole of the sewage system he had installed for Maroochy Shire Council. Boden realized that he could kill two birds with one stone, and get revenge on both Hunter Watertech and the Council.

Between February and April of 2000, Boden used his unauthorized access to issue forty-six commands to the sewage system gates. Boden leaked 800,000 litres of sewage water into local parks, rivers and businesses. The sewage killed the marine life and turned rivers black. The cost of the attacks has since been estimated to be around $1 million in damages.

Boden was a skilled technician and was able to mask the events as 'anomalous' events on behalf of Hunter Watertech. The relationship between Maroochy Shire Council and Hunter Watertech had become fraught as the Council blamed Hunter Watertech for installing faulty and destructive systems. It took extensive digital forensics to realise that these were not accidents, but were the malicious and deliberate attacks of a disenchanted ex-employee.

Boden was only caught when police officers pulled over his car for a routine stop. The officers found radio systems and computer equipment that looked out of the ordinary. Boden has since been sentenced to two years in prison.

7

Bullying versus Respect

It is the way one treats his inferiors more than the way he treats his equals which reveals one's real character.

REV. CHARLES BAYARD MILIKEN

I would rather be a little nobody, then to be an evil somebody.

ABRAHAM LINCOLN

Knowing what's right doesn't mean much unless you do what's right.

THEODORE ROOSEVELT

If you are neutral in situations of injustice, you have chosen the side of the oppressor. If an elephant has its foot on the tail of a mouse, and you say that you are neutral, the mouse will not appreciate your neutrality.

DESMOND TUTU

What if the kid you bullied at school, grew up, and turned out to be the only surgeon who could save your life?

LYNETTE MATHER

Introduction

Bullying is defined by the duration, frequency and intentionality of people in positions of power unduly accusing, criticizing or humiliating others. It is usually a psychological rather than a physical process, though of course it can be both. It can take many forms. Bullying can be emotion, physical and/or verbal. It can be done by groups or individuals.

We know that bullying is more likely to occur in some environments rather than others. Where there is role conflict or ambiguity; where there is acute or chronic work overload; where workers have little autonomy; where there is an atmosphere of fear or redundancy, or sacking or whole organization collapse – bullying is more likely. Anytime there is a win-lose and not a win-win philosophy there is conflict and often, in the shadows, lurks bullying. Some organizations require considerable self-control and discipline on the part of their members: those that fall out of line get clear feedback that could be seen as bullying.

Most agree on three issues: *First*, bullying is a serious problem that blights people's lives and affects work-place efficiency. *Second*, there are things we can do to prevent it, though some just mask it, others might increase it, while some genuinely help. *Third*, it is a multi-causal problem – that is it has multiple causes. It is likely to be due to various factors happening at the same time.

This chapter is about managers who bully their staff and work in organizations that turn a blind eye towards, or even encourage, bullying.

A culture of incivility

Every organization has a unique but palpable culture. From the lighting and office layout to the people that are employed, you start to get an understanding of a company's culture the moment you step over the threshold. Culture combines both the everyday feeling of 'the way that things are done around here', as well as a more visionary comprehension of what it means to work for the company. The impact of culture is significant, with numerous studies demonstrating how culture can be a propelling factor for greatness or what lets an organization sink into redundancy.

Good leaders are aware of the significance that culture can play. Good companies will ask themselves what type of organization they need to be in order to achieve their goals. Successful companies ask how they can implement changes to bring about the culture they believe is needed to succeed. CEOs and HR departments will often try to mould their organization into the type of culture that they think is best, outlining core values that employees should hold close as they go on with their daily work.

Despite most CEOs saying that their culture is unique and unlike any other in their industry, the same abstract terms are often repeated in company value statements. Maitland, a financial communications consultancy, found that FTSE 100 organizations seem to use the same three core values to define their culture: Integrity, Innovation, and *Respect*.

Respect as a value can have a profound impact on the disenchantment of employees. It is understandably a value that most organizations want attributed to them. They want to be known as a 'nice place to work'; that their employees are treated with dignity and consideration.

Whilst it sounds appealing, valuing *Respect* has no meaning unless it is given context: is respect contingent on hierarchy? Do employees show respect by deferring to those who are higher ranked than them? Or does it just refer to the polite treatment of your colleagues?

It is harder to hold *Respect* in high regard when it is unclear how and when you should be respectful. Without context and meaningful application, the question of 'What do we want to achieve?' will often supersede the answer to 'What type of organization do we want to be?' The prevalence of incivility at work offers an interesting paradox. Despite most companies now embracing a 'zero-tolerance to bullying' ethos, bullying and incivility are still commonplace for a large number of organizations. In order to defend against disenchantment, it is important to understand how managers can use respect to foster a motivated, happy and engaged workforce.

At Georgetown University, Christine Porath and her colleagues have been studying why it is that workplace incivility is so prevalent. Porath's research has unearthed some startling insights into the pervasive nature of incivility: one in two employees say they experience at least one instance of incivility every week, 98 per cent of employees have directly experienced some form of uncivil behaviour and 99 per cent have witnessed it happen to a colleague.

Porath noted that a common response was that employees had no time to be nice. Employees blame the modern, high-paced, technology-laden world of work for leaving them with little room for civility or pleasantries (Pearson and Porath, 2005). When asked why they treat others in their workplace with little respect, over 60 per cent of employees feel that they are too over-burdened to have the time to be nice.

The incivility paradox is prevalent for a lot of employees and ignored by a lot of managers. Being civil and respectful is too often seen as something that plays well on the company website, but is rarely put into practice. How far is a company willing to go in order to uphold these core values? When the pressure is on to be a commercially competitive company, does respect become less of a priority?

Incivility, disrespect and bullying

Every school had a bully. There was always one student who would parade the playground at lunchtime looking for a victim to persecute and belittle. They would pull pigtails, dish out dead-arms, and mock with mean names. They gossip and conspire, and giggle at viscous rumours.

Bullying is not a phenomenon that can be solely attributed to the callous nature of teenagers or later managers. We are always told that school is only temporary, that one day we will all grow up and everything will be better. But what happens when the thug from the playground grows up, gets qualifications and enters the world of work? When we are all grown up, how do we react to being belittled, besmirched and bullied?

The reality is that bullying does transcend the playground and is often present in the adult world of boardrooms, photocopiers and coffee machines. Similar to the schoolyard, bullying in the workplace comprises of both a physical and a psychological type of warfare, ranging from joking horseplay meant in good nature to hostile and intimidating acts.

However, bullying in the workplace does not always constitute the same overt shin-kicking, dirt-throwing tactics that the playground bully utilizes. Instead, a different arsenal of tactics are deployed in order mock and undermine: superiors deciding to criticize you in front of the whole team rather than in the privacy of their office; a colleague passive-aggressively CC-ing your boss into an email chain in attempt to highlight your ineptitude; and the inappropriate nicknames that are designed to reinforce the belief that you are not to be respected by your colleagues.

Modern research on workplace bullying exploded in the 1980s, with researchers focusing on different aspects, antecedents and attributes of disrespect. In a recent review, Hershcovis and Barling (2010) outlined some of the different types and definitions of disrespect that have been studied:

- *Incivility* – low intensity disrespect with ambiguous intent, including rude or curt verbal and non-verbal behaviours.

- *Bullying* – repeated and deliberate disrespect towards an employee over a period of time, including ridicule, slander, physical aggression and constant reminding of previous mistakes.

- *Social undermining* – disrespect with the intention to hinder the development of a positive social relationship, including insults, spreading rumours or openly questioning someone's work.

- *Dispute-related aggression* – when disrespect is the result of frustration over an incompatibility of views, wishes and desires that impact group outcomes.

- *Predatory bullying* – the victim has done nothing wrong, but the bully targets them to demonstrate social dominance or power over others.

- *Supervisor aggression* – when employees experience hostile and continued disrespect from another employee who has more power over them.

Psychologists have found that multiple factors can contribute to why bullying occurs. Job characteristics have been found to contribute to bullying, with envy and competition surrounding uncertainty of job status leading employees to undermine or sabotage each other. Additionally, managers who are uncertain of their position will often resort to harassment as a means to reassert authority. Psychologists have also analysed how the personality of the bully contributes to its prevalence. Research using the Big Five personality traits has shown that bullies are often characterised by lower agreeableness and conscientiousness, as well as high levels of extraversion and neuroticism (Mitsopoulou and Giovazolias, 2015).

There have also been attempts to identify a 'victim personality' in the workplace, with some evidence showing that victims of bullying are more likely to be highly neurotic but show lower levels of extraversion, conscientiousness and agreeableness (Nielsen et al., 2017). Perhaps even more curiously, there is evidence to suggest that bullies and victims display similar personality types. Psychologists have found that bullies are often bully-victims; they are both perpetrators as well as targets of bullying. It appears that bullies and bully-victims share the same 'dark' personality traits, indicating the possibility of a common dark core of psychopathy and Machiavellianism (Linton and Power, 2013).

However, there are people whose inherent 'darkness' causes them to be abusive leaders or callous colleagues. There is an extensive literature showing that bullies often possess 'dark' or malevolent traits. The 'Dark Triad' of psychopathy, Machiavellianism and narcissism is a particularly powerful instigator, with employees who are high on these traits being the most likely perpetrators of workplace bullying. It appears also that these 'dark' individuals use bullying as a mechanism to reinforce their darkness.

The tough and callous nature of psychopathy is linked to more direct and aggressive forms of bullying – i.e. predatory bullying, supervisor aggression and emotional abuse. Psychopaths are callous, lacking in remorse and excessively impulsive. They use bullying as a tool to assert social dominance over their colleagues.

Machiavellians, however, are strategic and long-term orientated. They are characterized by distrust and manipulation, wanting to be in control of information, power or money. As such, studies have shown that Machiavellians are more likely to bully as a method to either reinforce or help them achieve their position of power by undermining someone who is in their way – i.e. verbal aggression, control and manipulation of information, and professional discredit and denigration.

For years, the motivation behind bullying behaviour was thought to be the result of low self-esteem. The bully, feeling self-critical and insecure, would unleash torrents of abuse in an attempt to bolster their ego. Interviews with victims of workplace bullying reveal a common belief that the perpetrator is acting anti-socially out of jealousy. However, recent trends in psychological research have shown the opposite to be true. Instead, it is individuals who possess dangerously high levels of self-esteem that are found to be the instigators of unpleasantness in the workplace. A team of researchers at the University of Kentucky (Duffy et al., 2006) found that the inflated ego associated with narcissism played a key role in why employees engaged in undermining behaviours.

Narcissists think highly of themselves; they over-estimate their competence and fantasize about being in positions of power. As a result they become abrasive when this delusion is challenged. Narcissists have been found to use bullying and social undermining in order to elevate their own status within the group. Importantly, they have been shown to often utilize an indirect form of bullying – i.e. deception or social isolation (Baughman et al., 2012). This way it is harder to identify the bully, meaning the narcissist can maintain their social standing. As narcissists place a high value on their social status, they use more socially subtle forms of bullying to avoid the potential high cost of being aggressive and ousted as a bully. Researchers have outlined that there are six ways in which bullying can manifest:

1 *Social isolation* – acts that marginalize the individual, either through restricting their interactions with other co-workers or physically separating them from other employees.

2 *Control and manipulation of information* – selecting, manipulating and interfering with the information that an employee receives.

3 *Abusive working conditions* – changing the working environment for the employee to obstruct or hinder them from completing their tasks.

4 *Emotional abuse* – humiliation, insulting attacks directed at the person themselves, their personal life or their personal beliefs.

5 *Professional discredit and denigration* – belittling the knowledge, experience, effort or performance of the individual.

6 *Devaluation of professional role* – assigning the employee useless, impossible or overtly inferior tasks, undermining the importance of their job, or relieving them of their responsibilities without cause or foundation.

Epidemiological research shows that the number of employees who experience bullying, mistreatment and incivility within the workplace ranges from one in every twenty employees to nearly a third of an organizational workforce (Einarsen, 1999). What is most troublesome is that all too often these behaviours are accepted and encouraged by management, and inadvertently slip under the HR radar. One study found that 70 per cent of bullying involves management in some way, either as an active instigator or a complicit bystander (Van Fleet and Van Fleet, 2012).

Numerous studies have shown the detrimental effect that bullying can have, not only on an employee's performance, but also their physical health. Bullying puts the victim under a great deal of stress. When someone experiences stress as a result of incivility for too long or too often, it can start to erode away their mental well-being. Bullying has been found to: impair working memory, causing employees to absorb less information (Porath and Erez, 2007); damage an employee's immune system (Sapolsky, 2004); increase risk of heart disease (Slopen et al., 2012); and lower self-esteem, loss of confidence and an inability to cope (Coyne et al., 2000).

Treating others with disrespect has a powerful effect on an employees' sense of justice and disenchantment. Ohio University's John Schermerhorn outlined the particular importance of interpersonal justice: do employees feel that, when requests and decisions are communicated, they have been spoken to and treated with dignity?

Interpersonal justice is based on principles of social exchange – you treat others in the way that they have treated you. It is like receiving an unanticipated gift. There is an overwhelming urge to give a gift of equal magnitude in return. Employees who feel their working life has been made easier and more pleasant will feel the need to reciprocate. If treatment is fair, respectful and considerate, the returned response is likewise.

Choosing civility over competence

Competence is obviously vital for an organization to succeed. There have been no books, case studies or TedTalks on how picking the worst person for the job increases productivity. Competence is one of the most overt factors we can measure an employee on. Do they have the qualifications? A dazzling portfolio? The previous job experience? Managers look for any statistics and data to verify that this person has what is takes.

The problem is we forget that competence alone is not enough. When competence is prioritized at the expense of civility, we run the risk of hiring capable but caveated employees. One of the biggest issues of prioritizing competence over civility occurs when nasty employees are also high performers. Managers often unfortunately find it all too easy to turn a blind eye to a bully's misdemeanours when they are hitting their sales targets. The question then becomes this: What are the things that you would let slide if you know that this individual was competent? The occasional rude remark? An authoritarian approach to their colleagues? Them working entirely to the beat of their own drum?

It is an issue that has plagued business and sports for centuries. The best and brightest are heralded as 'übermensch' at the expense of other employees' well-being and happiness. Due to their high ability, they are allowed to be curt and scathing when interacting with others. Often in highly results-driven environments, it is the callous yet competent that excel. Something about the individual both propels them to success and disposes them to act in interpersonally disruptive ways. Instead of attempting to collaborate, these bullies end up aggressively perusing their own self-interests.

Robert Sutton, author of *The No Asshole Rule* (2007), has argued how able yet demanding employees are toxic for a successful workplace. Sutton stated that even if people 'win' and are uncivil, then they are still a bully and should be regarded as an 'office nuisance' and a hindrance rather than a star player. For Sutton, the key is to reject the potential bullies before they enter the organization at the recruitment stage.

Lars Dalgaard, who recently sold his HR company SuccessFactors for $3 billion, instigated Sutton's rule to try and solve this issue within his organization.

Dalgaard found that the 'no jerk' rule is the only way to effectively mitigate bullying. Lars argued that no matter how competent, skilled or experienced an individual is, there is no place for them in his organization if they are unpleasant and disrespectful. Whenever a new employee is hired at SuccessFactor, they are asked to sign a waiver that holds a specific clause around bullying: 'I will be a good person to work with – not territorial, not a jerk.'

Whilst these policies represent a step in the right direction, the reality is that 'jerks' and bullies still exist in most organizations. Inherent to most (if not all) organizations is also the concept of teamwork. Organizations are made up of people with a range of skills – sales, analysts, IT, human resources – all of whom have to work together effectively. Most of the time, companies will naturally form silos based on skill; analysts are sat with other analysts, whilst marketing sit separately in their own office. When working, these disparate factions need to come together and combine their skills to create a team that is greater than the sum of its parts.

When given the choice, people will often choose who they work with based on two criteria. Firstly, their competence: do they have the ability to get it done? How much does this person know about the job at hand? Are they an expert in this area or will the task demand more skills than they possess? Secondly, employees will evaluate potential collaborators on how likable they are: are they an enjoyable person to work with? Are they pleasant and respectful, or are they overly critical, patronising and blunt?

Two organizational psychologists, Casciaro and Lobo (2008), found that when employees consider what their colleagues would be like to work with, four different types emerge. Firstly, there are the *Lovable Stars*. These employees score highly on both dimensions, being both competent and a delight to have around. Secondly, there are the *Incompetent Jerks*; these employees are unfortunately simultaneously bolshie and idiotic. Then there are the *Competent Jerk*; they are experienced and educated in their field, can offer a large amount of insight, but can prove difficult to work with. Finally, there are the *Lovable*

Fools; they are the opposite of the *Competent Jerk* in that they are entertaining, engaging and enjoyable to work with. However, they lack the knowledge and skills that would make them highly competent for the given task.

Obviously, when the choice is available, everyone would opt for the *Lovable Star*. The *Incompetent Jerks*, with any luck, have been either effectively rooted out at the interview stage or exited from the company after their true nature had been discovered. However, what if there are only *Lovable Fools* and *Competent Jerks* to choose from? When asked, Cascairo and Lobo found that managers have often argued for the *Competent Jerk*: 'I can diffuse my antipathy towards the jerk if he gets the work done, but I can not work with someone who is incompetent.' 'All I really care about is the skills and expertise that you bring to the table. If you are a nice person on top of that, well it is an added bonus.'

Despite managers stating preference for competence over likability, the reality and consequence of this choice is somewhat startling. To demonstrate the impact of this, Casciaro and Lobo analysed whom it was that employees went to when they needed help or advice on a project. It was thought that employees would mirror the views of their managers and prioritize competence over civility, choosing colleagues who were skilled and able.

By analysing the co-operation, communication and interaction patterns within numerous organizations, they found the exact opposite to be the case. When it came to seeking advice, employees will choose the 'loveable fool' over the 'competent jerk'. In their paper, Cascairo and Lobo argued: 'If someone is liked, their colleagues will seek out every little bit of competence they have to offer.' If a colleague were considered unlikable, employees would refuse to work with them regardless of their ability or skill. Bullying and incivility causes communications to break down within an organization as employees actively avoid working with or talking to colleagues that are unpleasant.

Bullying has a cascading effect; once collaboration starts to decline, so too does the performance and effectiveness of the organization. A recent study demonstrated the powerfully detrimental impact that bullying, rudeness and incivility can have on performance. The study centred on training workshops for twenty-four paediatric medical teams working within intensive care units (Riskin et al., 2015). As a part of their workshops, the teams were placed in a simulated scenario where a premature infant needed treatment. The infant's health was rapidly deteriorating and the medical team were judged on how they responded. The aim of the exercise was to see how quickly, effectively and accurately the team could diagnose and treat the condition. During the training exercise, an expert would watch their progress and advise them on how they were doing (the 'expert' was secretly a member of the research team). The study wanted to see how team dynamics were affected when the 'expert' gave neutral comments compared to insults about their performance and the quality of their medical care.

The impact of being 'put down' and insulted was powerful. Teams who were exposed to the rude and uncivil 'expert' showed a sharp decrease in effectiveness across all medical criteria: their speed of diagnosis slowed, their accuracy plummeted and the effectiveness of their treatments decreased significantly. In these training scenarios, the infant was far less likely to survive when being treated by teams exposed to incivility and bullying.

This study illustrates that when the success of a team depends on collaboration and communication: bullying and incivility are its downfall. Teams that experience rudeness – either from an abusive supervisor, curtness from other teams or incivility from their own team members – stop sharing information and asking for help from their teammates.

Bullying causes employees to have a lower sense of psychological safety, making employees feel that their colleagues do not respect them or their contributions. When psychological safety is challenged, they shut down, no longer co-operating or communicating. As a result, teams become a group of disparate individuals rather than a harmonious network.

Recent studies have shown that once employees are exposed to bullying, they are three times less likely to co-operate and help their colleagues. Additionally, their willingness to share information and ideas decreases by more than half. Conversely, when teams experience civility and respect, employees are more likely to seek and accept feedback, experiment with new ideas, take risks, innovate, discuss errors and speak out against potential or actual problems (Porath and Gerbasi, 2015).

Valuing competence over likability can come at a steep price. When assessing competence, we look for the 'select in' criteria – what factors does this person need to have in this role? What managers also need to look for are their 'select out' criteria – what are the characteristics this person absolutely cannot have? Look for a person with the highest ability, but be prepared to rule them out if they do not have honesty or integrity. Having someone in the team who is willing to bully their teammates can have detrimental effects. A sub-par résumé might be unappealing, but a disenchanted employee or workforce is more so.

A culture of tolerance

There is a belief that being tough, cut-throat and competitive is the best way to get the best out of your employees. By bolting additional stress and pressure onto an employee's workload, this will ignite a fire within them and instil a motivation to achieve greatness. This is somewhat reflected in the popular HR trends and training modules. Training programmes around resilience, mindfulness and agility are designed to help employees cope as the organization slowly increases the pressure.

The reality is that these cut-throat and high-pressure environments come at a cost. In these aggressive environments, employees are left feeling disrespected, deflated and disenchanted. As time goes on, engagement becomes disengagement; a high-pressured work environment becomes a diagnosis of high blood pressure at the next doctor checkup; a fear-driven loyalty turns into wasting time searching for other jobs online. It is not enough to hope that employees will be able to cope with some additional training, but instead organizations need to be aware of how increasing the stress employees are put under can consequently foster long-term disenchantment.

Porath and her colleagues have been demonstrating the profound impact that civility (or a lack of it) can have on employee well-being, productivity and performance. In 2015, Porath polled around 20,000 employees from disparate and diverse industries in order to find out what their managers do that helps them become engaged at work. One leadership style emerged as the answer: *Respect.*

Respect went above and beyond employees being galvanized by inspiring visions, recognized for work, or opportunities for growth and development. The power of respect was profound: those employees who were respectfully treated in their organization had greater satisfaction with their work, displayed more focus and prioritization, and were more likely to stick with that organization.

However, research into the perceptions of managers reveals a different and warped view of what is important for leadership. Prominent social psychologist Denise Salin (2003) stated that managers can wrongly interpret workplace bullying as an efficient means of instigating increased performance. Some managers see and encourage bullying behaviour as examples of an employee's ruthless pursuit for excellence, regardless of the damage they do along the way. Certain organizations inadvertently promote bullying by encouraging employee 'toughness', where being confrontational and uncivil is mistaken for resilience.

Unsuccessful managers appear to trade respect for results. The research, however, shows that this style of management has the opposite effect to what is intended. Stress has been shown to act as a precursor to bullying, as employees in high strain jobs – including everything from high workload to low job autonomy – are more likely to engage in aggressive behaviours (Baillien et al., 2011). Additionally, employees who are stressed due to high job insecurity are more likely to act callously towards their colleagues (Silla et al., 2009). As managers prioritize results more than respect, the increases in employee stress translate to bullying and disenchantment.

Researchers have noted that bullying does not occur in isolation, but instead escalates and builds over time. It has a permeating effect on what is considered 'normal' by the employees of an organization. When employees believe that aggression is reinforced by managers, or leads to potential workplace advantages, bullying becomes a normal behaviour. Randall (2001) argued that employees do not need to witness these rewards or advantages first-hand, but merely see it happening to someone else. When bullying and aggression goes unchallenged (or worse, is encouraged), it becomes a norm within the organization. For instance, organizational cultures are defined by instrumental ethical norms – where employees are encouraged to act egotistical and in their own self-interest – these organizations were more associated with bullying (Bulutlar and Öz, 2009).

Often maladaptive norms will appear unintentionally and without malicious intent. A key example of this is the fine line between joking in good humour and bullying. There have been numerous studies that show humour and laughter have a positive influence in the workplace. A recent review found that employees who laugh together are more creative, collaborative, experience less burnout and are more productive at work (Mesmer-Magnus et al., 2012). Managers who are seen as good-humoured and tell funny (but appropriate) jokes receive greater support from their team, are better motivators, earn more and are promoted quicker (Bitterly et al., 2017).

However, humour can be a double-edged sword within the workplace. Getting it right can lead to a positive and energetic workplace. Getting it wrong can cause unintended but serious impact to the disenchantment of employees.

Peter McGraw (2014) developed the Benign Violation Theory in order to understand what it is that makes something funny. McGraw outlined three factors that make a situation humorous:

1 The situation needs to be seen as a *violation*; it has to go against the accepted norms of how things should be done.

2 The situation needs to be *benign*; it cannot be funny if it is seen as directly threatening.

3 The situation needs to be both a *violation* and *benign* simultaneously; it will not be funny it they occur separately.

A team of management academics in Singapore applied McGraw's theory to manager's humour and how joking at work can go horribly wrong (Yam et al., 2017). They found that employees interpret the jokes and actions of their manager, using these as cues for how to behave. Employees use this information to understand what behaviours are acceptable or benign, and which are malignant. When managers broadened the boundaries of what was seen as acceptable, this led team members to also push the boundaries of acceptable behaviour. When leaders used aggressive humour – such as teasing members of the team or telling dirty jokes – this was linked to employees becoming increasingly deviant. The misuse of humour saw an increase in chronic absenteeism, ignoring instructions, sharing confidential information, falsifying financial claims or getting drunk on the job.

This is not to say that humour should be banished from the workplace. Humour and laughing have been shown to be powerful tools in promoting success and motivating employees. The important factor to consider is when a joke is no longer just a joke. What employees consider 'normal' has a large impact on what behaviours they engage in. When managers are seen as good-humoured, but able to draw the line at what is unacceptable, they foster an environment where employees can strive. When managers are seen as covering callous remarks in the form of a joke, it encourages and normalizes bullying in the workplace. A culture of tolerance escalates to a disenchanted workforce.

Bullying and revenge

Employees who experience bullying and mistreatment become less satisfied with their jobs, less productive and more likely to leave their organization. Importantly, bullying is also a powerful motivator for revenge. Within the theory of disenchantment, bullying is the factor that appears to cause the most retaliated and targeted forms of revenge. Bullying and abuse are personal for the victim. It is an affront on the identity and ability of that employee.

Communication and interpersonal relationships centre on the principle of social exchange; people will treat others how they are treated. As a result, the victims of bullying will most often target their revenge or destructive behaviours towards the source; towards the colleague, team, or manager who is instigating the abuse. Research has shown this targeted destruction to be true. Victims of abusive supervision will engage in specific deviance acted towards the manager. They do so in outrage and as a form of retaliation. They are also trying to actively damage the organisation that the supervisor represents.

Recent research has shown that bullying diminishes the victim's sense of self, lowering their self-esteem, confidence, and ego. It is the response to this diminished sense of self that is key to understanding why victims are motivated to act destructively. Vogel and Mitchell (2015) found that employees respond destructively as a means of self-protection or self-presentation:

- *Self-protection*: Employees are motivated to 'balance the scales' in response to bullying. Counterproductive work behaviours – including fraud, theft and sabotage – are defensive tactics used to let employees stand up for themselves and demonstrate control over the situation. These behaviours will be targeted towards the abusive supervisor or colleague.

- *Self-presentation*: Employees are motivated to engage in destructive behaviours in order to present themselves as a 'good fit' with others in their social group, reducing the possibility that they could be a target. They therefore bully and victimize others in order to fit in with what is considered 'normal' in the workplace.

Vogel and Mitchell (2015) found that both self-presentation and defensive behaviours can work simultaneously in response to abusive supervision. The victim simultaneously looks to punish the source whilst endeavouring to appear to others as more likable (i.e. integration through behaving in similar ways). Victims who engage will often not consider the potential cost of their destructive behaviour. Their focus is solely on defending or standing up for themselves, looking to exact revenge on the source in a cathartic and self-gratifying manner. The act of revenge provides a form of release for the victim.

The actual behaviours employees use in response to bullying vary, with consequences ranging from reduced productivity and co-operation to aggressive retaliation and sabotage. To understand the range and reasons for responses, Beattie and Griffin (2014) surveyed employees of a security company for a year, asking employees to keep a record of any incidents of bullying they experienced, to rate its severity, and how they responded.

The most common response to incivility was to either ignore it or avoid the instigator. This was the response for 72 per cent of cases, with an overwhelming majority of employees admitting to using this tactic (96 per cent). The least common response was an employee retaliating by acting negatively towards another co-worker. One third of employees said that their response to bullying was to take their anger out on someone else. Direct revenge against the instigator was the result in nearly half of all bullying incidents, and was a tactic used by nearly three quarters of employees. As disenchantment progresses and the bullying continues, the responses from employees become more severe and destructive to those in the company.

The employee's commitment to the organization also plays a strong role in the effect of bullying, particularly from managers. Research has shown that bullying has the strongest effect when employees are still attached to the organization (Shoss et al., 2013). Bullying sparks the greatest source of injustice when an employee is still committed and engaged with the organization. Employees feel betrayed that their organization allows this behaviour, causing the injustice to be amplified.

As the employee's disenchantment grows, their commitment to the organization decreases. Consequently, this shift in commitment changes how employees respond to mistreatment. When an employee is committed to the organization, they are still dependent upon their manager for rewards and recognition. There is a power imbalance; the employee is at the mercy of the supervisor. As such, employees usually retaliate indirectly or look to harm the organization as a whole. Bennett Tepper, a leading academic in the field of bullying and mistreatment, found that when employees were actively looking for other jobs, this power imbalance shifts. Employees who are actively looking to leave the organization respond to abusive supervision by personally targeting the supervisor rather than at the organization as a whole (Tepper et al., 2009). The revenge becomes personal and employees disregard the potential consequences of targeting their manager.

Whilst the working world is becoming more fast-paced and technology-driven, it still fundamentally relies upon interconnectivity and interaction. It is not enough to just dismiss respectful interactions due to time-pressure and workload. A key element to building that spark within your team starts with self-awareness; knowing how your actions can make your team feel depreciated. As we move forward, civility becomes increasingly more important.

Conclusion

Bullying at work seems to be widespread. It has both long- and short-term consequences. It is of little use sending anti-bullying guidelines, particularly from HR. Paradoxically, this 'on-high', 'this-is-what-you-must-do approach' is once more often characterized by the bullying organization. The best way to do it is get the staff to develop their own guidelines. The staff need to agree what constitutes bullying and what to do about it. Make them feel part of the process and ensure they come up with sensible and useful guidelines. If you think bullying is happening to any noticeable extent, it is worth the effort.

Bullies are found in board rooms and boiler rooms. They lower morale and productivity and increase absenteeism and turnover. That fact alone merits serious investigation by any manager suspicious it may be occurring under his or her nose.

DISENCHANTMENT CASE 3: THE EMPLOYEE BEHIND THE WORLD'S BIGGEST DATA BREACH

The following comments are from former and current employees of large organizations, sourced from Glassdoor.

'I would advise that management/supervisory staff learn and action the BP Values and Behaviours before promoting it downstream.'

'Too much politics . . . Double standards between different assets in terms of benefits, salaries, promotions and career opportunities.'

'Middle management; very arrogant and incompetent, will do anything to get their bonuses including bullying their subordinates.'

'[Employees are] poorly paid, poorly rewarded for hard work and poorly rewarded when the company performs well due to the hard work of it's lowly employees.'

MOSSACK FONESCA (MF), A PANAMA-BASED law firm, must have been wondering when it was all going to stop. In 2016, MF experienced two major breaches in data security within just two months.

The first of these, occurring in April 2016 and dubbed the Panama Papers scandal, broke records as the largest leak in history: 2.6 terabytes of private data was leaked under the uninspired pseudonym 'John Doe'. To put the size of the leak into context, 2.6 terabytes would take somewhere close to sixteen months to download on a typical home broadband connection.

The data breach amounted to around 11.5 million documents, detailing the financially dubious activities of politicians, bankers and business people. The reputational fallout from the leaks was pervasive for those named in the documents. Geopolitical leaders have been pressured or forced to resign: Iceland's prime minister resigned after political protests and oppositional pressure while David Cameron was forced to defend his inheritance in parliament after his father was named in the papers.

MF vehemently ruled out the notion that an insider leaked the documents. Ramon Fonesca, one of the law firm's founders, stated that it was a hack from an external source. According to the firm, none of their employees could possibly be behind such a scandal.

Fast-forward to 15 June 2016. A mere two months after the Panama Papers scandal was publicized, MF experience their second data breach. An IT worker of MF's Geneva office was arrested on suspicion of data theft, unauthorized access and breach of trust. The big question surrounding the arrest still remains: did the same person commit these breaches? Was the Panama Papers scandal an insider attack committed by one of MF's IT workers?

Perhaps the answer is not important. If 'John Doe' was an external hacker, it is unlikely that he would have had such a level of access without the help of an MF employee. If 'John Doe' is the IT worker, then the man behind the world's biggest data breach acted with the intention to sabotage the organization he worked for. Whatever the case, the take-home message for MF stays the same; as an organization, MF are fostering an environment that is increasing their vulnerability to the insider threat.

Most insider threats are made, not born. The overwhelming majority of employees do not often join the world of work with overt intentions to steal from, damage or sabotage their organization. Instead they are jaded after a sequence of disenchanting events, leaving them cynical, angry and driven to balance the scales.

Disenchantment is not a solitary existence, but instead clusters around ineffective and damaging management practice. Research by Gallup, a performance management consultancy, has found that the behaviours and actions of managers explain up 70 per cent of why employees are engaged or disengaged. The same is true for the reverse, with managers being the key drivers for disenchantment within their teams. Organizations are often unaware of how their culture increases their vulnerability to the insider threat.

Ramon Fonesca was adamant that the Panama Papers scandal was not instigated by one of their employees. But what was the foundation of his certainty? Organizations often experience comparative-optimism when it comes to insider threat; this type of thing only happens to other companies, not to ours. It is unlikely that this is the only instance of MF employees intentionally harming their organization; it is merely the biggest and most public.

8

Trust and Distrust

It takes 20 years to build a reputation and five minutes to ruin it.

WARREN BUFFETT

Trust is like blood pressure. It's silent, vital to good health, and if abused it can be deadly.

FRANK SONNENBERG

The leaders who work most effectively, it seems to me, never say 'I'. And that's not because they have trained themselves not to say 'I'. They don't think 'I'. They think 'we'; they think 'team'. They understand their job to be to make the team function. They accept responsibility and don't sidestep it, but 'we' gets the credit. . . . This is what creates trust, what enables you to get the task done.

PETER DRUCKER

Trust is built when someone is vulnerable and not taken advantage of.

BOB VANOUREK

If you don't have trust inside your company, then you can't transfer it to your customers.

ROGER STAUBACH

Introduction

The word trust means 'reliance on the integrity, strength, ability, surety, etc., of a person or thing; confidence in them and what they say'. People say 'I trust him implicitly' or 'I don't trust a thing he says'. In this sense trust seems to have an all-or-nothing sense, yet it is possible to trust a person's judgement about some issues but not others.

Do you trust your neighbour with you house keys? Do you trust your friends to 'keep confidences'? Do you trust your MD, CEO or PR manager to tell the truth about the economic situation of your organization?

We will consider at least two types of trust. The first is whether an employer believes their colleagues and bosses are trustworthy. The second is reacting to managers who do not trust their employees or anyone else in the organization.

Would you let your employees post from the company social media account? It was an experiment conducted by a Canadian telecommunications company, who enlisted their 1,600 employees as 'brand advocates' for their social media accounts. Other than a few simple rules – use your best judgement, be respectful to competitors and do not say something you would not say in person – employees were given full access to write whatever they wanted on the company's behalf. From that point on, the company's public image and communication channels were in the hands of its employees; they had complete control over the messages that would be broadcast. The level of trust bestowed on those employees was huge.

Would you trust your team enough to do the same? Are you confident you know what it is that they would write? Conversely, would your manager trust you to post on behalf of the company? The exercise is less about what would be posted, and more about whether organizations are fostering a culture underpinned by trust.

Trust is a vital component of any business. The problem is that it is increasingly harder to find within the working world. In their 2017 Trust Barometer survey, Edelman – a global marketing consultancy – revealed that only 57 per cent of employees trust their organization to do what is right.

A practical and theoretical issue is that trust and distrust are often not thought of as separate issues. They are thought of as opposing ends of the same spectrum. When gauging public opinion with regards to trust – whether it is for politicians, businesses or the media – rarely do reports consider the possibility that distrust differs from trust.

Distrust is often seen as the absence of trust. This is happening particularly within the academic world, where researchers will too often assume distrust arises in the vacuum where trust no longer exists. This is not wholly the case. Whilst it is true that the factors that dispel trust are often the ones that build distrust, there are specific motivators that make distrust distinct. Distrust is a proactive phenomenon rather than an apathetic response. You only have to look to conspiracy theorists to find that this is the case. They actively try to find flaws in information they are presented with to either confirm their theories or disregard evidence to the contrary.

A waning trust has been shown to occur when there is no longer proof or reason to place your faith in that person, organization or institution any more. Distrust is instead underlined by an impetus to be suspicious. A growing distrust emerges when you are given reasons to re-evaluate the information you are presented with in light of your disenchantment.

Trust, trustworthiness and trust propensity

Trust is the foundation of any effective and meaningful relationship; whether it is between partners, the public and politicians, or within organizations. Trust is also something that everyone intrinsically understands, but can rarely put their finger on what it is or where it emerges. Even more apparent is when trust disappears; when the abstract bonds that hold a relationship together suddenly come apart.

Trust is a multi-faceted psychological concept to define. Throughout the previous decades, research has focused on the role of trust in its various applications. Trust has become blurred as research has focused on the cognitive processes, personal dispositions and individual differences associated with trust. As a result, the academic world has been left with a hodgepodge of definitions as each researcher has attempted to define trust anew.

At an employee level, trust is about uncertainty and vulnerability. Siegrist and Cvetkovich (2000), outlined trust as a 'willingness to rely on those who have responsibility for making decisions and taking actions'. In the workplace, trust plays a distinct role in co-operation and reliance on others. Rarely are employees in control of every aspect of their work. They therefore have to relinquish responsibility to other members of their organization: whether that is a manager giving autonomy to his team to act independently or employees having decisions made for them by senior members of staff.

There are those who find it inherently difficult to hand over any control. There are some employees who have such high levels of conscientiousness that their attention to detail starts to become maladaptive and obsessive. Dotlich and Cairo (2013) named these workers *perfectionists*: those who place unrealistically high standards upon themselves and others, and miss opportunities due to double- or triple-checking work. As a result, they will resort to micromanaging their peers as they become anxious when any aspect of the work is out of their control. Often, the *perfectionists* do not realize that they are doing this. The key is self-awareness. Nan Russell (2014) devised the following questions to help managers understand their trust attitudes:

1   Much of my time is spent on 'controlling' or monitoring staff communications, productivity or behaviour.   *True or False*

2 More often than not, I settle for mediocre talent to fill positions, or
   I cannot find the internal people to promote.   *True or False*

3 Disengagement or a lack of accountability is a problem I frequently
   encounter.   *True or False*

4 Since I want great results, I need to control and micromanage
   people.   *True or False*

5 I think policies and procedures should be designed to ensure
   employees do not break the rules or take advantage of the
   company.   *True or False*

6 It is hard to go on vacation, so most years I have time off
   remaining.   *True or False*

7 I think a needs-to-know communication approach works best with
   staff.   *True or False*

8 It is hard to be comfortable when people work from home/remotely
   since you do not really know what they are doing or where they
   are.   *True or False*

9 Monitoring staff interactions is critical to make sure customers,
   clients, and providers are treated well and with high service.
   True or False

10 People have to earn my trust.   *True or False*

Managers that build trusting cultures are those who make positive assumptions about their staff, communicate effectively and give their employees the freedom and autonomy to work. Think about a colleague or manager in your organization. Chances are that if they were to answer 'true' to more than three of these questions, it is possible that they are a *perfectionist* and a micromanager. Often the distrust that they project is not malicious, but instead represents a need for control.

There are also those who are overly eager to relinquish responsibility to anyone willing to make decisions for them. In the Hogan's (1997) terminology, these are the *cautious* and *dutiful* personality types. The *cautious* employee becomes avoidant, fearful and unassertive. They shut themselves off from their colleagues and will proactively delay decision making until they feel they have all possible information. Similarly, the *dutiful* employee becomes indecisive, ingratiating and conforming. They are overly eager to please and take pride in supporting their superiors. As a result, both the *cautious* and *dutiful* employee find responsibility and accountability overwhelming and will look to pass the buck as quickly as they can.

Distrust is a little bit different. Distrust is less about relinquishing control, and more about suspicion and scepticism. Fein and Hilton (1994) outlined distrust as 'actively entertaining multiple, possible rival, hypotheses about the motives and genuineness of a person's behaviour'. Employees who experience distrust become vigilant of their environment and the people they work with. The employee believes that their company assumes that they cannot be trusted with information, money or materials. This, of course, is a two-way street; when the employee feels distrusted, they become distrusting in return. Managers are seen as manipulators rather than mentors, colleagues as conspirators rather than collaborators.

There are two distinct aspects to distrust that are important to consider for understanding the process of disenchantment:

- **Trust propensity** – the qualities of the trustee that affect trust, i.e. the person that is trusting.

- **Trustworthiness** – the qualities of the trusted that affect trust, i.e. the target of the trust.

When it comes to understanding trust and distrust, these two factors play an important role in how experiences are processed and how trust can fall apart.

Trust propensity is a quality of the trustee (i.e. the person that is doing the trusting). Scholars have referred to this as personality-based trust, dispositional trust, or generalized trust. Trust propensity acts like a set of rose-tinted glasses. Whilst previous interactions are the best predictors for deciding whether to trust someone, propensity to trust appears to filter the information in a more positive light. Employees who are high on trust propensity actively reprocess information about their colleagues or managers to fit their trusting persona. They will continuously give the benefit of the doubt, even if a manager has undermined them or left them high and dry. The issue arises when they are overly trusting. Employees who are trusting – to the point of being maladaptive – are more likely to have their good nature taken advantage of.

Equally, there are those employees who see the world through dark-tinted glasses. These are the employees who are inherently negative about all decisions, behaviours or change. They see it as an affront to their status quo and respond with resistance and pessimism. Hogan calls these employees *Sceptical* or *Leisurely*. The *Sceptical* employee is cynical and mistrusting of others, holding powerful grudges against those who have wronged them in the past. The *Leisurely* employee treats information with passive-aggression and irritation. They will appear pleasant on the surface, but will be subversive and counterproductive once their manager's back is turned. These employees are the entire opposite of their rose-tinted counterparts. They are overly distrusting and will torpedo collaboration and communication due to their intrinsic negativity.

Trust propensity can also be altered by previous work experiences. There are employees who have become hardened and disenchanted over time due to poor management. A recent study analysed data from over 5,000 Australian workers to look at how demographics and job characteristics can change an employee's willingness to trust their manager. The study found that: distrust increased with age; distrust was greater for employees in the public sector than the private sector; distrust grew the longer an employee worked in the same place; and unionized employees were more distrusting than their non-unionized colleagues (Chang et al., 2016).

Trustworthiness instead is about the other person and what makes them inherently deserving of trust. There is some credit to the idea that some people have a trustworthy face. Face shape (Buckingham et al., 2006), eye colour (Kleisner et al., 2013) and body language (Brown and Moore 2002) have all been shown to influence our first impressions on someone's trustworthiness.

The distrusting, paranoid and vigilant manager

Clearly some people have very low trust in anyone. They appear mildly paranoid. What does the research on paranoid personality disorder teach us about interpersonal trust, or indeed the lack thereof? According to Oldham and Morris (2000:167–8) the old DSM-III-R describes paranoid personality disorder as:

A. A pervasive and unwarranted tendency, beginning by early adulthood and present in a variety of contexts, to interpret the actions of people as deliberately demeaning or threatening, as indicated by at least four of the following:

1. Expects, without sufficient basis, to be exploited or harmed by others.

2. Questions, without justification, the loyalty or trustworthiness of friends or associates.

3. Reads hidden, demeaning or threatening meanings into benign remarks or events, e.g., suspects that a neighbour puts out trash early to annoy them.

4. Bears grudges or is unforgiving of insults or slights.

5. Is reluctant to confide in others because of unwarranted fear that the information will be used against him or her.

6. Is easily slighted and quick to react with anger or to counterattack.

7. Questions, without justification, fidelity of spouse or sexual partner.

B. Occurrence not exclusively during the course of Schizophrenia or Delusional Disorder.

According to Oldham and Morris, the following six traits and behaviours are clues to the presence of what they call the *Vigilant* style. A person who reveals a strong *Vigilant* tendency will demonstrate more of these behaviours more intensely than someone with less of this style in his or her personality profile.

1. *Autonomy.* Vigilant-style individuals possess a resilient independence. They keep their own counsel, they require no outside reassurance or advice, they make decisions easily, and they can take care of themselves.

2. *Caution.* They are careful in their dealings with others, preferring to size up a person before entering into a relationship.

3. *Perceptiveness.* They are good listeners, with an ear for subtlety, tone, and multiple levels of communication.

4. *Self-defence.* Individuals with Vigilant style are feisty and do not hesitate to stand up for themselves, especially when they are under attack.

5. *Alertness to criticism.* They take criticism very seriously, without becoming intimidated.

6. *Fidelity.* They place a high premium on fidelity and loyalty. They work hard to earn it, and they never take it for granted. (pp. 151–2)

Vigilance can turn into paranoia and the latter to mistrust. Over time the vigilant leader can turn sub-clinically paranoid with disastrous effects for the organization.

Kets de Vries and Miller (1985) noted that whole organizations can become paranoid. They argue that when power is highly centralized in a leader with paranoid tendencies, there will tend to be a great deal of vigilance caused by distrust of subordinates and competitors alike. This may lead to the development of many control and information systems and a conspirational fascination with gathering intelligence from inside and outside the firm.

Paranoid thinking will also lead to a centralization of power as the top executive tries to control everything himself (no one can be completely trusted). The strategy is likely to emphasize 'protection' and reducing dependency on particular consultants, sources of data, markets or customers. There is likely to be a good deal of diversification, with tight control over divisions and much analytical activity. A leader who is obsessed with fantasies concerning distrust can set a very distinctive tone for the strategy, structure and culture of an organization.

The characteristics of these organizations are: suspiciousness and mistrust of others; hypersensitivity and hyper-alertness; readiness to combat perceived threats; excessive concern with hidden motives and special meanings; intense attention span; cold, rational, unemotional and interpersonal relations. The paranoid organization is defensive and hypervigilant. It is pervaded by an atmosphere of distrust. Distrust and suspiciousness of others at work is their abiding characteristic. The motives of all sorts of colleagues and bosses are interpreted as malevolent, all the time. The 'enemy' is both without and within.

They suspect, without much evidence, that others are exploiting, harming or deceiving them about almost everything both at work and at home. They are preoccupied with unjustified doubts about the loyalty or trustworthiness of subordinates, customers, bosses, shareholders, etc. on both big and small matters. They are reluctant to confide in others (peers at work) because of the fear that the information will be used against them: kept on file and used to sack them. They may even be wary of using email.

They read hidden or threatening meanings into most benign remarks or events from emails to coffee-room gossip, and then remember them. They are certainly hypersensitive to criticism. They persistently bear grudges against all sorts of people going back many years and can remember even the smallest slight. They perceive attacks on their character or reputation that others do not see and are quick to react angrily or to counterattack. They seem hyper-alert and sensitive. They have recurrent suspicions, without justification, regarding the fidelity of their sexual or business partner and can be pretty obsessed with sex.

Paranoid individuals are slow to commit and trust, but once they do so are loyal friends. They are very interested in others' motives and prefer 'watch-dog' jobs. They like being champions of the underdog, whistle-blowers on corruption. They are courageous because they are certain about their position. They are on the side of right: idealists striving for a better world. But they can be overly suspicious or fearful of certain people, which can manifest itself in an irrational hatred to certain race, religious or political groups.

They are not compromisers and attack attackers. Many of their characteristics make them excellent managers: alert, careful, observant and tactical. But they can have problems with authority; and in dealing with those who hold different opinions from their own. However, they are more sensitive to the faults in others than the faults in themselves. The business world, they believe (sometimes correctly) is full of danger, dishonest people and those that are untrustworthy and will let them down. Because they believe others are out to harm them they can be over-argumentative, bellicose, belligerent, hostile, secretive, stubborn and consumed with mistrust. They are not disclosive, are suspicious of others and are experts on projecting blame onto others.

Dotlick and Cairo (2003:53) see the paranoid leader as manifesting habitual distrust. They are 'inappropriately and egregiously suspicious' which has an insidious effect on all those around them. They tend to see downsides to every action; to see others exclusively acting politically or in their own self-interest or with ulterior motives. They are always critical in feedback and obsessed with what can (and will) go wrong. They identify three signs:

1   Relentless scepticism about other people's motives.

2   Their direct reports become more and more highly defensive.

3   They have increasing difficulty forging alliances with outside groups, companies and institutions.

They believe that, in certain occupations, people are trained to be distrustful and sceptical but that this can easily go too far. They believe the paranoid leader needs always to analyse the cause of their distrust and to recognize how much it is hurting their career. They need to be more positive and to imagine what effect their behaviour has on others.

Miller (2008) calls the paranoid leaders 'vigilantes' because of their 'watch your back', 'people can't be trusted' philosophies. They see deception, malevolence and persecution everywhere as their supersensitive and often malfunctioning radar is primed to pick up betrayal, duplicity and hostility. Of course, they project onto others those characteristics they do not like in themselves. They are often on a vendetta and should not be crossed lightly.

The war room mentality of paranoid leaders means they fit well in competitive and combatative sectors. Paranoid bosses demand total loyalty and surprising self-disclosure about the employee's private life. However, the smallest and most trivial thing can turn the supportive boss into a suspicious enemy. They brood, bide their time and remember. They keep records to take revenge. Interestingly they have got a good nose for insincerity and sycophants. They can be highly perceptive as to the motives of all those around them. Miller (2008) suggests they need to know who their enemies really are and beware black/white thinking.

Hogan and Hogan (2001) call this disorder 'Argumentative.' These types, they argue, expect to be wronged, to be betrayed, to be set up, to be cheated or to be deceived in some way. They see the world as a dangerous place, full of potential enemies; they enjoy conspiracy theories and are keenly alert for signs of having been mistreated. When they think they have been unfairly treated they retaliate openly and directly. This may involve physical violence, accusations, retaliation or litigation. Retaliation is designed to send the signal that they are prepared to defend themselves. They are known for their suspiciousness, their argumentativeness and their lack of trust in others. They are hard to deal with on a continuing basis because you never know when they are going to be offended by something (unpredictability), and because they are so focused on their own private agenda they do not have much time for others (unrewarding).

Paranoids mishandle stress by retreating, by withdrawing into their ideology and then attacking that which is threatening them. They are very persistent and tend to accumulate enemies. They are self-centred and ideology-centred – all information and experience is filtered through their odd world view and evaluated in terms of the degree to which it fits with, or threatens that view, which somehow reflects on them.

To work with them colleagues have no alternative but to agree with them, because they will defeat any objection in a way that makes sense to them. Colleagues will not be able to persuade them that they are wrong, and risk alienating them by challenging them, and once they decide people cannot be trusted, the relationship will be over. You are either for them or against them.

The bottom line? Some people (and organizations) are more paranoid than others. Some seem not to trust anyone or anything. Whilst there are times it pays to be vigilant a distrust, as of an untrustworthy manager, can quickly lead to disenchantment.

Competition and co-operation

The evolutionary psychologists have argued that it is socially advantageous to accurately make judgements about another person's trustworthiness from very little information. Neuropsychology studies have shown that trustworthy faces cause an increased activity in the limbic system – the emotional epicentre – lending credence to the theory of a dedicated 'social intelligence' function in our brain (Winston et al., 2002).

Additionally, abstract qualities such as personality traits are detectable and can influence a decision to trust someone. The evidence suggests that there is a certain facial geometry of people who have high levels of 'dark' traits – particularly psychopathy and Machiavellianism – causing our limbic system to implicitly identify that they should not be trusted (Gordon and Platek, 2009).

But how accurate are our initial predictions? There are those people who place great emphasis on their 'gut instinct' about others, making decisions on hunches rather than evidence. Frank (1988) wanted to test just how much our intuition affects our decisions to co-operate with someone else.

One of the more famous tests of co-operation is the Prisoner's Dilemma. Based on the economics of game theory, the task is based on the hypothetical scenario that the police have arrested two members of a criminal gang and placed them in separate cells. The police do not have enough evidence to prosecute but are hoping to catch them on a lesser charge. Each prisoner is given the opportunity to either remain silent or betray the other prisoner by testifying that they committed the crime. The officer presents each prisoner with a deal:

1   If you both betray each other, you will both get five years for the crime.

2   If you testify on the other prisoner, but they remain silent, then you will be set free while your colleague gets ten years.

3   If you both remain silent, then you will both only serve one year.

It is in both prisoners best interest to co-operate and remain silent. But by remaining silent, you leave yourself vulnerable to the possibility of being double-crossed by the other. Which option do you choose? How much should you trust the other prisoner?

In Frank's research two unknown players were pitched against each other in the game. Frank found that, when the players were given a brief time to socially interact before making their decision, the emotional connection and sense of trust had a significant impact on what the players decided to do next. After limited social interaction, players were able to accurately predict whether the other would choose to co-operate or betray them. When the opposite player was deemed as untrustworthy, people would choose to betray the other player in an attempt to protect themselves.

In the workplace, employees engage in the Prisoner's Dilemma more often than they realize. In every co-operative relationship, there is the opportunity to work together and receive mutual benefits or to renege and take it all. Each time both players experience the same vulnerability. The difference is that in the workplace each successive game is framed by the decisions of the last; the players remember what the other chose to do.

When co-operation is seen as an iterative trust exercise, it changes the way in which people 'play' the game of working together. *Trustworthiness* and *trust propensity* will frame the initial decisions made by the players, but each successive game becomes about the past behaviours of the other players.

If an employee chooses to renege and burn the other 'player' – whether that is going back on a promise to a client or stealing the credit from a colleague for a project – this has severe consequences. The next 'game' does not start anew, but is shrouded in what came before. In the workplace, colleagues are seen as more trustworthy if they work with a humble but high level of expertize (Marshall et al., 2013). Managers and colleagues who show greater honesty, behavioural consistency (i.e. fulfilling promises) and concern are more likely to be seen as trustworthy in the workplace (Sekhon et al., 2014). Employees who are once burned become twice shy when it comes to trust. Once the vulnerability has been exploited it becomes very hard to rebuild that trust.

When it comes to a trusting and co-operative relationship, there are often stark differences in what players see as 'winning'. What is the result that is

TABLE 8.1

		Team A	
		Co-operate	**Defect**
Team B	**Co-operate**	+£50 / +£50	−£50 / +£150
	Defect	+£150 / −£50	−£10 / −£10

deemed best? When we play a variation of the Prisoner's Dilemma in organizations, it becomes very clear how 'winning' differs between departments. In the variation, decisions are made for 'money' as opposed to jail time (as seen in Table 8.1), decisions are made in teams rather than individuals (with a representative showing a card that indicates their decision), and the objective is to *maximize the earnings of your group* over the course of eight rounds. After four rounds, the teams are allowed to communicate and discuss a strategy for the final four rounds.

The same thing happens every time. At some point in the first four rounds, one of the teams will defect and sell out the other. At that point, the trust is gone and both teams choose to defect and lose money until the negotiation stage. How do you bridge the gap and start to rebuild trust? In our consulting, we have seen a baffling range of tactics to try and guarantee co-operation for the final four stages:

- A common option is that teams decide to take it in turns being the co-operator and the betrayer. This is the most risky, but also the most short-sighted of the options. There is a mutual sense of justice and comfort that both teams will get the opportunity to burn the other team. However, it does not guarantee that both teams will stick to the arranged system. This is not so much an agreement to trust each other as much as it is an agreement of mutually assured destruction.

- Some teams draw up contracts to ensure that both teams will stick to the word and co-operate for the final four rounds. Despite the game being only for fun and demonstrative purposes, this is often the only way that two teams will trust each other once the trust has gone. There is a great (implied) dishonour in breaking the contract, but the reality is that neither team is willing to be vulnerable to the other without a legal framework in place.

- The smartest and most trusting option is when a team destroys their card for defecting. This leaves them with only one option; to co-operate. They display their willingness to be vulnerable and trusting and hope that the team does the same. In the majority of cases the other team reciprocates as trust begets trust.

This is also where a team's ethos comes to the fore. Some teams will have decided that they should adopt a strategy that secures their team's interest at the expense of the other team; an 'us versus them' mentality. These teams are generally distrusting of others around them. They assume that everyone else is out to get them and therefore they should act defensively as a form of defence.

The teams that show the greatest level of trust are the ones that see the 'group' as both teams. It is not a case of maximizing your team's earnings, but the earnings of both teams together. When distrust takes hold, employees and even whole departments will often forget that they are a part of a bigger mechanism. It is not about securing your own 'win', but making sure that you 'win' together.

Consequences of trust

Fehr has studied the economic and biological implications of trust for over 20 years. In one seminal paper, Fehr and his colleagues (Kosfeld et al., 2005) found that the neuropeptide Oxytocin is strongly associated with trusting behaviours.

In their experiments, participants who were given a drug to temporarily increase their Oxytocin levels were found to be significantly more trusting towards strangers; these people were more willing to trust strangers with larger sums of their own money.

Unfortunately, it is both impractical and unethical to administer doses of Oxytocin to staff as a means of building trust, so we cannot advize you to build trust in this way! However, Fehr's research has revealed an important insight into the consequences of trust. Fehr suggests people have an aversion to trust inequity (Fehr and Schmidt, 1999); *we re-evaluate how much we trust others based on how much they trust us.* His research has indicated that people are heavily influenced by reciprocity, wanting to balance the level of trust they express with what they experience. His experiments have led him to the conclusion that, in the workplace, trust begets trust: 'If you trust people, you make them more trustworthy and, conversely, sanctions designed to deter people from cheating actually make them cheat.' Fehr's work has highlighted a circular but highly important consequence of trust; that it results in increasingly more trust.

In an equally obvious fashion, a key consequence of trust is that employees start to feel trusted. Employees are socially astute to trust because of the social reality that emerges. Some scholars have argued that trust, for this reason, should be considered as a verb as opposed to a noun.

Currall and Inkpen (2006) state that trust is the *act* of relying on another person or party under a condition of risk. Additionally, Solomon and Flores (2003) argue that trust is not something we possess or 'have'. Instead it is an *action*; something that we do and make through our behaviours. Employees are aware of when they are truly trusted because of the consequential behaviour of their colleagues and managers. It is difficult to convince an employee that they are trusted if they are given no independence, hopeful initiatives, or assurance that they will do the right thing without being monitored.

When employees feel that they are trusted, their performance and commitment both increase. A recent study of schoolteachers in Macau assessed the exact impact of 'feeling trusted' (Lau et al., 2014). When employees felt trusted, they had greater self-confidence and self-belief in their ability. In turn, their supervisors considered them to be better performers and show greater organizational citizenship. Additionally, a recent survey of employees in eighty-eight retail outlets found that when employees felt trusted by their manager, this led to better performance and employees wanting to take on more responsibility.

Conversely, when employees feel distrusted their performance declines steadily. Distrust causes suspicion and scepticism. They feel as though their managers are waiting to catch them out by monitoring their every move. As a result, employees spend more of time covering their actions and preserving themselves than they do working (Mayer and Gavin, 2005). Trust allows employees more freedom to get on with the job at hand because they are no longer worrying that their colleagues or managers are out to get them.

There is both theoretical and empirical evidence to suggest that a team's trust in their manager is based on shared experiences (Ferrin et al., 2006). The employees within a team are likely to interact with each other far more often than each of them interacts with their manager. As a result, the perception – and consequential trust – of that manager is based on a collective appreciation of their previous experiences with that manager. As teams talk about examples of previous interactions, a perception starts to manifest itself. There are three aspects that contribute to a group's perception of their manager:

1   *Benevolence.* Do they show benevolence through supportive and sincere communications?

2   *Competence.* Do they appear skilful and able at what they do?

3   *Integrity.* Are they honest and do they adhere to ethical principles?

Once this perception is set, it is particularly difficult to shift. Disenchantment sets in and spreads as team members communicate and share stories. When the group is distrusting of their manager, there is evidence to show that they become less engaged and productive. Supporting this, disenchantment clusters appears to cluster and congregate around poor managers – the ones who show spite, incompetence and dishonesty.

The same is true in the opposite direction. When employees and teams consistently perform effectively and productively (*competence*), are honest and open with their supervisor (*integrity*), and communicate with respect and support (*benevolence*) then managers begin to develop a trusting and positive perception of their group. However, recent empirical evidence has shown that *competence* is the more salient feature for managerial trust in employees. When employees are effective in their role, managers show increased trust in them.

Despite Fehr arguing that we are averse to an inequity in trust, this is not always the case. Sometimes there is an imbalance or incongruence in trust between two people, with one demonstrating far more trust than the other. This can become particularly apparent in the early stages of a relationship. A clear example of this is an employee–supervisor relationship, where risk and responsibilities are different. As a manager or employee joins the organization, the relationship starts afresh. It is at this point when trust can be at its most incongruent.

When employees distrust their manager, they start to doubt the authenticity of their decisions and behaviours. When a supervisor distrusts their team, they become sceptical of the integrity, efficiency and effectiveness of their work. As time goes on and the two parties interact more, both manager and employee will infer trust and start to reciprocate.

The issue is when trust starts to coalesce and settle at a low level, with both parties distrusting each other. Distrust causes managers and employees to try and constrain their interactions. Managers start to hide information from their employees and monitor activity to catch social loafing or poor performance. Employees in turn communicate less with their manager and become demotivated due to the low expectations their managers have for them. As distrust and disenchantment spiral downwards, employees become increasingly motivated to hold up or sabotage their work.

Whilst distrust in general can be disastrous, incongruence can lead to greater senses of disenchantment on the losing side. When there is imbalance, one of the two is likely to have their vulnerabilities exploited time and time again. The question is which has the greater detrimental effect: is it more damaging for a manager to distrust their team, or for their team to have no trust in them? Evidence from a recent study (Carter and Mossholder, 2015) seems to suggest that performance suffers most when employees distrust their manager (but their manager trusts them). When the manager's trust was lower than the employees, performance was still affected, but not nearly as much.

In his book *Speed of Trust* (2006), Stephen Covey compared trust to a speedometer: when trust goes down in any context – between partners in a relationship, within a team or organization, or between businesses and clients – speed goes down and cost goes up. Covey's analogy demonstrates a simple truth. When trust is low, everything gets a little harder; processes become less efficient as employees or key stakeholders dig their feet in and resist being taken into something by someone they do not trust. The inverse of Covey's analogy is also true: when trust increases, speed goes up and costs decline.

The consequences of distrust can be severe. Disenchanted employees end up spending more time avoiding the surveillance that is put in place than they do working. Communication starts to break down as employees and managers no longer share important information with each other. On the other side of the coin, trust fosters productive, engaged, and happy employees. Trusted employees experience greater self-confidence, have higher self-confidence, and stay with their company longer. The question is this: what can you do to increase the speed of your company's trust-ometer?

Tackling trust and trust repair

The stark reality is that trust is a rare commodity within organizations. In their 2014 review, PricewaterhouseCoopers – a UK based professional services firm – found that 37 per cent of CEOs were concerned with the lack of trust within their organization. In 2017, that number rose to 55 per cent. With less than 50 per cent of non-executive or managerial employees trusting the company they work for, how does an organization start to tackle distrust and rebuild trust?

Bingham (2017), an HR consultant at the forefront of the positive psychology movement, has argued that the buck falls with managers and senior staff. Bingham wrote: 'if employees don't trust you, *it's up to you to fix it*'. Bingham recommended three strategies for managers and companies to start rebuilding trust in their culture:

1 *Hire for trust.* A common theme throughout business psychology is the issue of *select-in* versus *select-out* criteria. Managers will often focus on the skills they feel are needed for that role and neglect looking for attributes that make them unworthy. Bingham recommends asking questions that determine integrity and honesty as these will help build trust from the ground up. Ask when they have tackled extra work to help their organization or team meet critical goals. Or when they put their clients', co-workers' or company's interests ahead of their own.

2 *Make positive assumptions.* As mentioned before, trust begets trust in the workplace. Managers that work off negative assumptions – locking up supplies, withholding important information, or enforcing overbearing rules – project an assumption of distrust. Promote transparency, reject micromanagement, and assign challenges with affirmation that the goals will be reached. Bingham argued that

building trust comes through a culture of openness, where your team can ask 'through the grapevine' style information so that you can confirm or debunk the rumours.

3 *Zero tolerance towards deceit.* For trust to work, managers must clearly communicate that employees who actively undermine that trust are not welcome in the company. The flip side of this is that managers must be held to the same standard and admit when they have made mistakes. Bingham states all employees make mistakes, but the key to getting your team to trust you is to acknowledge your own shortcomings and accept responsibility.

It is also vital that these strategies are communicated effectively throughout the organization. Business ethics scholar Archie Carroll (2006) argues that ethical organizations drive enchantment and build trust by making the first steps to broadcasting that they are willing to engage in trust. Central to this is effective communication within the organization. Research at the North Carolina Management School found that internal communication has been shown to increase levels of trust between managers and employees (Mayer and Gavin, 2005).

When managers engage in undistorted communication this reinforces and builds upon the level of trust that an employee has for the manager. Face-to-face communication has been shown to be the most powerful method, as it is the clearest way to resolving employee ambiguity and uncertainty. Business academic Gail Thomas (2009) and her colleagues argued that specific aspects of communication can be vital. In particular, they stated: 'When employees perceive that they are getting information from their supervisors and co-workers that is *timely, accurate,* and *relevant,* they are more likely to feel less vulnerable and more able to rely on their co-workers and supervisors.'

Resolving distrust and building a trusting culture can be seen as a cycle. Lewicki and Bunker (1996) outline three phases when building and maintaining a culture of trust:

1   *Calculus-based trust.* This is the lowest level but most fundamental form. Calculus-based trust emerges when employees feel there are rules and policies in place to protect them from being taken advantage of – i.e. how we should treat each other and the consequence for violating those guidelines.

2   *Knowledge-based trust.* This level emerges when employees have the understanding and experience of their colleague or manager to anticipate how they will behave. Setting a precedent of being open, honest, and consistent in actions will reinforce a high level of knowledge-based trust in employees. Alternatively, acting deceitful and secretive reinforces distrusting knowledge.

3   *Identity-based trust.* This level involves understanding the visions and ambitions of colleagues and employees. It is supporting employees in their development and progression.

Developing a team identity (e.g. a motto or shared vision), creating joint goals, committing to commonly shared values, and working closely and communicating frequently are ways that are effective in building *identity-based trust* (Lewicki and Bunker, 1996).

Dumitru and Schoop (2016), found that building organizational trust starts at the team level. When employees had trusted their peers, they identified with their team and organization more. As a result, they had greater affective commitment and trust in their organization as a whole. Their study showed the potential cascading effect that trust can have when trying to build a culture of trust. Additionally, it shows how quickly it can go wrong. When employees lose trust in their team members, this can escalate and cause disenchantment.

It is easy to send employees away on countless team building days or exercises. But these will not have the desired effect if it is not reinforced at the managerial and organizational level. To avoid disenchantment and dislodge distrust, employees need to feel as though their colleagues are on their side. Trust is a two-person game. Employees are playing a version of their own Prisoner's Dilemma every day at work. The question is this: do employees feel they can be vulnerable around their colleagues, and do employees feel that their managers are willing to be vulnerable towards them? When one or both players distrust each other, everyone ends up the loser.

Conclusion

It must be very unpleasant to work in an organization or for a manager who is either untrustworthy or shows no trust in others: or both. There are good reasons to be vigilant at work: people have both internal and external competitors for resources and markets. And, we all know, that as adults people do not always tell the truth.

We have seen that there are different types of trust and different ways of establishing or breaking it. What is very clear however is that if distrust is a feature of people in an organization for good or no reason this will very soon lead to disenchantment.

DISENCHANTMENT CASE 4: TERRY CHILDS AND THE CITY OF SAN FRANCISCO

The following comments are from former and current employees of large organizations, sourced from Glassdoor.

'They lie just about anything to keep up the reputation they're bound to lose. They say the customer is at the heart of the business, the biggest lie ever. Money is at the heart.'

'[Advice to Management] get rid of the bullying culture and start hiring competent people.'

'[Advice to management] Let honest, truthful people run the company.'

IN 2008, A CALIFORNIAN JUDGE set the bail at $5 million for Terry Childs. Childs was arrested for deliberately locking the city out of the network – including access to city e-mails, payroll, police records and information on jail inmates – and refused to give out the passwords. Why? Because Childs felt that his supervisors were incompetent.

Childs was a network administrator for the city of San Francisco. He was particularly skilled at this job; he was one of only (at the time) 16,000 CISCO certified internetworking engineers in the world. As a result, he was entrusted with building and managing the city's networks, as well as the mammoth task of bringing together all of its disparate parts. Childs went on to develop a new, interconnected system that replaced most of the city's networks.

Childs was clearly proud of his accomplishments. He applied for, and was granted, a copyright for the design of his new network as a form of 'technical artistry'. Additionally, he became reluctant to hand over control. He was sceptical of the abilities of his colleagues, and ended up being the chief administrator for the network. Childs was the *head honcho* for anything and everything to do with his network; troubleshooting, changes and the overall management.

Childs held the position for five years, earning a basic six-figure salary to overlook his creation. The issue was that Childs had unprecedented and uncontrollable power over the network. He was the only one who had access, making him virtually indispensible. As a result, he was on call 24/7, 365 days a year. Childs became increasingly disgruntled, as ineffective communication and management within the city applied additional pressure to a man who was unwilling to relinquish control. Childs' disenchantment escalated when he heard that the city were reducing the budget by laying people off, and his job was one of those on the line.

The incident occurred when a colleague of Childs attempted to audit his system. An angered Childs confronted, harassed and photographed his colleague in attempts to not allow her in. Why was Childs so upset? It was reported that the source of Childs' rage was that no one had told him an audit was going to take place. Childs perceived this as an information-gathering mission to oust him from his position, seeing his auditing colleague as a threat and intrusion.

Two weeks later, the city asked that Childs relinquish control of all usernames and passwords for the system. Childs refused to do so, instead changing the passwords and not letting anyone have them. He viewed his managers and peers as ineffective and unfair in the way he had been treated up until that point. Childs claimed that no one in the city was capable or competent enough to manage the system.

Childs was subsequently arrested for tampering with the network and subversively avoiding checks. As a frame of reference, Childs' $5 million bail is nearly five times higher than the expected bail for a murderer. Why was Childs' bail set so high? Ron Vinson, deputy director of the city's Department of Technology and Information Services, stated there was a real fear that if he were released on bail Childs would permanently lock the system and erase the records.

What lessons can be learned from the disenchanted case of Terry Childs? The ultimate lesson is that disenchantment yields no winners. Despite Childs' unlawful – and ultimately petty – response, it is the management who let the situation escalate to the point it did. A lack of communication and oversight led to the rise of a superuser with unbridled power. Childs was increasingly pressured in his role, but equally was not pressed to delegate or bring in support around him. 'Superstars' in the organization should not be left to just 'get on with it'. No matter how brilliant or talented, every employee needs an environment where they can strive and continue to develop. Forgetting about these employees and leaving them in the corner will only foster disenchantment.

9

A Kept Word versus
A Broken Promise

Promises are only as strong as the person who gives them . . .?
STEPHEN RICHARDS

*Promises may fit the friends, but non-performance will turn
them into enemies.*
BENJAMIN FRANKLIN

There is no greater fraud than a promise not kept.
GAELIC PROVERB

*Between today and tomorrow are graves, and between promising
and fulfilling are chasms.*
AUTHOR UNKNOWN

Introduction

Whether they are called promises or not from the selection interview to the
retirement party people make statements about the future. They may be about

salary levels, promotion prospects, training opportunities, etc. Employees often hear these statements as promises: just as electors hear statements from politician as promises about what they will do when elected. Most of us have learned to be cynical with regard to politicians but less so with managers.

A major source of disenchantment at work occurs when a worker has expectations thwarted after what they believe is a broken promise. They were, they believe, promised certain things which never came to fruition. Some have records of these promises (like emails), but most do not, meaning they are very much open to dispute, discussion, and debate. This chapter is about what happens when promises are broken.

Generation Y and the workplace

There is an unofficial rule of the Internet known as Godwin's Law. It states that as an online discussion grows longer, so too does the probability of someone making a comparison involving Hitler, the Nazis or the Holocaust. Granted, the glibly called *reductio ad Hitlerium* is not a steadfast rule. But it is startling how often Godwin's perception is proven correct. You only need to spend a short time scanning the comments on articles about political figures for it to crop up.

Recently, it appears that a similar yet less macabre *reductio ad Millennium* rhetoric is occurring within most discussions of the 'future of the workplace'. These discussions primarily focus about how the working week will evolve due to huge advances in technology, and how our expectations and assumptions regarding work will evolve with it. But with *reductio ad Millennium,* as these debates on the future of the workplace go on, it is the probability of Generation Y being referenced that increases exponentially.

Perhaps HR experts are right to engage in *reductio ad Millennium*; it is now estimated that 75 per cent of the world's employees are Millennials, with

50 per cent of leadership positions being help by under thirty-five-year-olds. Generation Y represents the most educated and technologically immersed generations the world has ever seen. The question becomes this: what do Millennials expect from the workplace? What do they believe they are entitled to and what do they understand they are being offered?

Previous generations had developed an intuitive, generally accepted 'system of expectations' that they all appeared to agree on. An organization was for life, not just for this financial year. You joined an organization at the bottom and meandered your way up the hierarchical ladder over the course of fortyish years (if you were fortunate). In exchange for pitching-up and pitching-in, you were guaranteed job security, financial progression and personal development. When the day came to hang up your hat, the organization would throw a party in your honour and present you with an engraved gold watch. These were apparently simple times. Employees believed (and most experienced) that if you demonstrated loyalty, your organization would see that you were well looked after.

Enter Generation Y. Many now argue that Generation Y have ripped up the rulebook and entirely rejected this notion of what work should be. Millennials have been described as lazier and more entitled than previous generations, as well as being hyperbolically diagnosed as suffering from deeply unattractive, entitled, narcissism. As a result, Millennials are thought of as less committed to their job, less engaged at work and more likely to pack it all in after a few years. But is this the case? Do the current batch of twenty-one-year-old graduates hold fundamentally different expectations about work?

Deloitte's 2016 Millennial survey uncovered certain trends in their thinking. Young workers believe a company's success needs to be measured on more than just their financial performance. Generation Y wants to work for companies who focus on people – their customers, employees and society as a whole. Millennials choose to work for employers that value professional development and progression, 'flexitime', and a sense of meaning from work. Keeping young workers around is a function of leadership; Millennials who feel overlooked and underutilized for leadership positions have one foot out of the door.

But, are these values really unique to Millennials? Are workers under the age of thirty-five the only people who value working for an ethical organization or having a job that has purpose? It seems to be a consistent attribution error on behalf of HR gurus. Millennials are actually quite similar to older workers, with psychological and government statistics finding that young people share very similar expectations of work as their parents and grandparents. When it comes to tenure, Millennials are statistically no different to young workers in previous generations.

Changes in what we expect from work are not due to Millennials demanding something different, but are due to the workplace evolving for all generations. Advancing technology and busier commutes build the value of working remotely from time to time. Globalization and technology have made the world a smaller place. The 'job for life' has been retired, making way for faster-paced, 'higher flow-through' organizations where the workforce is more fluid than stagnant. Stock options and a company car are now less enticing than cultural fit and personal development opportunities. What can be expected from the workplace is not what was desired before.

Unwritten expectations

Expectations play an important role at work. When expectations are met and promises kept, employees are motivated and driven. When promises are broken or tracks forced in another direction, it can be an incredibly derailing experience. People say they feel cheated, lied to and psychologically abused.

In the workplace, unwritten expectations are ubiquitous. These unwritten expectations form the basis of the *psychological contract*. In an important paper,

Edgar Schein (1988) defined the psychological contract as: 'the unwritten expectations operating at all times between every member of an organization and the various managers and others in that organization.... Each employee has expectations about such things as salary or pay rate, working hours, benefits and privileges that go with a job' and 'the organization also has more implicit, subtle expectations that the employee will enhance the image of the organization, will be loyal, will keep organizational secrets and will do his or her best.' It is an implicit agreement about the reciprocal obligations between employee and employer. It is not legally binding, nor does it exist anywhere formally. But the psychological contract has a firm grip over the enchantment and motivation of employees.

Denise Rousseau (1995), went on to distinguish between four different types of unwritten contract:

- *Psychological*. This contract is within the individual. It contains a set of beliefs regarding the promises made, accepted, and relied upon between themselves and their organization.

- *Normative*. The shared psychological contract that emerges in a work group. It reflects the fact that individuals interpret their situation in the same way.

- *Implied* . These are the interpretations of third parties regarding what the explicit and legal contract means for individuals in the organization.

- *Social*. There are general beliefs in mutual work obligations associated within a particular culture or society. It is what general society expects from work: 'a fair day's work for a fair day's pay'.

Different jobs can demand different expectations. The teenager who delivers the daily paper desires a dissimilar set of values and behaviours in their employer than the middle-aged financial analyst. Regardless, the unwritten presumptions that an employee has about their job mould the framework in which they view their motivations and outcomes.

Some employees only expect one thing from their employer – a regular and reliable pay cheque. Think about the job that lets employees save up for their first car or put students through university. It is likely to be a menial Saturday job or working behind the bar at the local pub. The implicit agreement is 'a fair day's work for a fair day's pay'. These are known as *transactional contacts* and serve a simple purpose. The obligations between the employee and employer revolve around materialism: how much will the employee get paid for how many hours?

These types of contracts can be very useful when there is no long-term plan surrounding the work. High-tech firms or temporary-recruitment agencies have built their business model around these types of expectation. These companies will often hire individuals on a short-term contract or for a specific project based on certain skills that they have. This is a very economical model of what people expect from work. The only things that matter to the employer and employee are that the task is finished in exchange for an agreed amount of pay.

But this is not what often goes on in the world of work. Employers often want their employees to be more than task-completing automatons. They want people who contribute meaningfully to the culture of the organization, people who help create a pleasant working environment.

Similarly, employees often need more than just a payslip from their employer. Whilst the 'job for life' is following a similar path to fax-machines, pagers and VHS, it does not mean that employees are not looking for meaningful progression within their organization. Employees want to develop professionally and personally, and hope that the organization will support them with this. Organizations know that creating talented employees will allow the business to progress.

Understanding why employees are motivated to progress and develop is often key to ensuring that this is done effectively. MacRae and Furnham (2017) outline six types of employee motivation. They differentiate between the *intrinsic* motivators – when employees are driven by internal rewards, and the *extrinsic motivators* – when employees are driven by rewards that are external to them:

Intrinsic motivators

- *Autonomy* – valuing engagement, active stimulation, participation, and development at work. These employees want the freedom to do their work their way.

- *Competence* – valuing achievement, status and recognition. These employees strive to be good at what they do.

- *Affiliation* – prioritizing working with others, passing on knowledge, and social responsibility. These employees want to feel as though they belong.

Extrinsic motivators

- *Security* – prioritizing job security, stability and regularity. These employees want to know that they will be with their company for the long haul.

- *Compensation* – valuing salary, bonuses, insurance and job perks. These employees work for the rewards.

- *Comfort* – enjoying personal convenience, flexibility and a calm job. These employees want a job that fits with their personal lifestyle.

For employees to be able to feel connected to their organization, an interpersonal connection needs to form with their employer: the employee needs to know how they want to develop; the employer needs to be clear on how they can facilitate this. The contract goes beyond being *transactional,* and starts involving *relational* expectations.

Relational contracts describe a more in-depth, interpersonal psychological contract that can exist between employer and employee. Instead of being founded in materialism, *relational contracts* are socio-emotional. They encompass expectations of how the organization will help you develop as an individual, as well as how you can help contribute back into the organization. At the recruitment stage, organizations will often talk of development opportunities or chances to progress.

The recent surge of graduate jobs are tailored around this model; two to three years of loyalty will often provide new recruits with the personal development, training and mentoring from a more senior member of the organization. For employees, this experience is invaluable and provides them with the opportunity to improve and excel. For the employer, their employees are now well trained, invested in the organization and enchanted.

Building expectations

At some point, these expectations have to be built. There has to be a point when the person and the company begin to form ideas about what can be expected from the other. Most often, the genesis of the psychological contract will occur at the very first meeting. Getting this first meeting right is vital from both sides, as it sets the precedent for the working relationship. Luckily, it is a meeting that can be planned and strategized, as expectations are often shaped in the interview.

The selection process is where the company and the candidate begin to size each other up, delving into the details of what the other is like. Interviews can be over in ten minutes, or stretch on for hours. They can compose of a rigid and unwavering set of questions, or differ with each candidate. Do you use a single interviewer or a present panel? Do you interview the candidates individually, or lump them together and force them to co-operate on a task?

It can take place in an unused, windowless meeting room, or in more unconventional settings – one is to interview a candidate whilst going for a walk around the organization. Whatever the case, every interview usually has a primary purpose; the interviewer is analysing whether the candidate has what it takes, whilst the candidate is measuring whether this is the sort of place they want to spend thirty plus hours a week for the foreseeable future.

What most people do not realize is that *the interview also begins to set the stage for the psychological contract*. Whilst the interviewer and candidate are looking for what they want (or do not want) in the other, they are inadvertently building an idea of what they can expect. What type of work ethic will this person bring? Does the candidate show interest in development and growth? Does the company value having a social impact? Does the company have dress-down Fridays?

However, issues start to emerge when initial impressions do not match reality. The selection process will often see two interesting psychological phenomena that cause an incongruence to grow between what was said and what can be expected: impression management and self-deception.

Impression management

Much like a first date, it is generally assumed that neither party wholly presents their true self in an interview. At first, the majority of people will present a version of themselves that they feel is most interesting, engaging and attractive to the other person. You love cooking, enjoy travelling and take delight in long walks on the beach. You leave out the part where you confess your unwavering dedication to collecting model train sets. It is a case of *impression management*; making sure that you portray selected aspects of yourself that you think the other party will like.

A similar process occurs in the interview. Cynics say the interviewee lies about themselves and the interviewer about the job and the organization. Both the interviewer and candidate will engage in a form of impression management, it is just that the overall image presented is slightly different. Impression management is something that everyone expects to see at interviews. It is widely assumed that what is said in an interview cannot be taken as gospel. Many people have noted that the selection interview features a lot of 'smoke and mirrors'; the interviews make the organization seem better than it potentially is, whilst the interviewee overstretches the truth about some of their abilities.

Max Eggert (2007), an expert on selection, has argued that there are many different types of lies. They make a good checklist for the potential interviewer.

1 **White-lies**. These are found in the 'puff' statement some people are encouraged to write on their CV. 'I am a totally committed team player'; 'I have excellent social skills and the ability to read people'; 'I am utterly trustworthy and loyal'. The question of course is 'who says?' Where is the evidence? The best solution is to ignore all this flim-flam and say 'I will be the judge of that, thank you'.

2 **Altruistic lies**. These are lies that attempt a cover-up, but look as if they are helping others. So rather than say they left their last job because their manager was a bully, or the company was patently dodgy, they say they resigned to look for new challenges.

3 **Lies of omission.** For many these are the most frequent and easiest of lies. People might omit details of school or university grades because they had poor marks. Whole periods of their life are obfuscated. The most common lie concerns dates, often to disguise the fact that the candidate seemed to spend a surprisingly short amount of time in a succession of jobs. It is no more nor less than concealment.

4 **Defensive lies.** The defensive lie is one that conceals by generalizations or vagaries. Ask a person about their previous boss's management style, their reason for leaving or their health record and you are often faced with a string of vague expressions such as

'like others in the company'; 'much the same as my co-workers'; 'at that time'. Ask vague questions you get defensive lies.

5 **Impersonation lies.** This is also called the transfer lie and occurs mostly where people take credit for others' work. Statements such as 'I doubled sales over the year'; or 'I was responsible for a budget of over three million'. All others in the hierarchy are forgotten in these lies. And it is difficult to establish the facts often as to who exactly was responsible for particular successes (and disasters which are, of course, omitted).

6 **Embedded lies.** This is a clever subterfuge to confuse the interviewer. So 'I really enjoyed my time in Oxford' could refer to a first job in the city of dreamy spires where s/he was a mere underling. The idea is to suggest than an experience, qualification or achievement was very different from the actuality. 'It was good fun being with the BBC/CNN' could mean practically anything from 'I once went to a show there' to 'they filmed at my school'.

7 **Errors of commission or fact.** This is lying 101. They are explicit, verifiably false claims. It is about claiming qualifications you do not have; starting up or working for companies that never existed; skills that do not exist. It is the most blatant form of lie.

8 **Definition lies.** This is the sport of lawyers and of presidents. What precisely does it mean 'to have sex with' someone; what is a company turnaround; what does it mean to be in the 'talented' group? This approach involves working with a very specific and obscure definition so that for all intents and purposes you are telling the truth.

9 **Proxy lies.** This is where the candidates get others to lie for them. It is usually referees but could be former teachers. They may skilfully work on their previous employers' poor memory, vanity or other bribes to persuade them to obfuscate.

The smart suit, the carefully crafted CV and specifically selected referees are all impression management tools used by the candidate. The organization will do the same, handing out glossy brochures and giving tours of only the best parts of the office. These are all part of the impression management processes, used as 'spin' for both the employer and the candidate. It is a selective and carefully presented version of reality, advertizing the facts in a particular way.

Often, impression management does not harm anyone. It is a way of rewording and framing certain attributes or achievements to be slightly more dazzling than they actually are. Most interviewers and candidates are aware of this, and start to decode the jargon by reading between the lines. 'Proficient in elementary French' usually means the candidate has not spoken a word since their Year 11 school trip to Lyon. Job descriptions that state 'along with other admin duties, to support senior staff' really mean that the candidate will be at mercy of any one in a more senior position to them.

Interviewers want to filter the brightest from the brainless, and will study HR best sellers on 'Killer Questions to ask at the Interview' or 'How to Read People Like a Book'. Candidates will counter by memorizing passages from 'Great Answers to Tough Interview Questions'. The whole process becomes a charade, with both parties building loosely formed expectations from the tidbits of truth that they detected.

Whilst mostly harmless, it is important to distinguish the line between managing impressions and being authentic. For candidates, being upfront and direct about potential limitations will set certain expectations for the employer. It is better to undersell and exceed expectations than to come up short. When employers expect candidates to demonstrate a certain level of *finesse*, poor performance is seen as a lack of motivation on the part of the employee. The same is true for organizations. If the company is expected to be an energetic and innovative workplace, the spark is lost if the culture is more akin to David Brent's department in 'The Office'.

Self-deception

The second psychological phenomenon is *self-deception*. Self-deceptions are untruths told by people who wholly and genuinely believe them. Most of us will know someone who sincerely believes that they are funny, or believes that they have the makings of an Olympic athlete based on their Year 9 sports day performance. Yet it is painfully apparent to their friends, family and colleagues that they are mistaken. Despite the gentle hints that this is not the case, it does not shatter their belief. Alas, the delusions persist as they continue behaving and boasting that they have this ability.

However, to be deluded about your sense of humour or athletic prowess is relatively inconsequential, bar the potential jibes you may receive from your friends. A candidate who imagines they are bright when sub-par, or a company believing they are ground breaking when commonplace, these are more serious. For people, there are a number of traits that are particularly prone to self-deception: possessing courage, intuition, creativity, emotional intelligence and drive. Organizations can become deluded with their core values, priding themselves on honesty, integrity or respect when in reality they are the opposite of these.

In building expectations, the keen-eyed observer must be wary that positive self-deception can be symptomatic of something darker. Certain 'dark' personality traits are characterized by self-deception, particularly narcissism. Narcissists will hold delusions of grandeur, believing that they are truly special and gifted when it is not the case. When put under pressure or moved out of the spotlight, they will belittle the efforts of others and champion their own stories in order to reinforce their ego. Usually, this type of delusional self-promotion is something that puts people off.

However, it actually has the opposite effect in interviews. The arrogance and need for admiration that is associated with narcissism is also coupled with charismatic self-promotion. Having an outgoing and confident personality is something that pays dividends in the interview.

Paulhus et al. (2013) have studied the impact that 'dark' personality traits such as narcissism can have in social situations. 'A job interview is one of the few social situations where narcissistic behaviours such as boasting actually create a positive impression.' In their research, they noted: 'Narcissists tended to talk about themselves, make eye contact, joke around and ask the interviewers more questions. As a result, the study found that people rated narcissists as more attractive candidates for the position.'

But problems begin to emerge when these initial impressions are just a charade. The positive expectations that the interviewer has of the candidate will soon crumble under the slightest pressure. Dark traits, such as narcissism, can be self-serving up until the point of disaster. Most often, those who derail as managers are chronic self-deceivers. The same effect can occur for organizations. Interviewers who are charming and upbeat can make the organization seem a far more fun and vibrant place to work than it actually is.

Building expectations can be a potentially disastrous period for both the employee and the organization. Enchantment is contingent on a close alignment between expectations and reality. When initial expectations are left unmet and promises of potential broken, disenchantment can spark.

But it does not have to be this way? Organizations need to reflect on what type of company they are and how they want to be perceived by outsiders. If it is the case that they need to force the candidate to wear rose-tinted glasses to get them in the door, something needs to change. Focusing on person–organization fit is a powerful tool to help foster enchantment:

- What does the organization expect from a new employee?
- What does the candidate expect from the organization they work for?

Providing answers to these questions will build more accurate expectations and maintain the spark between employee and employer.

When expectations go awry

The key to winning a political campaign, it seems, is to make highly desirable promises. Promises to build a better economy; to improve national education; to put support mechanisms in place to help those who are in need. It seems that the bigger the size of the political position, the bigger the size of the promise. Promises of a better tomorrow lead to more votes, and a greater chance of winning that coveted seat.

Most people have come to expect that politicians will break most of the promises they make. However, the biggest reputational damage comes when voters believe that politicians will improve their lives, but five years pass and nothing has changed. When this happens, it sparks outrage and discontent. We want to hold the liars accountable and remove them from their post. Depending on the magnitude of the broken promise, it could spell their political demise come the next election.

In the workplace, it is unfortunately commonplace for managers not to keep promises made to their employees. Employees feel let down when the promised rewards are smaller than expected, when promotions vanish, and training opportunities never materialize. Unlike politics, if expectations are not met at work, it is not possible for employees to democratically oust their managers in the next financial year. So what happens when expectations go awry, when promises are broken and employees are left empty handed?

Different academics have used a range of terms to describe the different concepts involved with regards to the psychological contract:

- *Contract fulfilment* – when the employee perceives that the organization has committed and satisfied their obligations.

- *Contract breach* or *discrepancy* – when the employee believes that the organization has not done what was agreed. This could be that the organization has either under-fulfilled or over-fulfilled their promise.

- *Contract violation* – the employee's emotional reaction to a breach in psychological contract.
- *Contract abandonment* – when the employee or organization decide to simply no longer acknowledge the 'agreed contract'.
- *Contract reneging* – when either the employee or organization attempts to go back on the agreement.
- *Contract incongruence* – when the employee or organization perceive the contract to have been breached due to a misunderstanding of what it was supposed to involve.

Unmet expectations spark outrage, cynicism and apathy. When what we were promised fails to materialize, we become deflated and demotivated. There will unfortunately be employees who this happens to more than others. But it is not because their managers or organization have failed them with greater frequency. Simply, these employees will feel that the organization owes them a great deal more than their colleagues. These employees are entitled; they believe that they are special or gifted, and their talent deserves to be recognized by the organization. Entitlement can skew what an employee can realistically expect from their team, managers and organization.

A frequently posed question around entitlement is whether it has any relation to performance. Is it the great who become entitled as their previously normal expectations grow with success? Or are the entitled usually the epitome of mediocrity? The answer is that both are true. Ackerman and Donnellan (2013) investigated the subtleties of entitlement. They established two types of entitlement:

- *Normal* – entitlement as a result of previous performance and success.

- *Narcissistic* – entitlement as a result of an overinflated sense of self-worth.

Certain employees do possess a great deal of talent. However, whilst their esteem can be humble initially, as they continually succeed their expectations will grow as well. They begin to expect to win or to get a raise, not because others should bow to their greatness, but because they are genuinely good at what they do. This is termed *normal entitlement*. An employee could grow to expect that they be placed on key projects because they have the ability to close the deal and the track record to support it. However, they are under no delusion that for different tasks, other employees may be picked before them based on their skills. They distinguish between their abilities – what they are good at, and what they are average at – and can differentiate their expectations accordingly.

Narcissistic entitlement, however, does not make that distinction. These employees expect more in all areas of their life, regardless of their ability. Narcissistic entitlement is thought to be a defence mechanism, projecting expectations of winning and being the best as a mask for their inferiority. As a result, these employees are disappointed more often. When they fall short or do not receive what is expected, they place the fault on others; they believe it could not possibly be their fault. A recent psychological paper provided support for this reactionary mechanism. Narcissistic employees that are fired for poor performance place blame on their superiors, believing that their superiors are intimidated by their ability.

Entitled employees, narcissistic or normal, are more likely to experience disenchantment due to their sky-high expectations and standards. However, that is not to say that unmet expectations do not harm the non-entitled. Even when we hold realistic expectations, disenchantment can still spark; and there is neurological evidence to support this. In particular, the neurotransmitter dopamine has been shown to play a critical role in fostering disenchantment.

Dopamine is the neurotransmitter of pleasure and desire, being linked to all of the fun things that we experience in life: laughing with friends; seeing your sports team win the championship; eating a large amount of cheese at the weekend. It not only provides us with pleasure for specific experiences, but also motivates us to go and seek out more of these rewards. Consequently, people who are predisposed to higher dopamine activity are more likely to experience addiction; they are continually looking for that next pleasurable experience.

Rutledge, a computational neuroscientist at UCL, has been researching how levels of dopamine change influence our decision making, happiness and well-being. He found that expectations play a critical role in the amount of dopamine our brain releases. Thus, he inferred that happiness is not dependent upon how well things are going, but on whether they are going *better or worse than expected* (Rutledge et al., 2015).

When we achieve what we expect, our brain rewards us by releasing dopamine. Whether it is working towards beating the personal best on your 10 km. run, winning a project proposal that you were particularly proud of, or finally finishing the book that you had always wanted to write, once we achieve what we expected our brain rewards us with dopamine. It is a powerful surge, overwhelming you with a sense of accomplishment, happiness and, in a lot of cases, relief.

The same occurs when we receive a reward that we did not expect: discovering a five-pound note in an old pair of jeans; acknowledgement for work that you thought went unnoticed; your favourite café giving you an extra chocolate muffin on the house. These unexpected rewards are slightly different; there is no sense of relief or accomplishment, just a complete sense of pleasure. In actuality, these unexpected surprises cause a greater dopamine release compared to rewards that are expected. Finding the five-pound note in our jeans or coat causes us to light up. Yet we do not become so giddy when we receive our pay cheque each month, which is sizably more than five pounds. As we expect our pay cheques but not the surprise five-pound note, our dopamine release and subsequent happiness is different.

However, when we do not receive what we have come to expect, it causes our dopamine levels to plummet dramatically. Not getting the bonus that you worked hard all year for can leave a dark cloud over our mood for several days – perhaps even weeks. *The neurological fallout from broken promises can cause frustration, anger and apathy.* Employees become demotivated and disenchanted by their work. When expectations go awry, the resultant feeling is deeply unpleasant, and employees will want to avoid experiencing it a successive time.

The dangerous part for organizations becomes how their employees strive to avoid this feeling. What happens to the organization if employees no longer work with ambition because they feel it will never be rewarded? What if employees begin to leave and join competitors who reciprocate their effort? The worst, but very realistic, scenario is that the employee responds to their broken promise by rebalancing the scales; taking what they feel they are owed out of the company or manager, either through theft, fraud, or sabotage.

Sadly, breaking promises is something that every manager will have to do at some point. Realistically employees cannot expect to receive everything that they want, nor is that recommended. However, it is possible to prevent plummeting dopamine and rising disenchantment. The solution lies in managing expectations, making sure that as an employee you are aware of what you can realistically achieve. Great managers also actively and carefully manage the expectations of those they lead, so that no one experiences disenchantment when things do not turn out how they were originally thought. Regulating your dopamine, staying happy, and fostering spark can depend on getting your expectations right.

Managing expectations

Since its foundation in 1940, the McDonald's franchise has been littered with comical characters: the Hamburglar, Grimace, Birdie, Mayor McCheese, and of course Ronald McDonald. But in 1961, when an Illinois based businessman by the name of Ray Kroc bought the McDonald's franchise for $2.7 million, things started to get a little more serious.

After the purchase, Kroc had a grand of vision for the McDonald's franchise; to become the number one fast-food chain in the US. Kroc knew that to get there he had to invest in the employees and get them to invest in the company. Shortly after Kroc's takeover, McDonald's built the Hamburger University; an in-house training capability for employees. Scratch beneath the humorous name, and you will realise that this school is no joke.

The current selection criteria for the Hamburger University are rigorous, with as few as 1 per cent of applicants making it into some programmes. That makes it more exclusive than the most over-applied courses at Oxford (8.2%), Cambridge (9%), and Harvard (5.9%). Students at the Hamburger University can take modules on 'Advanced Restaurant Management', 'Business Consultancy' and 'Developing a Global Mind-set'. Completing modules will either earn you credits towards a Hamburgerology degree, or towards a certified bachelor's degree from one of over 1,600 US universities and colleges.

Due to the assumption that working in the fast-food industry is a dead end career or temporary employment for hard-up university students, it is becoming increasingly more difficult for companies like McDonald's to hire talent into their ranks. The Hamburger University provides a two-fold solution: not only does it legitimize the sector as a form of professional career, it also helps develop and train their own internal employees to fill the leader positions. It is estimated that more than 40 per cent of senior leaders in McDonald's currently are graduates from the Hamburger University.

The first graduating class had just fourteen employees. Today, more than 7,500 students attend Hamburger University each year. Since 1961, more than 275,000 McDonald's employees have graduated. McDonald's and the Hamburger University is a serious establishment designed to educate and up-skill their most dedicated and ambitious staff.

Development opportunities and the possibility to progress in the company are common expectations for employees. In fact, a lack of development or progression is one of the key reasons that people quit their jobs. From the start, new employees – particularly graduates – want to know that they are not only contributing to the organization, but that they are developing their own skills and career paths. If employees do not feel that the company is invested in them, their spark fades and their performance begins to reflect that attitude.

Finkelstein (2016) has long studied how managers develop and create great employees. During his research, he stumbled across an interesting phenomenon. He noted that if you look at the top cohort of any industry, up to half of them would have all worked for the same great leader at some point in their career. Finkelstein called these leaders 'Superbosses'; managers who have the ability to nurture brilliance. In his research, Finkelstein outlines numerous themes of the Superboss:

- *Taking a chance on unconventional employees* – Superbosses look for employees who can drive the performance of the business, but are capable of redefining what it means to be successful in that industry.

- *Adapting the job to fit the talent* – when you come across a talented employee, find ways to give them the opportunity to grow and develop.

- *Accept churn* – the reality is that flexible, intelligent and talented employees are likely to look for the best opportunities that are out there. The job of a Superboss is to create the environment that lets them have the greatest impact whilst they are there.

But within it all, these Superbosses set sky-high expectations for their protégés. Superbosses will deliberately hire exceptional employees; Lorne Michaels, creator and producer of 'Saturday Night Live', said: 'If you look around the room and think, "God, these people are amazing", then you are probably in the right room.'

Superbosses help set and manage the expectations of their team, providing them with the resources and autonomy to revolutionize the business they are in. The professional advancement they offer is beyond what could be considered traditional. These leaders will condense the learning and development of their team by assigning them projects way beyond their current capabilities. The steep learning curves and freedom to make errors fosters enormous personal and professional development. These employees become dedicated, driven, and enchanted in their careers. So much so, that most of these protégés go on to cause paradigm shifts within the company, or are helped by their Superboss to set up ground breaking ones of their own.

Sadly, not all leaders will become Superbosses. But that is not to say that strides cannot be made towards becoming brilliant. The key to fostering and maintaining your team's spark is to help manage and grow their expectations. A great example of this comes from Chris Resto, founding director of the MIT internship and professional development programme. Resto found that one leader at Johnson & Johnson had a particular skill for managing the expectations of his interns.

The leader would always start the internship the same way: getting the interns to list the skills they want to develop, any academic material they wanted to apply, and what their expectations were of the project and him as a manager. Separately, the manager would create his own list. Once they had finished, the two lists were compared, and comprises made for any expectations that did not overlap. The result? Each year, these interns left feeling as though they had been encouraged to push themselves. They left with a spark.

Resto's message is both simple and powerful. To effectively manage expectations and build spark, employees need to know what is expected of them. Do they know that the bar has been set high, or do they feel they can just coast along? If certain projects have been specifically designated to help develop an employee, are they aware of what skills they can get from the assignment?

Beyond this, managers need to know what the employees expect. If employees have a drive to take on challenging projects and stretch their ability, can the manager help facilitate this? It is often the case that the employee does not know what they do not know. Managers should have the experience and hindsight to understand what can be learnt from certain projects. Building spark is a two-way street: managers should not only be aware of what the employee expects, but also help identify areas of growth that they have not thought of.

Keeping promises: who should go first?

For the psychological contract to build spark and deter disenchantment, both parties need to be assured that the other will hold up their end of the deal. These promises are founded on a sense of trust; that the other party will feel obliged to reciprocate once you have done your part. It is an exchange relationship: I scratch your back, and you scratch mine.

But does it matter who goes first? If the employee goes first, there is a perceived risk that the spark might be lost when the hard work of one person is lost in the crowd. Conversely, organizations that are seen as faceless can become humanized by making the first move, but with no guarantee that the employee will act in kind.

Coyle-Shapiro and Conway (2005) wanted to understand whether it mattered as to who went first: was it the employees' performance that made the organization keep their promises, or did the organization drive better performance through making the first move? For sixteen months they analysed the sales performance and subsequent psychol-fulfilment of nearly 200 UK bankers. The financial services industry posed an appropriate backdrop for this investigation. No other industry is quite as aware or sensitive to this type of reciprocal exchange. As the saying goes, you will never see a happy banker on bonus day; they are either relieved at having been paid what they expected, or they are explosive with anger at having received less than their fair share.

Once their research was collected, the results were clear. It did not appear to matter who went first, just as long as someone did. The hard work and enthused performance of the individual lead to kept promises and a greater spark. On the other hand, when performance was slightly sub-par, a socio-emotional offering from the organization caused a large change in performance from the individual. Over time, the power of this relationship grew stronger; good performance was met with bigger and better promises, and initial offerings were responded to with greater shifts in dedication.

Coyle-Shapiro and Conway had tapped into something quite profound. They had demonstrated that sparking enchantment is not a one-way process. It is not a case of workers slogging away in the hope that they are remembered. Building an enchantment through kept-promises is a two-way process.

Conclusion

A good organization understands that the key to getting that spark lies in understanding the ambitions of their workforce. An organization blindly offering promotion packages and development opportunities is not the magic dust to secure employee enchantment. Instead, it is about interpreting their teams' desires and expectations, and helping them achieve those realities.

One of the most important things any manager does is *manage expectations*. Put another way, they make the *implicit contracts explicit*. And they keep their word as much as possible. If for one reason or another an employee believes they have been cheated, lied to or bamboozled by a manager or series of managers in an organization the process of disenchantment is likely to begin.

DISENCHANTMENT CASE 5: MATTHEW KEYS AND ANONYMOUS

The following comments are from former and current employees of large organizations, sourced from Glassdoor.

'Stop patronising employees with talking the values if you can't walk the walk.'

'Very great sense that the company care far more about money than about people.'

'... they are bullying their teams to deliver unreasonable objectives and the worse is that they promote non collaborative work amongst the team'

'Advancement based on friendships and contacts rather than achievement and potential.'

Matthew Keys has held many job titles – blogger; social media agent; network administrator; web producer; journalist – but hacker was not one of them. In fact, he admits this himself. 'I'm not a hacker ... I'm an ex-employee.' However, in 2016, Keys was charged with enabling the world's largest hacktivist organization, Anonymous, with unrestricted access to his former employer's network.

This disenchantment case starts in 2010. At that time Keys was the social media agent for Fox-40, a TV station that was owned by the Tribune Company. However, in October of 2010 Keys and his employer parted ways. The parting had not been amicable; Keys was not supportive of the news organisation's values nor the way it treated its employees. Shortly after leaving Fox-40, he wrote on his personal blog that the Tribune Company was a 'bankrupt news organization that didn't value its employees on the assembly line'.

After Fox-40, Keys joined Reuters news agency where he was the deputy social media editor. In the successive years, Keys started to build clout on social media. *Times* magazine named him as one of 2012's top 140 people to follow on Twitter. In the same year, the *Huffington Post* named him as one of the top 50 people to subscribe to for news on Facebook. However, this all came undone in April 2013. Keys was charged under the Computer Frauds and Abuse Act (CFAA) for providing Anonymous with log-in details to the Tribune Company.

Evidence had emerged that Keys, two months after leaving Fox-40, had aided Anonymous in hacking the *LA Times* online site. The FBI recovered archived logs of conversations between Keys and members of Anonymous on an online chat-room. The conversations showed that Keys had specifically asked if anyone was interested in defacing Fox or the *LA times*. When members voiced their interest and Keys had passed on details, Keys told the hackers to 'go fuck some shit up!'

Keys initially faced up to twenty-five years in prison and fines of up to $750,000. In October 2016, Keys was sentenced to two years in prison. In response, the Electronic Frontier Foundation – a not-for-profit organization that defends digital civil liberties – claimed the sentence was an example of 'prosecutorial discretion run amok'. The foundation of their dismay comes from the fact that the damage done by Anonymous was minimal; they posted a fake news article, which was removed forty hours later. However, the possible actions that Anonymous could have taken were enormous.

Matthew Keys was not a malicious man, nor was he an adept hacker with a motivation to politically protest against big business. In fact, Keys was clearly talented at his job. However, Keys represents one of the many cases of a disenchanted and disgruntled employee who becomes blinded in the pursuit of revenge.

10

Implications of Disenchantment and Case Studies

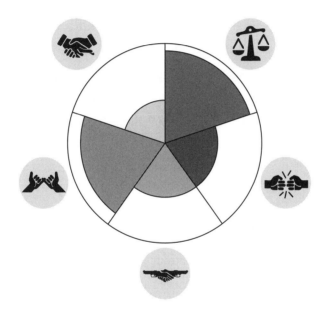

Introduction

We have argued that few people start work in an organization with a negative mind-set. Most are optimistic, hopeful and even enthusiastic. They know, as Freud pointed out, that the two most important determinants of health and happiness are to have good work and good relationships (*Arbeit* and *Leiben*).

However, things go wrong which leads them to become far less happy. We have suggested that there are various typical causes of disenchantment which can lead to alienation and revenge. In this chapter, we consider what occurs when there is considerable disenchantment in an organization.

Disenchantment profiles

One of the applications of the disenchantment model is to understand the *culture* of your organization, particularly how organizational processes and management practices influence the sentiment and commitment of its employees. The reality is that the best organizations are those who possess very low levels of the five disenchantment factors. However, that is often not the case. In fact, there are particular disenchantment profiles that appear with regularity. Below we discuss two of the most common and the implications of these profiles.

Organization A – High inequity and broken promises

Organization A depicts the typical profile of a highly competitive and results-orientated culture. In these organizations, employees are hired, rewarded and promoted based on their results rather than their collaboration, effort or good citizenship. Each employee is made crystal clear about what should be achieved, and is 100 per cent accountable for, and 100 per cent autonomous in, their work. Managers become delegators of work rather than leaders or supporters of their staff. The resulting culture is one that fosters perceptions of unfairness and broken promises.

In organizations where competition is promoted, employees become particularly sensitive to the success and failings of their colleagues. Employees are usually able to assess the inputs and efforts of others as well as what they

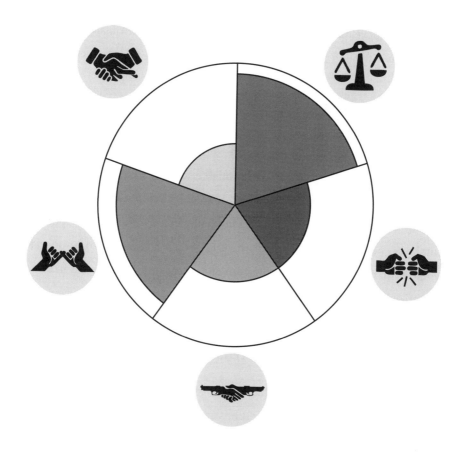

receive. The problem is that not everyone can be a winner. Employees become disenchanted as they start to doubt the fairness of allocation decisions.

Perhaps the 'star' employee is handed warm leads that are easy to secure whilst everyone else in the team are made to win sales from cold calling. The problem is that everyone is judged on the end result rather than the effort that was put in. The star employee continues to be seen as the golden child; the rest of the team are seen as lazy. These employees quickly become disenchanted as they realize that others are receiving unfair or beneficial treatment.

Additionally, when results are prioritized over efforts, the rewards become equally salient for employees. Bonus day is never a happy day; employees are either relieved that they received what they anticipated, or infuriated that it is lower. These employees feel they have been promised promotions, bonuses or development opportunities in return for their hard work and results. When the end reward falls short of what was expected, disenchantment is rife.

Disrespect and distrust frequently occur but have not permeated the whole organization. Instead, disenchanting factors will exist in severe pockets dotted throughout. In a reward-driven culture, disrespect becomes a way of doing business. Employees are taught to be tough and aggressive in the pursuit of sales. Most see this as a part of the job description; others become disenchanted as they are belittled and bullied. Additionally, in this individualist pursuit, employees become sceptical and distrusting of their colleagues. To co-operate would be to help someone else come out on top, meaning you are less likely to be noticed and rewarded for the job.

Organization B – High distrust and broken promises

Organization B is the typical profile for a resistant, reluctant and avoidant work culture. Employees in these organizations are often deeply rooted in their roles, having been there for many years, and prioritize the status quo. These cultures fail to reward success but are quick to criticize and punish failures. Employees are expected to conform and are deterred from innovation. Additionally, employees quickly become defensive, avoiding confrontation and falling back on the rules when things get tough. As a result, these organizations end up being defined by high distrust and behavioural inconsistency.

In organizations where these passive-defensive styles are expected, distrust becomes a key issue. Companies like Organization B are often typified by an approval culture where employees avoid confrontation and try to emphasize pleasant but superficial interpersonal communication. As a result, employees adopt passive-aggressive tactics; they show support and commitment in one scenario, whilst actively undermining or criticizing behind the scenes. Employees become distrusting of each other, not believing the genuineness of

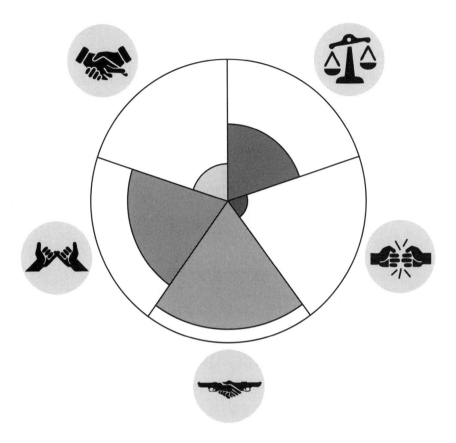

others' actions. Decisions are promoted as being in everyone's interest, but rarely do people believe this to be so. As distrust grows, employees become more possessive over their roles and responsibilities, speaking out against anyone who tries to do anything that falls within their remit without their blessing.

As innovation and co-operation is stifled, opportunities to progress become 'muffled'. Companies like Organization B have an issue of 'waiting for a dead man's shoes'; employees become deeply embedded in their positions, meaning that promotion or development opportunities are hard to come by. Employees become disenchanted because their hard work and loyalty is not reciprocated. Instead they have to wait for another employee to retire or be promoted out of their position before their opportunity comes up.

Respect and organizational lying, however, are not issues in Organization B. Employees are often deeply committed to the cause or philosophy of the organization and are highly motivated by the good they do. Additionally, these employees are neither competitive nor callous. The nature of Organization B means that it does not emphasize profits or sales. As a result, employees are often even-tempered and civil to each other. However, that is often purely on the surface. Underneath is a passive-aggressive core that is driving the distrust and unmet expectations.

Disenchantment and bad apples: protecting against the insider threat

Why do employees do bad things? Why do they steal from their company, commit fraud, or deliberately sabotage work? These are important questions for managers and organizations worldwide. The 'Insider Threat' is a growing risk. In their *2015 Global Economic Crime Survey*, PricewaterhouseCoopers reported that 75 per cent of organizations suffered from at least one instance of fraud. In 2016, this number rose to 86 per cent. Importantly, 81 per cent of these cases involved an inside employee. Employees can be an organization's greatest resource, but they can also represent the greatest source of liability. The average financial cost to an organization from an external attack is £44,000; the average cost of an insider attack is £2.1 million. So why do employees become insiders?

The 'insider threat' is a sensationalized term used within businesses to define what psychologists call Counterproductive Work Behaviour (CWB), which is any behaviour at work that goes counter to the short- and long-term interests and success of all stakeholders in an organization.

People steal at work. They take part in 'the unauthorized appropriation of company property for personal use, unrelated to the job'. They steal from their employer, their boss and their customers. It is all too common and can be costly. We have a range of words to disguise the issue: *pilfering* and *shrinkage*, *nicking* and *liberating items*. Many people think that taking home a few pens and envelopes does not count.

There is a long list of CWBs including deceit, espionage, fraud, sabotage and substance abuse. There are, for the politically correct, other things such as 'low personal standards', 'work avoidance' and 'indolence'. Counterproductive Work Behaviour also includes:

- **Antisocial behaviour**; usually restricted to the workplace.

- **Blue-collar crime**; everything from theft, property destruction and record fabrication to fighting and gambling by semi-skilled, often non-salaried staff.

- **Dysfunctional work behaviour**; intentional, unhealthy behaviour that is injurious to particular individuals who do it either to themselves or to others.

- **Employee deviance**; unauthorized but intended acts that damage property, production or reputations.

- **Employee misconduct**; the misuse of resources, from absenteeism to accepting backhanders.

- **Non-performance at work**; both not performing that which is required, while also performing acts not at all desirable.

- **Occupational aggressive crime deviance**; negative, illegal, injurious and devious behaviours conducted in the workplace.

- **Organizational misbehaviour**; behaviour that violates societal and organizational norms.

- **Organizational retaliative behaviours**; this is deliberate organizational behaviour based on perceptions of unfairness by disgruntled employees.

- **'Political' behaviour**; self-serving, non-sanctioned, often illegitimate behaviour aimed at people both inside and outside of the organization.

- **Unconventional work practices**; simply odd and unusual, but more like illegal and disruptive, behaviours.

- **Workplace aggression, hostility, obstructionism**; personally injurious behaviours at work.

- **Unethical work place behaviour**; behaviour that deliberately and obviously infringes the accepted ethical/moral code.

The term CWB is often used synonymously with anti-social, deviant, dysfunctional, retaliative and unethical behaviour at work. It costs organizations billions every year and many of them invest in ways to prevent, reduce or catch those who are most likely to offend. It is a multi-faceted syndrome that is characterized by hostility to authority, impulsivity, social insensitivity, alienation and/or lack of moral integrity. People feel frustrated or powerless, or unfairly dealt with, and act accordingly.

Psychologists broadly distinguish between two types of CWB:

- *Interpersonal deviance* – behaviours directed at other members of the organization, ranging from physical abuse to verbal and psychological abuse.

- *Organizational deviance* – behaviours intended to harm the organization the employee is a part of, ranging from taking elongated lunch breaks to fraud, theft, and sabotage.

Counterproductive Work Behaviour, however, is intentional and contrary to the interests of the organisation. It may not, in the short term, be reflected in counterproductivity which is the ultimate cost of CWBs. The essence of a CWB is wrongdoing. Thus, taking sick leave when not sick may be a common occurrence, indeed the norm, yet it is still a CWB.

Employees are the largest resource available to a company, yet they can also be the greatest source of liability. Organizations want to be able to find the *bad apples* and attribute all potential risk to them. The truth is that this is misguided and unhelpful. It is not the case that bad things are only done by bad people. It is more often the case that good employees are motivated to turn bad as a result of disenchantment.

Our research has supported this notion. When employees feel disgruntled and demotivated as a result of poor management and culture, they are far more likely to commit CWB. In particular, we have found that disenchanted employees use *personal abuse* (e.g. being nasty to colleagues or clients), *product deviance* (e.g. purposefully doing work incorrectly), *sabotage* (e.g. purposefully destroying company resources or materials), *theft* (e.g. stealing company materials or information), and *withdrawal* (e.g. coming in late and leaving early) as means to get revenge on their colleagues and organization as a whole. *Disenchantment has the power to turn a good-natured employee into a potential liability for their organization.*

Conversely, disenchantment (or a lack of it) has the power to temper the bad apples. There is ample psychological research to show that employees are more likely to engage in CWB when they are high on dark personality traits such as psychopathy and Machiavellianism. However, what we have found is that disenchantment can either *negate or amplify* their potential risk. When disenchantment was low, it did not matter whether an employee was high or low on psychopathy. It had little to no impact on how likely they were to engage in CWB. Enchantment tempers the impulsive and revenge-seeking nature of psychopaths. As disenchantment increased, however, the effect of psychopathy escalated rapidly. When both disenchantment and psychopathy were high, employees were the biggest risk for damaging behaviour.

Employees are at their most dangerous when they are *dishonest, devious and disenchanted.* They are already one step ahead of external threats; they are within the barricades and know exactly where is most sensitive. They can bide their time, wait to strike, and inflict damage that far exceeds what any external hacker can do.

The problem is that the inside threat is being seen as a technological problem by most companies in the security industry. The reality is that this is a human issue. Employees are deeply affected by the culture they work within. An organization's cyber infrastructure can be secure, but when a disenchanted employee operates it the threat remains. These employees are not inherently malicious, but have become disenchanted over time due to the factors that we have discussed in this book. The evidence has shown that they resort to CWB as a means to rectify the injustice that they have experienced.

Detecting the insider should not be a witch-hunt, but an investigation into how the organization is inspiring resentment within its employees. It comes down to this: how do you know which of your employees are Red Riding Hood and which have become wolves in Grandma's nightie? Protection against the wolves lies in rooting out the causes of disenchantment and making it right before it comes back to bite you.

The divisive power of disenchantment: social network analysis

What happens to an organization when its employees are disenchanted? So far, we have talked about the impact of disenchantment on the individual; how the behaviours, emotions and motivations shift in response to mistreatment and injustice. What we have not talked about is how disenchantment affects how and whom employees socialize with at work. On an individual level if our behaviours, emotions and motivations all shift, will this have a cascading effect on the social connections and networks formed in the workplace?

This is the backdrop to Company X. We were asked to consult with Company X to investigate their concerns around teamwork, communication and management culture. Being a small financial services firm, effective collaboration and interaction between employees is vital. Their success relies on employees working as a gestalt machine; what can be achieved as a cohesive unit is greater than the sum of the individual efforts of employees.

Building a 'team of teams' was something that the board at Company X had invested serious time, effort and infrastructure in. Managers threw team-building events to build and reinforce connections within departments. Employees were encouraged to regularly brief each other on new projects and leads. The office had been rearranged to emphasise an open and dynamic workspace. Understanding what factors were aiding an interconnected 'team of teams' – and removing those barriers that were holding it back – was at the forefront of Company X's working mind-set. The question was if, and how, any of this was actually working.

To answer this, we needed to look under the surface and see their social network. Social network analysis (SNA) uses network and graph theory to provide psychologists and social scientists with immense insight into the social structure and groupings of an organization. It reveals the informal structure of your organization, showing how knowledge, information and advice flows through the workplace. Organizational psychologist Simmy Grover (2016) described SNA as an echocardiogram for the organization, uncovering the heartbeat and blood flow of the workforce. Grover stated that success is dependent on the organizational network beating in rhythm.

Understanding the organizational network is something that the more politically savvy of us will do implicitly. It is an astute appreciation of how things get done in the company. Who likes and trusts whom? Who is the first person to know about a new business lead? Who do you need to get on board in order to persuade the CEO? Does the CEO go to their Head of Finance for advice or place more stock in what their executive assistant thinks? Social network analysis quantifies this informal network and reveals the informal structure. The key is then to know which players hold influential roles in that network.

In his book *The Tipping Point*, Malcolm Gladwell (2006) outlined that central to any successful epidemic were a handful of exceptional people. Gladwell called it 'The Law of the Few'. These were people who, due to their unique social position, could propel a new fashion trend, social movement or disease to the masses. These influential people were known as: *Connectors*, who seem to know everyone; *Mavens*, who retain exceptional amounts of knowledge; and *Salesmen*, who are capable of persuading anyone. According to Gladwell, the inclusion of these three types of people is vital for any social epidemic. In organizational networks, the gifted few are the people whose social position makes them influential beyond what their job perhaps would suggest.

Firstly, there are the Central Connectors. Like Gladwell's Connectors, these people are well-known faces in the organization. They seem to have a personal association with everyone, remembering birthdays and the names of their colleagues' children. Central Connectors fall right in the middle of an informal network, with large amounts of the workforce interacting with them on a daily basis. As such, their influence emerges due to the level of control they have over information in the company. They know who the right people are for a particular job. They are the first to know about new developments and are able to distribute information rapidly across their highly connected network. They are astutely aware of the comings and goings of the company. Usually this role is regarded as an extremely positive position to hold. However, being highly visible and overly popular can lead to overload. The ability to be adaptable, extraverted and emotionally stable is core to a successful Central Connector.

Then there are Brokers. These are people who position themselves in the structural holes and bridge a gap between two previously unconnected groups. Due to their strategic position, Brokers have control over the information that flows between groups of people, granting access to new ideas and opportunities. Ronald Burt (2000) has extensively studied the way a social network position can be advantageous for an individual's career. Burt argued that because Brokers stand in the gaps of a network, they are at a higher risk of receiving positive performance evaluations, promotions and having good ideas. Whilst Brokers may not be the most highly connected employees, they have made their connections count. The information and resources they have access to because of their positioning makes them a key player in any organization.

In most cases, the uncovered network is neither what the organization expected nor what they wanted it to be. Managers hope to be Central Connectors and self-assured stars believe they are Brokers. It all comes as a shock when the reality does not match the evidence. Company X was no exception. The daily calls and office 'feng shui' had not created a perfectly interconnected workforce. Instead the company seemed to be siloed, with employees talking mostly to those in their department. Inter-department communication was limited, with only a select few employees bridging the gaps. The Central Connectors had also become the Brokers, acting as confidants and primary contacts for every department. Company X had hoped that their central players would be the senior members of the company or rising stars they had marked for development. The shock came when these individuals were identified as disconnected and on the periphery of the network structure.

Company X was mystified. They thought that they had done everything right, and were disappointed to realize that their efforts had not built an idyllic 'team of teams'. The reality is that building a cohesive unit is more than changing the office layout and away days. It is about building an organizational culture that motivates employees to communicate. The question therefore becomes: 'What factors are bringing people together – or pulling them apart – in our company?'

Within SNA, there is a concept called *assortativity* – the preference to connect with others who are similar to you in some way. We like people who share the same interests, hobbies and values as us. Cooing romantics will profess that 'opposites attract', but the reality is better represented as 'birds of a feather flock together'. The question is what similarities are drawing groups of people together and building clusters.

In the case of Company X, office demographic variables seemed to play a leading role. Employees were clustered tightly together in their departments, primarily talking to their colleagues who have a similar job role to them. It is an obvious similarity – it is easy to talk about the work you are doing, and there is no one better to do that with than someone with a similar job to you.

However, there were some employees who were bridging the gaps between departments. These employees were acting as Brokers, seeking out other colleagues who were outside of their usual milieu and connecting previously detached parts of the organization. The problem was there were too few of these employees to build the 'team of teams' culture that Company X coveted. Instead of a symbiotic unit of highly interconnected employees, Company X was made up of disparate areas that were held together by a few core workers. To improve their culture and increase collaboration, it was vital to understand what motivated the rogue employees to bridge the gaps. This is where we discovered the divisive power of disenchantment and the influence it has on office dynamics.

There are always a few in every organization: their infectious smile, positive disposition, and humorous anecdotes make them a delight to have around. You know that if you are in need of a laugh, or just want a light-hearted break for 15 minutes, they are the person to go to. But you are not the only one with this idea. Others in the workplace who want to bask in the jovial glow of their quips and comments will rendezvous at this employee's desk or congregate to where they are stood in the kitchen. Employees will even transcend departmental barriers just to chat with this person knowing that it will brighten up their day.

In our research at Company X we discovered that employees cluster based upon the similarity of their disenchantment. Those who were enchanted at work, and wanted to remain that way, interacted with other enchanted employees.

They sought them out for advice, communicating with them more frequently and being more likely to consider them a friend. Whilst there is no overt indicator or organizational title that can declare who these people are, employees seem to know who their enchanted and engaged colleagues are. We found that the feeling is mutual – the happy-go-lucky individuals are more likely to seek out others who they believe to have outlooks that are similar to theirs.

But what of the disenchanted? The employees that are disaffected and resentful towards their organization? They certainly have no interest in those who believe the organization is fair and just. Importantly, the disenchanted also do not just stew in solitary. There is an assumption in HR that the jaded are lone wolves, keeping to themselves as well as being left alone by their colleagues. They are thought to just gently stew in solitary, with the occasional muttered comment of discontent. But this is not the case. When looking at advice networks, the *disenchanted cluster together*. As with the enchanted, the disenchanted attract other like-minded individuals to them. Disenchantment can form pockets that are hard to break up. As the disenchanted congregate, their symptoms worsen.

The problem within Company X was that there was a diverse range of disenchantment levels throughout the workforce. When the disenchantment levels between two employees were disparate, they rarely asked each other for help or advice, they avoided seeing each other, and they definitely did not consider their relationship anything more than trivial. The consequence? A breakdown in communication and a dissolution to the 'team of teams' ideal.

The impact did not just stop at an individual level, but scaled up in how whole departments were communicating. In Company X, communication between disparate departments is vital. The problem was that disenchantment was having a powerful derailing effect on how the departments worked together. Departments would be consistent in their disenchantment; there were very few enchanted outliers in a department marked by disenchantment. Yet departments would vary on their baseline enchantment levels. Information flowed freely within the enchanted and disenchanted, but there were very little pathways out into the rest of the organization. As the enchantment levels varied dramatically across departments, effective communication started to fail.

For instance, within Company X the Sales and Analysts departments needed to communicate effectively to generate revenue. Analysts needed to relay their new research to the Sales team for it to be marketed to clients. And Sales needed to interact with the Analysts to answer the technical questions that their clients have. For Company X, the Sales team were severely more disenchanted than the Analysts. The Analysts no longer wanted to actively interact with them; they only did it when they absolutely had to. Until then, the Analysts remained in their cubicles talking amongst themselves.

But what is the cost of this disrupted dialogue? Whilst Company X's dream of a 'team of teams' is a nice ambition, does it really matter if the company culture falls short? When we looked at the impact of disenchantment, it was more disruptive that we had initially predicted.

The problem is that disenchantment starts to impact a company's profits after a fairly short amount of time. In fact, we have been able to consistently predict a department's profit–loss ratio in the following quarters based on how their disenchantment compares to others. When departments are similar, they generate significantly more profit for their company. These are departments that want to interact, collaborate and secure new clients. They are happy to have conversations about things other than work, and end up interacting more as a result. Their frequent and friendly interaction leads to successful and profitable business. Yet, when disenchantment levels are disparate, this cohesive working environment falls away.

Disenchantment is more than identifying management swamps. It is more than identifying and rectifying areas where there are risks that counterproductive work behaviour may emerge. It influences how your organization interacts, connects and collaborates. And this can have a big impact. If teams are communicating frequently, you tap into the full range of talent and skill that your company has to offer. Yet, when a key element of your organization is resentful and angry, this all comes to a halt. And the cost to your bottom line could be more than you expect.

How disenchantment undermines personal success and well-being

The reality of success is that it is hard work. The success stories of entrepreneurs tell us about the countless hours, perseverance and stress that it takes. Importantly, successful people need to be able to carry on with the same passion when the pressure becomes overwhelming and they feel that their goal is unobtainable. But what is it that makes someone able to persevere?

There are countless blog articles that attempt to depict the traits of successful people to help others emulate these habits in the hope that they too will become successful. However, being successful is more than making sure you 'prepare for the journey' or 'ask important questions'. Sometimes people also have the right 'stuff' or 'what it takes' to reach greatness.

When employees experience prolonged interpersonal and emotional stress at work, employees can experience 'burnout'. Burnout has been defined by psychologists as an internal and emotional response to external stressors that consume, exceed and deplete our personal and social resources. It represents the metaphorical incapacity for the fire within us to continue burning brightly. Three types of burnout have been identified:

- *Personal burnout* – the exhaustion a person is experiencing on a day-to-day basis. 'How often do you feel physically exhausted?'; 'How often do you think "I cannot take it anymore"?'

- *Work burnout* – exhaustion that is a direct result of work. 'Do you feel that every working hour is tiring for you?'; 'Do you feel worn out at the end of a working day?'

- *Client burnout* – exhaustion that is a result of clients or 'people work'. 'Clients' is a broad term that covers patients, inmates, children, students, etc. 'Does it drain your energy to work with clients?'

Conversely, under immense stress some individuals demonstrate resilience and persevere in a relatively unwavering manner. Resilience is defined as the ability to recover from setbacks, adapt well to change, and keep going in the face of adversity. It is a dynamic process, allowing people to effectively respond to stress by allocating the psychological resources needed to cope. Resilience has often been positioned as a self-righting mechanism and buffer to negative psychological outcomes; the ability to effectively and dynamically respond to stress prevents psychological resources from 'running dry' and causing burnout. A recent paper demonstrated how resilience plays both a mediating and moderating role in how personality affects burnout (Treglown et al., 2016).

Most companies recognise that resilience is an important factor success. It helps employees survive and thrive in the turbulent conditions of the workplace. Organizations are building resilience from the bottom up by investing more in developing their employees' resilience. The approach is to help employees cope and maintain their well-being.

However, what companies often forget is how the culture they have fostered can play a part in determining their employees' resilience. By investing in resilience training, there is the hope that employees will be able to cope with whatever is thrown at them. What organizations rarely do is look internally to understand how their processes and practices are fostering unnecessary additional stress.

Our recent research has found that disenchantment has a profound effect on employees. Disenchantment has the power to thwart the effectiveness of our good habits, undermine our resilience and foster burnout. When employees feel disgruntled and downtrodden, they are more likely to experience personal, work and client burnout. The management practices and organizational processes that cause an employee to feel cynical and angry also have the power to negatively affect their psychological well-being. Disenchantment drains the cognitive resources of employees, as well as providing them with little respite to recover. When employees no longer have the psychological resources to deal with pressures in the workplace, they are more likely to burn out. Employees become less attentive, productive and effective as their mental health declines. They are absent and ill more often because their body no longer has the resources needed to cope.

Additionally, disenchantment was found to negate the protective power of resilience. Our analysis found that disenchantment moderated the effect of resilience on burnout. That is, even if employees initially possess high levels of resilience, disenchantment shackles its dynamic ability to buffer against burnout. Disenchantment saps the drive and determination from employees, leaving them at a far greater risk of mental illness.

Organizations that are serious about the success and well-being of their employees need to consider how disenchantment is undermining their best efforts. Whilst resilience and mindfulness training will help provide employees with the tools they need to strive, disenchantment has the power to disarm employees of these protective skills.

Conclusion

Everyone probably has the experience of disenchantment at work. To recap, we believe the five factors that make up the dynamic disenchantment experience are:

Organizational lying/Hypocrisy. This is the perception by the employee that what the organization says about itself in public and even to its employees is a pack of lies. There is an inconsistency between the words, actions and decisions in the workplace. The organization is seen as deceitful and lacking integrity. Employees become disenchanted when they realize their workplace is nothing like how it appears on the corporate website.

Perceived inequity. The idea that some people in the organization are treated very differently from others. The hottest word at work is fair: that people are fairly assessed, promoted and rewarded. Yet it can seem to some that loyalty, hard work and productivity have less to do with success than some other attributes such as demography, brown-nosing or particular experiences.

Bullying and mistreatment. This is the belief that some senior people are callous, uncaring and nasty. The organization is a place where being tough and ruthless is encouraged. Employees feel downtrodden and belittled each day as they fall victim to continuous incivility.

Distrust. The feeling that the organization does not even trust its own employees. Employees grow suspicious of their managers and colleagues, questioning the genuineness of their behaviour. Employees look over their shoulder, vigilant that a colleague might stab them in the back. Disenchantment grows in two directions: managers are unwilling to let employees work without being monitored or scrutinized, while their colleagues are secretive and un-cooperative.

Broken promises. This is all about expectations not being met, or that the organization has not held up their end of the bargain. For some, the selection interview and the induction period are where people set their expectations about working for the organization. They tell you what they stand for, what they expect and how things work. Employees become disenchanted when these expectations are broken.

When these phenomena occur frequently and intensely, partly because they are part of the corporate culture, people react. Some simply resign, others take revenge. The latter can take many forms. There is a large cost to the individual employee as well as the organization as a whole. For organizations to effectively manage motivation and demotivation, they need to be aware of how they could be fostering *disenchantment*. Measuring disenchantment is simple and has a profound impact. But organizations need to be prepared to cast the mirror upon themselves in order to understand how their processes and practices are driving *disenchantment*.

BIBLIOGRAPHY

Ackerman, R. A., & Donnellan, M. B. (2013). Evaluating self-report measures of narcissistic entitlement. *Journal of Psychopathology and Behavioral Assessment, 35*(4), 460–74.

Amiot, C. E., Vallerand, R. J., & Blanchard, C. M. (2006). Passion and psychological adjustment: a test of the Person–Environment Fit hypothesis. *Personality and Social Psychology Bulletin, 32*, 220–9.

Anderson, N. (2004). *Work with Passion*. New York: New World Library.

Babiak, P., & Hare, R. (2006). *Snakes in Suits: When the Psychopath Goes to Work*. New York: Regan Books.

Baillien, E., De Cuyper, N., & De Witte, H. (2011). Job autonomy and workload as antecedents of workplace bullying: a two-wave test of Karasek's Job Demand Control Model for targets and perpetrators. *Journal of Occupational and Organizational Psychology, 84*(1), 191–208.

Baucus, M. S., & Near, J. P. (1991). Can illegal corporate behaviour be predicted? An event history analysis. *Academy of Management Journal, 34*, 9–36.

Baughman, H. M., Dearing, S., Giammarco, E., & Vernon, P. A. (2012). Relationships between bullying behaviours and the Dark Triad: a study with adults. *Personality and Individual Differences, 52*(5), 571–5.

Beattie, L., & Griffin, B. (2014). Accounting for within-person differences in how people respond to daily incivility at work. *Journal of Occupational and Organizational Psychology, 87*(3), 625–44.

Bingham, S. (2017). If employees don't trust you, it is up to you to fix it. *Harvard Business Review*, 2 January.

Bitterly, T. B., Brooks, A. W., & Schweitzer, M. E. (2017). Risky business: when humor increases and decreases status. *Journal of Personality and Social Psychology, 112*(3), 431.

Bradburn, N. M. (1969). *The Structure of Psychological Well-Being*. Chicago: Aldine.

Brayfield, A., & Rothe, H. (1951). An index of job satisfaction. *Journal of Applied Psychology 35*, 307–11.

Briner, R. B., & Denyer, D. (2012). Systematic review and evidence synthesis as a practice and scholarship tool. Handbook of evidence-based management: Companies, classrooms and research, 112–29.

Brown, W. M., & Moore, C. (2002). Smile asymmetries and reputation as reliable indicator of likelihood to cooperate: an evolutionary analysis. *Advances in Psychology Research, 11*, 59–78.

Buchanan, B. (1974). Building organizational commitment: the socialization of managers in work organizations. *Administrative Science Quarterly, 19*, 533–46.

Buckingham, G., DeBruine, L. M., Little, A. C., Welling, L. L., Conway, C. A., Tiddeman, B. P., & Jones, B. C. (2006). Visual adaptation to masculine and feminine faces influences generalized preferences and perceptions of trustworthiness. *Evolution and Human Behavior, 27*(5), 381–9.

Bulutlar, F., & Öz, E. Ü. (2009). The effects of ethical climates on bullying behaviour in the workplace. *Journal of Business Ethics, 86*(3), 273–95.

Burke, R., & Fiskenbaum, L. (2009). Work motivations, work outcomes, and health: passion versus addiction. *Journal of Business Ethics, 84*, 257–63.

Burt, R. S. (2000). The network structure of social capital. *Research in Organizational Behavior, 22*, 345–423.

Carroll, A. B. (2006). Trust is key when rating great workplaces, in Mishra, K., Boynton, L., & Mishra, A., 'Driving Employee Engagement: The Expanded Role of Internal Communications'. *International Journal of Business Communication, 51*(2), 2014, 183–202.

Carter, M. Z., & Mossholder, K. W. (2015). Are we on the same page? The performance effects of congruence between supervisor and group trust. *Journal of Applied Psychology, 100*(5), 1349–63.

Casciaro, T., & Lobo, M. S. (2008). When competence is irrelevant: the role of interpersonal affect in task-related ties. *Administrative Science Quarterly, 53*(4), 655–84.

Chang, J., O'Neill, G., & Travaglione, A. (2016). Demographic influences on employee trust towards managers. *International Journal of Organizational Analysis, 24*(2), 246–60.

Cleckley, H. (1941). *The Mask of Sanity*. St Louis: C.V. Mosby.

Colella, A., Paetzold, R., Zardkoohi, A., & Wesson, M. (2007) Exposing pay secrecy. *Academy of Management Review, 32*, 55–71.

Cooke, R., & Lafferty, J. (1989). *Organizational Culture Inventory*. Plymouth, MI: Human Synergistic.

Coyle-Shapiro, J. A., & Conway, N. (2005). Exchange relationships: examining psychological contracts and perceived organizational support. *Journal of Applied Psychology, 90*(4), 774.

Coyne, I., Seigne, E., & Randall, P. (2000). Predicting workplace victim status from personality. *European Journal of Work and Organizational Psychology, 9*(3), 335–49.

Covey, S. (2006). *The Speed of Trust: The One Thing That Changes Everything*. New York: Simon & Schuster.

Csíkszentmihályi, M. (1975). *Flow*. San Francisco: Jossey-Bass.

Currall, S. C., & Inkpen, A. C. (2006). On the complexity of organizational trust: a multi-level co-evolutionary perspective and guidelines for future research. *Handbook of Trust Research*, 235–46.

De Haan, E., & Kasozi, A. (2014). *The Leadership Shadow: How to Recognize and Avoid Derailment, Hubris and Overdrive*. London: Kogan Page.

Deci, E. L., & Ryan, R. M. (1985). *Intrinsic Motivation and Self-determination in Human Behavior*. New York: Plenum Publishing Co.

Dotlich, D., & Cairo, P. (2003). *Why CEOs Fail*. New York: Jossey-Bass.

Duffy, M. K., Shaw, J. D., Scott, K. L., & Tepper, B. J. (2006). The moderating roles of self-esteem and neuroticism in the relationship between group and individual undermining behavior. *Journal of Applied Psychology, 91*(5), 1066–77.

Dumitru, C. D., & Schoop, M. A. (2016). How does trust in teams, team identification, and organizational identification impact trust in organizations? *International Journal of Management and Applied Research, 3*(2), 88–97.

Eggert, M. (2007). *Perfect Interview*. Random House.

Einarsen, S. (1999). The nature and causes of bullying at work. *International Journal of Manpower*, *20*(1/2), 16–27.

Feather, N. T. (1975). *Values in Education and Society*. New York: Free Press.

Fehr, E., & Schmidt, K. M. (1999). A theory of fairness, competition, and cooperation. *Quarterly Journal of Economics*, *114*(3), 817–68.

Fein, S., & Hilton, J. L. (1994). Judging others in the shadow of suspicion. *Motivation and Emotion*, *18*(2), 167–98.

Ferrin, D. L., Dirks, K. T., & Shah, P. P. (2006). Direct and indirect effects of third-party relationships on interpersonal trust. *Journal of Applied Psychology*, *91*(4), 870.

Finkelstein, S. (2016). *Superbosses: How Exceptional Leaders Master the Flow of Talent*. London: Penguin.

Frank, R. H. (1988). *Passions Within Reason: The Strategic Role of the Emotions*. New York: W.W. Norton & Co.

Friedman, M. (1980). *Free to Choose*. New York: Harcourt.

Furnham, A. (2010). *The Elephant in the Boardroom*. Basingstoke: Palgrave Macmillan.

Furnham, A. (2015). *Backstabbers and Bullies*. London: Bloomsbury.

Furnham, A., & Taylor, J. (2011). *Bad Apples*. Basingstoke: Palgrave Macmillan.

Gladwell, M. (2006). *The Tipping Point: How Little Things Can Make a Big Difference*. Little, Brown.

Gordon, D. S., & Platek, S. M. (2009). Trustworthy? The brain knows: implicit neural responses to faces that vary in dark triad personality characteristics and trustworthiness. *Journal of Social, Evolutionary, and Cultural Psychology*, *3*(3), 182.

Gorgievski, M., & Bakker, A. (2010). 'Passion for work: work engagement vs workaholism'. In S. Albrecht (ed.), *Handbook of Employee Engagement*. London: Edward Elgar.

Grover, S. (2016, 17 August). How can network analysis help you? [Blog post]. Retrieved from https://medium.com/@SciTechGeekette/how-can-network-analysis-help-you-655facceedaa

Hare, R. (1999). *Without Conscience*. New York: Guilford Press.

Harpaz, I., & Snir, R. (2003). Workaholism: its definition and nature. *Human Relations*, *56*(3), 291–319.

Hershcovis, M. S. (2011). 'Incivility, social undermining, bullying . . . oh my!': a call to reconcile constructs within workplace aggression research. *Journal of Organizational Behavior*, *32*(3), 499–519.

Hershcovis, M. S., & Barling, J. (2010). Comparing victim attributions and outcomes for workplace aggression and sexual harassment. *Journal of Applied Psychology*, *95*(5), 874–88.

Herzberg, F., Mausner, B., & Snyderman, B. B. (1959). *The Motivation to Work*. New York: Wiley.

Hogan, R. (2006). *Personality and the Fate of Organizations*. New York: LEA.

Hogan, R., & Hogan, J. (1997). *Hogan Development Survey Manual*. Tulsa, OK: Hogan Assessment Centres.

Hogan, R., & Hogan, J. (2001). Assessing leadership: a view from the dark side. *International Journal of Selection and Assessment*, *9*, 40–51.

Holland, P. J., Cooper, B., & Heckland, R. (2015). Electronic monitoring in the workplace: the effects on trust in management, and the moderating role of occupational type. *Electronic Monitoring and Surveillance*, *44*, 161–75.

Hui, H. (1992). 'Values and attitudes'. In R. Westwood (ed.), *Organizational Behaviour*, 63–90. Hong Kong: Longman.

Kets de Vries, M., & Miller, D. (1985). *The Neurotic Organization*. San Fransisco: Jossey-Bass.

Kleisner, K., Priplatova, L., Frost, P., & Flegr, J. (2013). Trustworthy-looking face meets brown eyes. *PLoS One*, *8*(1), e53285.

Kohn, A. (1993). Punished by rewards. *Harvard Business Review*, September/October.

Kosfeld, M., Heinrichs, M., Zak, P. J., Fischbacher, U., & Fehr, E. (2005). Oxytocin increases trust in humans. *Nature*, *435*(7042), 673–6.

Lafreniere, M-A., Belanger, J., Sedikides, C., & Vallerand, R. (2011). Self-esteem and passion for activities. *Personality and Individual Differences*, *51*(4), 541–4.

Lau, D. C., Lam, L. W., & Wen, S. S. (2014). Examining the effects of feeling trusted by supervisors in the workplace: a self-evaluative perspective. *Journal of Organizational Behavior*, *35*(1), 112–27.

Lewicki, R. J., & Bunker, B. B. (1996). Developing and maintaining trust in work relationships In T. Tyler & R. Kramer's (eds), *Trust in Organizations: Frontiers of Theory and Research*, pp. 114–39. California: Sage Publications.

Linton, D. K., & Power, J. L. (2013). The personality traits of workplace bullies are often shared by their victims: is there a dark side to victims? *Personality and Individual Differences*, *54*(6), 738–43.

Lodahl, T., & Kejner, M. (1965). The definition and measurement of job involvement. *Journal of Applied Psychology* 49, 24–33.

London, M., & Howat, G. (1978). The relationship between employee commitment and conflict resolution behavior. *Journal of Vocational Behavior*, *13*(1), 1–14.

Lykken, D., & Tellegen, A. (1996). Happiness is a stochastic phenomenon. *Psychological Science*, *7*(3), 186–9.

Machlowitz, M. (1980). *Workaholics*. New York: Mentor.

Mageau, G. A., & Vallerand, R. J. (2007). The moderating effect of passion on the relation between activity engagement and positive affect. *Motivation and Emotion*, *31*, 312–21.

Marshall, A. P., West, S. H., & Aitken, L. M. (2013). Clinical credibility and trustworthiness are key characteristics used to identify colleagues from whom to seek information. *Journal of Clinical Nursing*, *22*(9–10), 1424–33.

Mayer, R. C., & Gavin, M. B. (2005). Trust in management and performance: who minds the shop while the employees watch the boss? *Academy of Management Journal*, *48*(5), 874–88.

McGraw, A. P., & Warren, C. (2014). Benign violation theory. *Encyclopedia of Humor Studies*, *1*, 75–7.

McManus, I. C., & Furnham, A. (2010). 'Fun, Fun, Fun': types of fun, attitudes to fun, and their relation to personality and biographical factors. *Psychology*, *1*, 159–68.

MacRae, I., & Furnham, A. (2017). *Motivation and Performance: A Guide to a Diverse Workforce*. London: Kogan.

Mesmer-Magnus, J., Glew, D. J., & Viswesvaran, C. (2012). A meta-analysis of positive humor in the workplace. *Journal of Managerial Psychology*, *27*(2), 155–90.

Miller, L. (2008). *From Difficult to Disturbed*. New York: Amacom.

Millon, T. (2004). *Personality Disorders in Modern Life*. Hoboken, New Jersey: John Wiley & Sons, Inc.

Mitsopoulou, E., & Giovazolias, T. (2015). Personality traits, empathy and bullying behavior: a meta-analytic approach. *Aggression and Violent Behavior*, *21*, 61–72.

Moscoso, S., & Salgado, J. (2004) 'Dark side' personality styles as predictors of task, contextual and job performance. *International Journal of Selection and Assessment*, *12*, 356–62.

Myers, D. (1993). *The Pursuit of Happiness*. New York: Avon.

Ng, T. W. H., Sorensen, K. L., & Feldman, D. C. (2007). Dimensions, antecedents, and consequences of workaholism: a conceptual integration and extension. *Journal of Organizational Behavior*, *28*, 111–36.

Nielsen, M. B., & Knardahl, S. (2015). Is workplace bullying related to the personality traits of victims? A two-year prospective study. *Work & Stress*, *29*(2), 128–49.

Nielsen, M. B., Glasø, L., & Einarsen, S. (2017). Exposure to workplace harassment and the Five Factor Model of personality: a meta-analysis. *Personality and Individual Differences*, *104*, 195–206.

Oates, W. (1971). *Confessions of a Workaholic: The Facts about Work Addiction*. New York: World Publishing Company.

Oldham, J., & Morris, L. (2000). *Personality Self-portrait*. New York: Bantam.

Ouimet, G. (2010). Dynamics of narcissistic leadership in organizations. Towards an integrated research model. *Journal of Managerial Psychology*, *25*, 713–26.

Paulhus, D. L., Westlake, B. G., Calvez, S. S., & Harms, P. D. (2013). Self-presentation style in job interviews: the role of personality and culture. *Journal of Applied Social Psychology*, *43*(10), 2042–59.

Paullay, I., Alliger, G. & Stone-Romero, E. (1994). Construct validation of two instruments designed to measure job involvement and work centrality. *Journal of Applied Psychology*, *79*, 224–8.

Pearson, C. M., & Porath, C. L. (2005). On the nature, consequences and remedies of workplace incivility: no time for 'nice'? Think again. *The Academy of Management Executive*, *19*(1), 7–18.

Pech, R., & Slade, B. (2007). Organizational sociopaths: rarely challenged, often promoted. Why? *Society and Business Review*, *2*, 254–69.

Phillipe, F. L., Vallerand, R. J., & Lavigne, G. L. (2009). Passion does make a difference in people's lives: a look at well-being in passionate and non-passionate individuals. *Applied Psychology: Health and Well-Being*, *1*, 3–22.

Pink, D. (2010). *Drive: The Surprising Truth About What Motivates Us*. New York: Riverhead Books.

Porath, C. L. (2015). The leadership behavior that's most important to employees. *Harvard Business Review* (digital article).

Porath, C. L., & Erez, A. (2007). Does rudeness really matter? The effects of rudeness on task performance and helpfulness. *Academy of Management Journal*, *50*(5), 1181–97.

Porath, C. L., & Gerbasi, A. (2015). Does civility pay? *Organizational Dynamics*, *44*(4), 281–6.

Randall, P. (2001). *Bullying in Adulthood: Assessing the Bullies and Their Victims*. London: Brunner-Routledge.

Riskin, A., Erez, A., Foulk, T. A., Kugelman, A., Gover, A., Shoris, I., & Bamberger, P. A. (2015). The impact of rudeness on medical team performance: a randomized trial. *Pediatrics*, *136*(3), 487–95.

Rousseau, D. (1995). *Psychological Contracts in Organizations: Understanding Written and Unwritten Agreements*. California: Sage Publications.

Rousseau, F. L., & Vallerand, R. J. (2008). An examination of the relationship between passion and subjective well-being in older adults. *International Journal of Aging and Human Development*, *66*, 195–211.

Russell, N. S. (2014). *Trust, Inc*. Career Press.

Rutledge, R. B., Skandali, N., Dayan, P., & Dolan, R. J. (2015). Dopaminergic modulation of decision making and subjective well-being. *Journal of Neuroscience*, *35*(27), 9811–22.

Salin, D. (2003). Ways of explaining workplace bullying: a review of enabling, motivating and precipitating structures and processes in the work environment. *Human Relations*, *56*(10), 1213–32.

Sapolsky, R. M. (2004). *Why Zebras Don't Get Ulcers: The Acclaimed Guide to Stress, Stress-related Diseases, and Coping – now Revised and Updated*. New York: Macmillan.

Schaufeli, W., Taris, T., & Bakker, A. (2006). 'Dr Jekyll or Mr Hyde? On the differences between work engagement and workaholism.' In R. Burke (ed.), *Research Companion to Working Time and Working Addiction*. Cheltenham: Edward Elgar.

Schein, E. H. (1988). *Organizational Culture*. Sloan School of Management, Massachusetts Institute of Technology.

Schmitt, M., Baumert, A., Gollwitzer, M., & Maes, J. (2010). The Justice Sensitivity Inventory: factorial validity, location in the personality facet space, demographic pattern, and normative data. *Social Justice Research*, *23*, 211–38.

Sekhon, H., Ennew, C., Kharouf, H., & Devlin, J. (2014). Trustworthiness and trust: influences and implications. *Journal of Marketing Management*, *30*(3–4), 409–30.

Shirom, A. (2011) Vigor as a positive affect at work. *Review of General Psychology*, *15*, 50–64.

Shoss, M. K., Eisenberger, R., Restubog, S. L. D., & Zagenczyk, T. J. (2013). Blaming the organization for abusive supervision: the roles of perceived organizational support and supervisor's organizational embodiment. *Journal of Applied Psychology*, *98*(1), 158.

Siegrist, M., & Cvetkovich, G. (2000). Perception of hazards: the role of social trust and knowledge. *Risk Analysis*, *20*(5), 713–20.

Silla, I., De Cuyper, N., Gracia, F. J., Peiró, J. M., & De Witte, H. (2009). Job insecurity and well-being: moderation by employability. *Journal of Happiness Studies*, *10*(6), 739.

Slopen, N., Glynn, R. J., Buring, J. E., Lewis, T. T., Williams, D. R., & Albert, M. A. (2012). Job strain, job insecurity, and incident cardiovascular disease in the Women's Health Study: results from a 10-year prospective study. *PLoS One*, *7*(7), e40512.

Smilor, R. (1997). Entrepreneurship, reflections on a subversive activity. *Journal of Business Venturing*, *12*, 341–6.

Snir, R., & Harpaz, I. (2011). Beyond workaholism. *Human Resource Management Review*,

Solomon, R. C., & Flores, F. (2003). *Building Trust: In Business, Politics, Relationships, and Life*. Oxford: Oxford University Press.

Spector, P. E. (1988). Development of the work locus of control scale. *Journal of Occupational Psychology*, *61*, 219–30.

Spence, J., & Robbins, A. (1992). Workaholism: definition, measurement and preliminary results. *Journal of Personality Assessment*, *58*, 160–78.

Spreitzer, G. M., Sutcliffe, K., Dutton, J. E., Sonenshein, S., & Grant, A. M. (2005). A socially embedded model of thriving at work. *Organization Science*, *16*(5), 537–50.

Sutton, R. I. (2007). *The No Asshole Rule: Building a Civilized Workplace and Surviving One That Isn't*. Hachette UK.

Tepper, B. J., Carr, J. C., Breaux, D. M., Geider, S., Hu, C., & Hua, W. (2009). Abusive supervision, intentions to quit, and employees' workplace deviance: a power/dependence analysis. *Organizational Behavior and Human Decision Processes*, *109*(2), 156–67.

Thomas, G. F., Zolin, R., & Hartman, J. L. (2009). The central role of communication in developing trust and its effects on employee involvement. *Journal of Business Communication*, *46*(3), 283–310.

Treglown, L., Palaiou, K., Zarola, A., & Furnham, A. (2016). The dark side of resilience and burnout: a moderation-mediation model. *PloS One*, *11*(6), e0156279.

Vallerand, R. J. (2008). On the psychology of passion: in search of what makes people's lives most worth living. *Canadian Psychology*, *49*, 1–13.

Vallerand, R. J., & Houlfort, N. (2003). 'Passion at work: towards a new conceptualization.' In S. Gilliand, D. Steiner & D. Skarlicki (eds), *Emerging Perspectives on Values in Organizations*. Greenwich, CT: IAP, pp. 187–204.

Vallerand, R. J., Salvy, S-J., Mageau, G. A., Elliot, A. J., Denis, P. L., Grouzet, F. M., & Blanchard, C. (2007). On the role of passion in performance. *Journal of Personality*, *75*, 505–34.

Vallerand, R. J., Paquet, Y., Philippe, F., & Charest, J. (2010) On the role of passion for work in burnout. *Journal of Personality*, *78*, 290–311.

Van Beek, I., Taris, T., & Schaufeli, W. (2011). Workaholic and work engagement employees. *Journal of Occupational Health Psychology*, *16*, 468–82.

Van Fleet, D. D., & Van Fleet, E. W. (2012). Towards a behavioral description of managerial bullying. *Employee Responsibilities and Rights Journal*, *24*(3), 197–215.

Vogel, R. M., & Mitchell, M. S. (2015). The motivational effects of diminished self-esteem for employees who experience abusive supervision. *Journal of Management*, *43*(7), 2218–51.

Weihrich, H. & Koontz, H. (1993). *Management: A Global Perspective*. New York: McGraw Hill.

Winston, J. S., Strange, B. A., O'Doherty, J., & Dolan, R. J. (2002). Automatic and intentional brain responses during evaluation of trustworthiness of faces. *Nature Neuroscience*, *5*(3), 277–83.

Yam, K. C., Christian, M., Wu, W., Liao, Z., & Nai, J. (2017). The mixed blessing of leader sense of humor: examining costs and benefits. *Academy of Management Journal* (online).

INDEX

3/18